AF404513

PETE CHANDLER

DESIGN MANAGEMENT HANDBOOK

TRAINEE TO DIRECTOR

novum pro

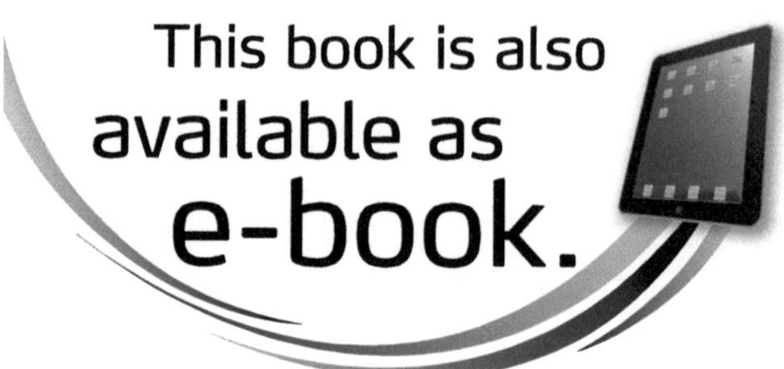

© 2025 novum publishing gmbh
Rathausgasse 73, A-7311 Neckenmarkt
office@novum-publishing.co.uk

ISBN 978-3-99146-320-7
Editing: Chris Beale
Cover photo:
Molotok007 I Dreamstime.com
Cover design, layout & typesetting:
novum publishing
Internal illustrations: Pete Chandler

The images provided by the author
have been printed in the highest
possible quality.

www.novum-publishing.co.uk

All rights of distribution,
including via film, radio, and television,
photomechanical reproduction,
audio storage media, electronic data
storage media, and the reprinting of
portions of text, are reserved.

Printed in the European Union on
environmentally friendly, chlorine- and
acid-free paper.

CONTENTS

INTRODUCTION

**Tell us about your time with the Company,
from the day you joined to becoming a Director**

- September 5th 1994 was a big decision day for me; do I accept my University place or do I accept a Job Offer of Trainee Draughtsperson at, then a small cladding company?

- The thought of gaining knowledge and experience whilst having a salary was a key influence, and upon reflection, was a monumental decision that set the path for my working career.

- My part-time attendance at College whilst working at the cladding company was an intense but exciting time; getting paid whilst learning was amazing!

- Working on a number of projects across all parts of the UK as a Designer and Senior Designer, with key Clients and Architects, required a high level of technical skills, robust planning and programming and commercial awareness, which cemented my promotion to Design Manager in April 2000.

- With the successful delivery of complex projects and managing the design process for multi-million pound, prestigious and award-winning developments, I became part of a Senior Management Team in April 2006.

- Hard work and determination, coupled with enthusiasm and a positive attitude, were fundamental to my rapid progression through defined Design roles within a fast-growing Company.

- I have excellent attention to detail, build relationships with integrity and thrive on providing innovative and practical solutions to complex projects.

- I was appointed as Design Director in April 2014.

- I have experienced a few different role changes within different companies since that time due to Company Insolvencies but have always managed to continue to operate at a Senior level.

Why do you think your team is great?
[Also, tell us a bit about the diversity within the team]

- I have always had a fantastic Design Team! My teams have been hardworking, conscientious and very experienced in all aspects of the building envelope.

- My teams have been very reliable and passionate in what they do; they consistently exceeded my expectations and delivered high quality designs. They all continue to do so today!

- My teams have always been well structured with the correct balance of Apprentices, Graduate Design Trainees, Assistant Designers, Designers, Senior Designers and Design Managers with opportunities to grow and develop within the Business.

- All Trainees within my Department have undertaken my Design Training Programme, which was supplemented by specific external training courses, internal 3D training and regular CPDs to further enhance themselves as individuals and contribute further to the team's success.

- It has been very much about the people, not only in my teams, but throughout the Company. Relationships are fundamental within any business, especially in the high demands of the Constructions Industry.

- We have always had a diverse range of skills, knowledge and abilities within my teams, and we were all constantly developing. There is a range of 2D and 3D capabilities.

- My teams have always been a pleasure to work with; they all understood and supported each other to reach greater goals, demands of the business and the ever-growing Company.

- They all "pulled-together" when times are tough.

- I have only been successful because of the good people around me.

What were the most exciting projects
that you got to work on and why?

- I provide bespoke total design solutions to suit Clients and architects' needs. Offering vast technical knowledge and commercial expertise, I guide and advise main contractors, architects and installers in all elements of the building envelope design and build.

- There are a number of projects that have been enjoyable, exciting, tough and difficult. It is not possible to name them all as there are now over 100 projects I have been involved with over my career.

What advice would you give to aspiring designers?

- Relationships are fundamental and it is essential that as much contact is made with people, whether it be internal or external. Building these relationships will further enhance the delivery of projects within all disciplines of the business.

- Respect for your team and peers is important, and it is essential that they respect you. A Director's position naturally commands a level of respect and authority, but ensure that you talk to your staff and ask "how are they getting on" and "how they are feeling."

- Live the Company Values within the business and promote them through your teams. I am very passionate about what I do, and people "feed" off this.

- "Deliver what you promise" may seem a cliché, but it is true. Do not promise something that you cannot deliver, whether to a team member or client, and when you promise something make sure you deliver it.

- Be influential and make "things happen" even though it may be a difficult decision. Make sure the decision is in the best interest of the Company.

- Believe in your ability to take on the role. You will often find yourself carrying out the role or part of the role prior to taking it on officially and being "awarded the title."

- Be the Leader and make sure you "step back" and look at the "bigger picture" in the best interest of the Company. Be strong, believe in yourself and people will follow you.

- It is fine to focus on your areas of development to enhance your career further, but do not forget the skills you have gained and the areas which "got you to where you are."

- Make sure you understand succession and where people can grow, where they can further enhance your team and Region.

- Enjoy it.

This Management Handbook has been produced in a bullet point format. I believe in short, sharp sentences identifying the key issue or point being raised as opposed to lots of text. There are images of relevant supporting documents throughout.

My First Letter

- This is where it all began:

Friday - 26
9am

Southampton,
Hants.,

13th August, 1994.

To Miss Smith,

I am writing with regards to the advert I saw asking for a trainee draughtsperson / designer.

I have recently left Barton Peveril College on completion of two A-level courses in English Literature and Graphical Communication both of which I am awaiting results. I have also completed four G.C.S.E's within the two years in Physics, Computing, Law and Business Studies.

I have been interested in technical drawing ever since starting school and especially since I went out on work experience to a drawing office where I carried out technical drawings of heating and ventilation systems, as well as general office duties such as photocopying and printing.

I would very much like to work in a drawing environment as I am very interested and enjoy technical drawing,

Yours Sincerely

(PETER CHANDLER)

PRE-CONSTRUCTION

Tender Checklist

- It is essential to understand the documents available at BID stage, and a 'Tender Checklist' should be completed to ensure the relevant and appropriate information is available.

PC | TENDER CHECKLIST		
No.	**Item**	**Responsibility**
1.1	Scope of works	
1.2	Cladding Specification	
1.3	Roofing Specification	
1.4	Door Type Spec	
1.5	Acoustic Report	
1.6	Wind Load Report	
1.7	Fire strategy drawing	
1.8	Movement and Tolerance and Report	
1.9	Fire Engineering Report	
1.10	Cleaning and maintenance Report	
1.11	Employers Requirements Report	
1.12	BREEAM Assessment and Reports	
1.13	Security Related Reports	
1.14	3D Delivery Plan	
1.15	Door schedule	
1.16	Window schedule	
1.17	Louvre Schedule	
1.18	Curtain Wall Schedule	
1.19	Flashing and Cill details	
1.20	Model in suitable format	
1.21	dwg	
1.22	pdf	
1.23	Construction Programme	
1.24	Access & Methodology	

- Tender deliverables need to be identified with clear actions.

<table>
<tr><th colspan="3">PC | TENDER DELIVERABLES</th></tr>
<tr><th>No.</th><th>Item</th><th>Responsibility</th></tr>
<tr><td>1.1</td><td>Model/Drawing Review</td><td>Estimating / PC</td></tr>
<tr><td>1.2</td><td>Drawing Mark-up</td><td>Estimating / PC</td></tr>
<tr><td>1.3</td><td>Identify & issue RFI's</td><td>Estimating / PC</td></tr>
<tr><td>1.4</td><td>Project programme and Sequencing</td><td>Estimating / Ops</td></tr>
<tr><td>1.5</td><td>Steelwork Review [high level]</td><td>Estimating / PC</td></tr>
<tr><td>1.6</td><td>Design Budget and Price</td><td>PC</td></tr>
<tr><td>1.7</td><td>Specification Review</td><td>PC</td></tr>
<tr><td>1.8</td><td>Specification Commentary</td><td>Estimating / PC</td></tr>
<tr><td>1.9</td><td>Summary of Key Issues</td><td>Estimating / PC</td></tr>
<tr><td>1.10</td><td>Risk / Challenges Register for Design & Technical</td><td>Estimating / PC</td></tr>
<tr><td>1.11</td><td>Door schedule Review</td><td>Estimating</td></tr>
<tr><td>1.12</td><td>Glass Matrix / Summary sheet</td><td>Estimating / PC</td></tr>
<tr><td>1.13</td><td>Identify and Produce Principle details / Buildability</td><td>Estimating</td></tr>
<tr><td>1.14</td><td>Procurement List</td><td>Estimating</td></tr>
<tr><td>1.15</td><td>Technical Review [complicated]</td><td>PC</td></tr>
<tr><td>1.16</td><td>3D Strategy Review</td><td>PC</td></tr>
<tr><td>1.17</td><td>Secondary Steel work requirements</td><td>Estimating / PC</td></tr>
<tr><td>1.18</td><td>Glass and panel replacement</td><td>Estimating / Ops</td></tr>
<tr><td>1.19</td><td>U values - Calc as part of tender submission</td><td>Estimating / Suppliers</td></tr>
<tr><td>1.20</td><td>Materials and Finishes Schedule</td><td>Estimating / PC</td></tr>
<tr><td>1.21</td><td>Updated record of design Information</td><td>Estimating</td></tr>
<tr><td>1.22</td><td>Monitor changes during the bid process</td><td>Estimating</td></tr>
</table>

Establish Roles and Responsibilities

- Tender Launch Meeting to be held by BID Manager.
- Agree level of input required by Pre-Construction Team.
- Identify any further resources required during the Tender.

PC | DESIGN RESPONSIBILITY MATRIX

Project: xxx — Pre-Tender [Estimating Led]

Tender Process Stage	ID	Design Deliverables	Include in Technical Handover Pack	Estimating	Pre-Con Design	Technical Compliance	Design	Buying	Construction	Commercial	Date Planned	Date Complete
Start												
Week 1 / Week 2	1	Project Launch or Pre-Handover	✗	Estimating	Pre-Con Design							
	2	Establish Roles, Responsibilities & Programme	✗	Estimating	Pre-Con Design	-	-	-	-	-		
	3	Scope / Bid Review	✗	Estimating	Pre-Con Design	-	-	-	Construction	Commercial		
	4	Produce & Issue Info Required Schedule [IRS]	✓	Estimating	Pre-Con Design	-	-	-	-	-		
	5	Establish Design Responsibility	✓	Estimating	Pre-Con Design	-	-	-	-	Commercial		
Hold Point 1												
Main Bid Period	6	BIM Review [Execution Plan or LM Default]	✓	Estimating	Pre-Con Design	-	-	-	-	-		
	7	Mark Up of Client Drawings	✓	Estimating	Pre-Con Design	-	-	-	-	-		
	8	Produce & Issue Design Deliverables	✓	Estimating	Pre-Con Design	-	-	-	-	-		
	9	Establish Site Programme & Sequencing	✓	Estimating	Pre-Con Design	-	-	-	Construction	Commercial		
	10	Produce & Issue Design Programme	✓	Estimating	Pre-Con Design	-	-	-	-	-		
	11	Establish Design Budget & Price	✓	Estimating	Pre-Con Design	-	-	-	-	-		
	12	Specification Review	✓	Estimating	Pre-Con Design	-	-	-	Construction	Commercial		
	13	Produce Specification Commentary	✗	Estimating	Pre-Con Design	-	-	-	Construction	Commercial		
	14	Risk & Opportunities Schedule	✓	Estimating	Pre-Con Design	-	-	-	Construction	Commercial		
	15	Door Schedule Review	✓	Estimating	Pre-Con Design	-	-	-	-	-		
	16	Produce Glass Matrix / Summary Sheet	✓	Estimating	Pre-Con Design	-	-	-	-	-		
	17	Establish Fire Strategy	✓	Estimating	Pre-Con Design	-	-	-	-	-		
	18	Glass / Panel Replacement Strategy	✓	Estimating	Pre-Con Design	-	-	-	Construction	-		
	19	Technical Checklist [1 - Structure]	✓	Estimating	Pre-Con Design	-	-	-	-	-		
	20	Technical Checklist [2 - Performance]	✓	Estimating	Pre-Con Design	-	-	-	-	-		
	21	Technical Checklist [3 - Design]	✓	Estimating	Pre-Con Design	-	-	-	-	-		
	22	Technical Checklist [4 - Maintenance]	✓	Estimating	Pre-Con Design	-	-	-	-	-		
	23	Initial Value Engineering Review	✗	Estimating	Pre-Con Design	-	-	-	Construction	Commercial		
	24	Identify & Produce Principle Details	✓	Estimating	Pre-Con Design	-	-	-	-	-		
	25	Buildability Review of Key Interfaces	✓	Estimating	Pre-Con Design	-	-	-	Construction	-		
	26	Identify & Issue Requests For Information [RFI]	✓	Estimating	Pre-Con Design	-	-	-	-	-		
	27	Issue Supplier & Materials Schedule	✓	Estimating	Pre-Con Design	-	-	-	-	-		

Phase	Stage	No.	Task	Hold Pt	Estimating	Pre-Con Design		Design	Buying	Construction	Commercial
			Hold Point 2								
Pre-Tender [Estimating Led]	Post Tender / Pre-Order	28	Material Selection & Samples	✗	Estimating	Pre-Con Design	-	-	-	Construction	-
		29	Allocation of Resources	✗	Estimating	Pre-Con Design	-	-	-	Construction	Commercial
		30	Value Engineering Review	✗	Estimating	Pre-Con Design	-	-	Buying	Construction	Commercial
		31	Establish Approval Process & Timescales	✓	Estimating	Pre-Con Design	-	Design	-	Construction	Commercial
			Hold Point 3								
Pre-Tender [Estimating Led]	To Project Award	32	Produce & Issue CDM Assessment	✓	Estimating	Pre-Con Design	-	-	-	Construction	-
		33	Identify Off-site Manufacture / Pre-Assembly	✓	Estimating	Pre-Con Design	-	-	Buying	Construction	Commercial
		34	Establish Contractual Documents	✗	Estimating	Pre-Con Design	-	-	-	-	Commercial
			Hold Point 4								
Pre-Tender [Estimating Led]	Post Award	35	Final Sub-Contractor & Supplier Selection	✗	Estimating	Pre-Con Design	-	Design	Buying	Construction	Commercial
		36	Design Intent Review / Can We Start	✗	Estimating	Pre-Con Design	-	Design	-	Construction	Commercial
		37	Produce Handover Packs	✗	Estimating	Pre-Con Design	-	-	-	-	-
			Hold Point 5								
Pre-Tender [Estimating Led]	Post Award	38	Produce Technical Handover Pack	✗	-	Pre-Con Design	-	-	-	-	-
		39	Handover Meeting	✗	Estimating	Pre-Con Design	-	Design	Buying	Construction	Commercial
		40	Technical Handover	✗	-	Pre-Con Design	-	Design	-	Construction	Commercial
			Hold Point 6								
Post-Tender [Operational Team Lead]	Operational Delivery Design Teams	41	Strategy Meeting	✗	Estimating	Pre-Con Design	-	Design	Buying	Construction	Commercial
		42	Issue Info Required Schedule [IRS]	✗	-	Pre-Con Design	-	Design	-	Construction	Commercial
		43	Review & Issue Design Resource Programme	✗	-	Pre-Con Design	-	Design	-	Construction	-
		44	Design Adjudication	✗	-	Pre-Con Design	-	Design	-	Construction	Commercial
		45	Review Global Orders Required & Dates	✗	-	-	-	Design	Buying	Construction	Commercial
		46	Material Application For Warranty Forms	✗	-	-	-	Design	Buying	-	Commercial
		47	Review Movement & Tolerances	✗	-	-	-	Design	-	Construction	-
		48	Establish Technical Submittals	✗	-	-	-	Design	-	Construction	-
		49	Produce Design Quality Plan [Where Required]	✗	-	-	-	Design	-	-	-
		50	Review CDM Assessment	✗	-	-	-	Design	-	Construction	-
		51	Buildability Review of Key Interfaces	✗	-	-	-	Design	-	Construction	-
		52	Engineering & Calculation Review	✗	-	-	-	Design	-	-	-

Continuation by Operational Design Delivery Teams

- Design Issue Tracker to be populated and launch Meeting to be held by BID Manager. Priorities should be defined using the red, amber and green [RAG] principle.

	PC	DESIGN ISSUE TRACKER										
Area	**27/06/2023**	**Owner**		**Drawing or**	**Building or**	**Status**	**1**			**Potential Costs**		
	Item	**Company**	**Person**	**RFI Reference**	**Area Code**		**Description**	**Date**	**Saving**	**Neutral**	**Additional**	
1.00	**General Issues**											
1.01	Design Freeze	PC	PC		General	✓	PC stated in meeting that the Stage 4 design will be frozen on -/--/--.					
1.02	Air Test	PC	PC	TQ-024	General	☹	PC stated in meeting that the building may be air tested and that a figure of 5Pa/m2 is to be achieved.					
1.03	Testing & Compliance	PC	PC / PC		General	☹	PC stated in meeting that Scope of testing, samples and benchmarks is still to be determined.					
1.04	Suppliers	PC	PC		General	☺	PC to issue list of preferred suppliers for craneage, scaffold and access plant.					
1.05	RFI				General	✓	PC Design / RFI action tracker to be created.					
1.06	Document Control Training	PC	PC / PC		General	☺	PC to issue list of names required for training.					
1.07	Material Submittals				General	✓	PC to issue format / template for material submittals.					

Information Required Schedule [IRS]

- Refer to Programme ID.
- Show Priority [1, 2, 3 and in red, amber, green].

IRS No	Programme ID	Priority	Information Description	Date Required	Comments	Date Received	Closed Out
			PC | INFORMATION REQUIRED SCHEDULE [IRS]				
1	59	1	Construction status Architect drawings	--/--/--	Should be stated in order		
2	59	1	Construction status Engineers drawings	--/--/--	Should be stated in order		
3	59	1	Consultant design team residual Risk Register	--/--/--			
4	59	1	Construction status project Specifications	--/--/--			
5	74	2	Building movement and tolerances report	--/--/--			
6	74	2	Wind load report	--/--/--			
7	74	2	Acoustic report	--/--/--			
8	74	2	Building Design Life	--/--/--	Should be stated in order		
9	74	3	Agreed samples	--/--/--			
10	-	3	Agreed mock-ups	--/--/--	There are no mock-ups requirements on this project		
11	120	2	Secure by design requirements	--/--/--			
12	-	1	Agreed Value Engineering schedule	--/--/--	Commercial input required		
13	-	1	Agreed Extra-Over requirements	--/--/--	Commercial input required		
14	-	1	Agreed air sealing responsibilities	--/--/--			
15	-	1	Confirmation of guarantees required	--/--/--			
16	120	1	Louvre classification	--/--/--			
17	74	1	Gutter category confirmation	--/--/--			
18	74	1	Fire strategy	--/--/--			
19	-	2	Construction status Steelwork fabrication drawings	--/--/--	Review to be carried out to identify differences from Engineers drawings		
20	-	2	Construction status M & E drawings	--/--/--			
21	164	2	Glass photometric [solar control / g-value]	--/--/--			
22	164	2	Guarding requirements [roof edges / barrier loads / balustrades]	--/--/--			
23	154	2	Door and ironmongery schedule	--/--/--			
24	-	3	3D Architectural model [in Revit or AutoCAD]	--/--/--	Should be stated in order		
25	-	3	3D Structural model [in Revit or AutoCAD]	--/--/--	Should be stated in order		
26	-	3	Agreed BIM requirements / strategy	--/--/--	There are no mock-ups requirements on this project		
27	-	3	Cleaning and maintenance strategy	--/--/--			
28	179	3	Manifestation requirements	--/--/--			
29	74	3	Lightning protection requirements	--/--/--			

Marked Up Drawings Required

- Add North, East, South and West.
- Add main grid lines [at corners].
- Cross reference ID number to Deliverables Schedule.

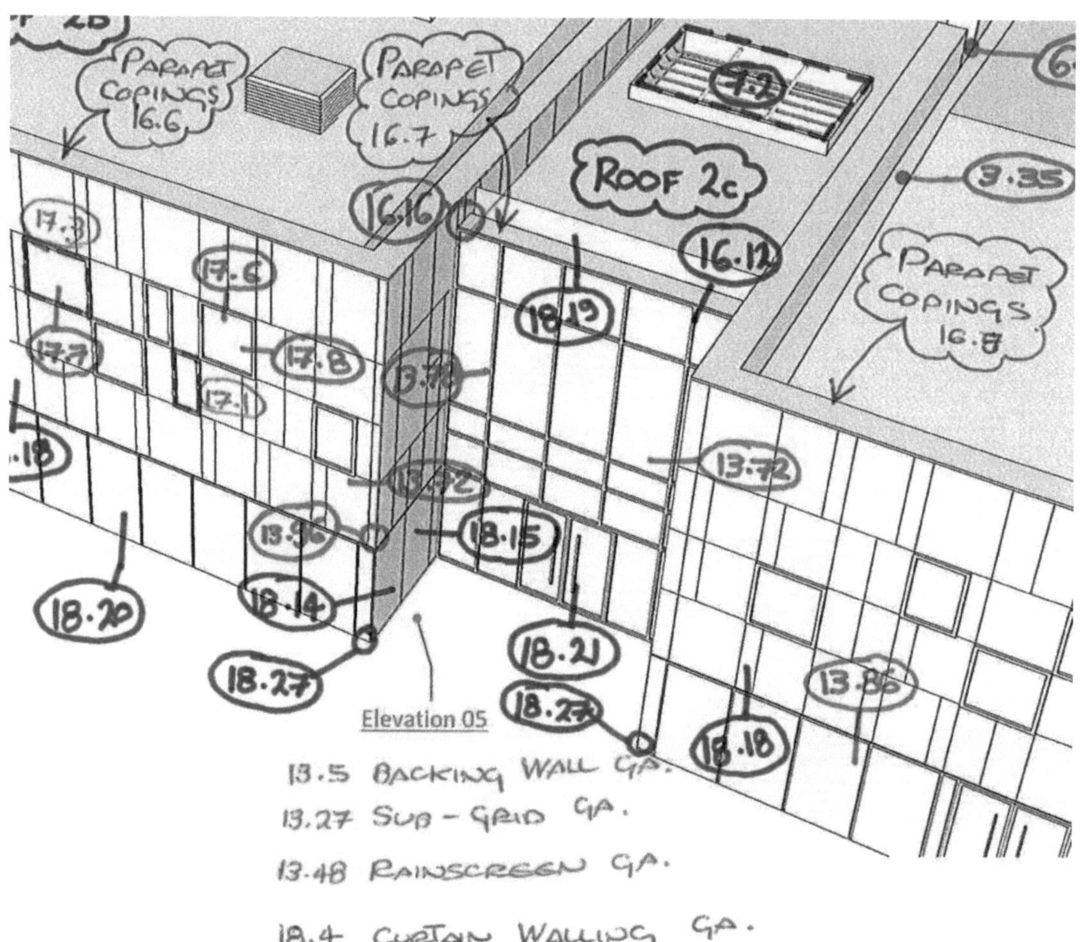

13.5 BACKING WALL GA.

13.27 SUB - GRID GA.

13.48 RAINSCREEN GA.

18.4 CURTAIN WALLING GA.

Produce and Issue Design Deliverables

- Produce complete list of drawings required.
- Design Manager to be allocated for 100% of duration of project.
- Senior Design Manager to be allocated for 50% of duration of project.
- Add number of drawings.

ID	Area / Drawing Title / Location	Type	Level	No. Drawings	Notes	Resource	1	2	3	4	5
	PC | DESIGN DELIVERABLES										
0.0	Project Value as %	71.0	£ 124,171.06	275			0.00	0.00	0.00	0.00	0.00
	£ 1	General	0 [Adm]		Admin / Co-ordination	Design Manager					
5%	£ 0	GA	0 [Adm]		2D Low Level Design	Assistant Designer					
6%	£ 0	Spec Drawing	1 [2DL]		2D Medium Level Design	Designer					
7%	£ 0	Detail	2 [2DM]		2D High Level Design	Senior Designer					
8%	£ 0	Schedule	3 [2DH]		2D+ / 3D Low Level Design	Designer					
9%	£ 0	Sundry	4 [3DL]		2D+ / 3D Medium Level Design	Senior Designer					
10%	£ 0		5 [3DM]		3D Modelling / Geometry	Senior Designer					
11%	£ 0		6 [3DH]		Engineering	Structural Engineer					
12%	£ 0		7 [Eng]		Document Control	Document Controller					
01.00	General | Project Start Up			0							
01.01	Information Review / Handover / Technical Review	General	0 [Adm]	0		Design Manager					
02.00	General | Setting Out & Principle Detailing			0							
02.01	Models / Grids / Building Lines / Levels / Sections	General	3 [2DH]	0		Senior Designer					
03.00	Design | Roof	28		27							
03.01	Low Level Liner Layout	GA	2 [2DM]	1		Designer [Cladding]					
03.02	Low Level Top Hat & Clip Layout	GA	2 [2DM]	1		Designer [Cladding]					
03.03	Low Level Top Sheet Roof Plan	GA	2 [2DM]	1		Designer [Cladding]					
03.04	Low Level Gutter Support Layout	GA	2 [2DM]	1		Designer [Cladding]					
03.05	Low Level Gutter & Outlet Plan	GA	2 [2DM]	1		Designer [Cladding]					
03.06	High Level Liner Layout	GA	2 [2DM]	1		Designer [Cladding]					
03.07	High Level Top Hat & Clip Layout	GA	2 [2DM]	1		Designer [Cladding]					
03.08	High Level Top Sheet Roof Plan	GA	2 [2DM]	1		Designer [Cladding]					
03.09	High Level Gutter & Outlet Plan	GA	2 [2DM]	1		Designer [Cladding]					
03.10	High Level Gutter & Outlet Plan	GA	2 [2DM]	1		Designer [Cladding]					
03.11	Specification Sheet	Spec Drawing	2 [2DM]	1		Designer [Cladding]					
03.12	Ridge Detail	Detail	2 [2DM]	1		Designer [Cladding]					
03.13	Top Sheet Fixed Point Detail	Detail	2 [2DM]	1		Designer [Cladding]					
03.14	High Level Eaves Detail [GL A & D]	Detail	2 [2DM]	1		Designer [Cladding]					
03.15	Low Level Eaves Detail [GL D]	Detail	2 [2DM]	1		Designer [Cladding]					
03.16	Low Level Eaves Detail [GL H]	Detail	2 [2DM]	1		Designer [Cladding]					
03.17	High Level Eaves Detail [GL 1 & 14]	Detail	2 [2DM]	1		Designer [Cladding]					
03.18	Low Level Eaves Detail [GL 1 & 14]	Detail	2 [2DM]	1		Designer [Cladding]					
03.19	Outlet / RWP Connection Detail	Detail	2 [2DM]	1		Designer [Cladding]					
03.20	Gutter Corner Detail	Detail	2 [2DM]	1		Designer [Cladding]					
03.21	Gutter Joint Details	Detail	2 [2DM]	1		Designer [Cladding]					
03.22	Overflow Detail	Detail	2 [2DM]	1		Designer [Cladding]					
03.23	Fixing Schedule	Spec Drawing	2 [2DM]	1		Designer [Cladding]					
03.24	Lap Details / Installation Guide	Detail	2 [2DM]	1		Designer [Cladding]					
03.25	Low Level Hip Detail	Detail	2 [2DM]	1		Designer [Cladding]					
06.02	High Level Hip Detail	Detail	2 [2DM]	1		Designer [Cladding]					
03.27	Lightning Protection Detail [VO]	Detail	2 [2DM]	1		Designer [Cladding]					
03.28	Construction Issue	Detail	2 [2DM]	0		Designer [Cladding]					

- If time does not allow then the following should be considered as a minimum.

PC | DESIGN DELIVERABLES

ID	Area / Drawing Title / Location	Type		No. Drawings
1.0	**Design | Wall Cladding | Building 1**	9		**74**
1.1	GA's - Plans	GA	2	
1.2	GA's - Sections	GA	4	
1.3	GA's - Elevations	GA	4	
1.4	Details	GA	16	
2.0	**Design | Wall Cladding | Building 2**	4		**48**
2.1	GA's - Plans	GA	4	
2.2	GA's - Sections	GA	6	
2.3	GA's - Elevations	GA	8	
2.4	Details	GA	30	
				122

- Type of deliverable to be identified.

	PC | DESIGN DELIVERABLES		
	Type		
1	General		
2	GA		
3	Spec Drawing		
4	Detail		
5	Schedule		
6	Sundry		

- Complexity to be indicated to allow for resource planning.

	PC | DESIGN DELIVERABLES		
		Level	**Notes**
		0 [Adm]	Admin / Co-ordination
		0 [Adm]	Admin / Co-ordination
		1 [2DL]	2D Low Level Design
		2 [2DM]	2D Medium Level Design
		3 [2DH]	2D High Level Design
		4 [3DL]	2D+ / 3D Low Level Design
		5 [3DM]	2D+ / 3D Medium Level Design
		6 [3DH]	3D Modelling / Geometry
		7 [Eng]	Engineering

- Produce Drawing Deliverable Schedule showing number of drawings.
- Ensure there is a cumulative sum of drawings.
- Ensure the 'week-xx' principle is used from the project start date.

PC | DRAWING SCHEDULE					Week -24	Week -25	Week -26	Week -27
Drawing Number	Drawing Title	Resource	Drawing Status	Progress	-/-/-	-/-/-	-/-/-	-/-/-
Roofing Works			6					
1001	Drawing Title	Pete	01 | In Progress	30%	x			
1002	Drawing Title	Pete	02 | GA & Details Complete	40%	x			
1003	Drawing Title	Pete	03 | Issued For Initial Approval	50%		x		
1004	Drawing Title	Pete	06 | Revise Drawings	60%		x		
1005	Drawing Title	Pete	05 | Issued For Final Approval	70%			x	
1006	Drawing Title	Pete	05 | Issued For Final Approval	80%			x	
Cladding Works			6					
2001	Drawing Title	Pete	06 | Revise Drawings	80%				x
2002	Drawing Title	Pete	06 | Revise Drawings	80%			x	
2003	Drawing Title	Pete	07 | Issued For Construction	90%		x		
2004	Drawing Title	Pete	07 | Issued For Construction	90%		x		
2005	Drawing Title	Pete	08 | Complete	100%	x			
2006	Drawing Title	Pete	08 | Complete	100%	x			
Check 12		Total	12		4	4	3	1
			Cumulative Production		4	8	11	12
		Sub-Total [x]	12					

Establish Site Programme and Sequencing

- Set week numbers to Access Date [start on site].
- Construction works are week number 1, 2, 3...
- Pre-construction works are week numbers -3, -2, -1...

- Ensure activity gaps are added in programme so ID numbers remain the same throughout the life of the project.
- Baseline – save Baseline once programme is complete.
- Samples – add samples and sample approval on programme.

- Float – is owned by the project [do not mention to Client].
- Time Risk Allowance [TRA] is owned by the Sub-Contractor [ideally this should be shown on programme].

Under the Contract the programme submitted must show:

- The starting date, access dates, key dates and completion date.
- Planned completion.
- Order / timing of operations.
- Order / timing of work the employer and any others?
- Dates when the contractor plans to complete various tasks required?
- The dates when the contractor plans to meet each condition stated for the key dates.
- Dates when the contractor needs access to part of the site if later than its access dates.
- Acceptances, plant, materials and other things to be provided by the employer and information from others.
- For each operation, a statement of how the contractor plans to do the work [including equipment and resources].

Provisions for Float, Time risk allowances, Health and Safety requirements, contract procedures and information showing how each activity on the activity schedule relates to operation.

Legends

Baseline Summary		Manufacture		Cladding Work			
Receipt of Construction Status Information		Construction		Partial Cladding Weathertight			
Review of Construction Status Information		Overall Construction Duration		Delivery of Key Glazing Materials			
Hold Point		Site Set Up / Decamp		Glazing Work			
Design		Netting		Partial Glazing Weathertight			
Engineering		Edge Protection		Envelope Complete			
Sub-Contractor Design		Scaffolding		Key Date			
Scheduling		Steelwork Handover		Work By Others			
Sub-Contract Scheduling		Delivery of Key Roofing Materials		Summary			
First Issue Date		Roofing Work		Baseline			
Approval		Partial Roof Weathertight					
Latest Order Date		Delivery of Key Cladding Materials					

Overall Sub-Contract Works

- Sub-Contract Order Date [Assumed].
- Issue of Information Required Schedule [IRS] *[day after Order Date]*.

ID		Task Name	Start	Duration	Finish	% Complete	Design Activity	Week 173							
								M	T	W	T	F	S	S	M
1		**Overall Sub-Contract Works**	**Fri 14/09/18**		**Fri 14/09/18**	**0%**									
2		Overall Sub-Contract Works | Sub-Contract Order [Assumed]	Mon 06/02/23	0 wks	Mon 06/02/23	0%	01 | Contract								
3		Overall Sub-Contract Works | Start Date [Commencement of Design] [Assumed]	Mon 06/02/23	0 wks	Mon 06/02/23	0%	01 | Contract								
4		Overall Sub-Contract Works | Issue of Information Required Schedule [IRS]	Mon 06/02/23	0 wks	Mon 06/02/23	0%	03 | Information								
5		**Sub-Contract Site Works**	**Mon 06/02/23**	**0 wks**	**Mon 06/02/23**	**0%**									
6		Sub-Contract Site Works | Access Date [AD?]	Mon 06/02/23	0 wks	Mon 06/02/23	0%	01 | Contract								
7		Sub-Contract Site Works | Temporary Weathertight of Roofing Works [KD?]	Mon 06/02/23	0 wks	Mon 06/02/23	0%	01 | Contract								
8		Sub-Contract Site Works | Temporary Weathertight of External Cladding [KD?]	Mon 06/02/23	0 wks	Mon 06/02/23	0%	01 | Contract								
9		Sub-Contract Site Works | Temporary Weathertight of Glazing [KD?]	Mon 06/02/23	0 wks	Mon 06/02/23	0%	01 | Contract								
10		Sub-Contract Site Works | Completion of Roofing Works [KD?]	Mon 06/02/23	0 wks	Mon 06/02/23	0%	01 | Contract								
11		Sub-Contract Site Works | Completion of External Cladding [KD?]	Mon 06/02/23	0 wks	Mon 06/02/23	0%	01 | Contract								
12		Sub-Contract Site Works | Completion of Glazing [KD?]	Mon 06/02/23	0 wks	Mon 06/02/23	0%	01 | Contract								
13		Sub-Contract Site Works | Envelope Complete [KD?]	Mon 06/02/23	0 wks	Mon 06/02/23	0%	01 | Contract								

Sub-Contract Site Works [key dates only at top of programme]

- Ensure 'over-arching' summary of Design and Procurement Off-Site Activities.
- Start Date [Commencement of Design] [Assumed].
- Access Date [Week 1] – commencement of External Envelope [Assumed].
- Completion of Sub-Contract Works [Assumed].

Produce and Issue Design Programme

- Design and Procurement Off-Site Activities.
  - General | Management.
  - General | Receipt of Construction Status Information [Start of Design].
  - General | Review of Construction Status Information.
  - General | Hold Point – can we proceed?
  - General | Models / Grids / Building Lines / Levels.
  - General | First Issue Drawing Date [FIDD].

ID		Task Name	Start	Duration	Finish	% Complete	Gantt
1		General | Design & Procurement	Thu 23/03/23	1 wk	Wed 29/03/23	0%	General | Design & Procurement
2		General	Thu 23/03/23	1 wk	Wed 29/03/23	0%	General
3		General | Design Manager	Thu 23/03/23	0 wks	Thu 23/03/23	0%	23/03
4		General | Receipt of Construction Information [Start of Design]	Thu 23/03/23	0 days	Thu 23/03/23	0%	General | Receipt of Construction Information [Start of Design]
5		General | Review of Construction Information	Thu 23/03/23	1 wk	Wed 29/03/23	0%	General | Review of Construction Information
6		General | Hold Point - can we proceed?	Thu 23/03/23	0 wks	Thu 23/03/23	0%	General | Hold Point - can we proceed?
7		General | Models / Grids / Building Lines / Sections / Levels	Thu 23/03/23	1 wk	Wed 29/03/23	0%	General | Models / Grids / Building Lines / Sections / Levels
8		General | First Issue Drawing Date [FIDD]	Thu 23/03/23	0 wks	Thu 23/03/23	0%	General | First Issue Drawing Date [FIDD]

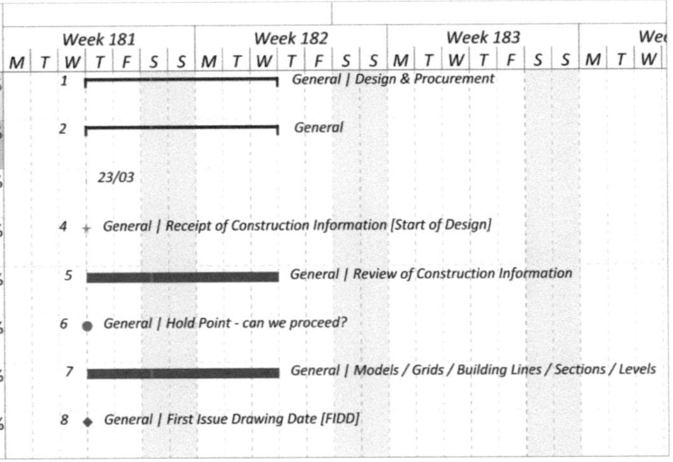

- Reserve Key Material
  - Reserve Key Material | Composite Panels [+Flat Sheet].
  - Reserve Key Material | Rainscreen [+Flat Sheet].
  - Reserve Key Material | Curtain Walling.
  - Reserve Key Material | Louvres.

ID		Task Name	Start	Duration	Finish	% Complete	Design Activity
1		General | Design & Procurement	Thu 23/03/23	14 wks	Wed 28/06/23	0%	
2		Reserve Key Material	Thu 23/03/23	14 wks	Wed 28/06/23	0%	
3		Reserve Key Material | Composite Panels	Thu 23/03/23	12 wks	Wed 14/06/23	0%	10 | Procurement
4		Reserve Key Material | Rainscreen	Thu 23/03/23	14 wks	Wed 28/06/23	0%	10 | Procurement
5		Reserve Key Material | Curtain Walling	Thu 23/03/23	14 wks	Wed 28/06/23	0%	10 | Procurement
6		Reserve Key Material | Louvres	Thu 23/03/23	12 wks	Wed 14/06/23	0%	10 | Procurement

- Key Design Date Matrix
  - Refer to Programme ID.
  - Refer to week numbers [-3, -2, -1, 1, 2, 3].
  - Show responsibilities.

						PC | KEY DESIGN DATE MATRIX			
Matrix No.	Programme ID	Deliverables ID	Week Number	Date	Area	Task Name	Responsibility	No. of Drawings	Comments
1	19	-	-11	--/--/--	Area 1	General | Hold Point - can we proceed?	Design Manager	0	
2	21	-	-10	--/--/--	Area 1	General | First Issue Drawing Date [FIDD]	Senior Designer 1	0	
3	23	-	-14	--/--/--	Area 1	Global Orders | Composite Roof Panels [+Flat Sheet]	Purchasing	0	
4	24	-	-14	--/--/--	Area 1	Global Orders | Composite Wall Panels [+Flat Sheet]	Purchasing	0	
7	29	3.0	-10	--/--/--	Area 1	Roof | Design | Details	Designer 1 [Cladding]	0	
8	41	4.0	-9	--/--/--	Area 1	Access Hatches | Design	Designer 1 [Cladding]	0	
9	47	5.0	-9	--/--/--	Area 2	Parapet Cladding | Design	Designer 1 [Cladding]	0	
10	55	6.0	-8	--/--/--	Area 2	Parapet Coping | Design	Designer 1 [Cladding]	0	
11	61	7.0	-8	--/--/--	Area 2	Terrace | Design	Designer 1 [Cladding]	0	
12	69	8.0	-8	--/--/--	Area 2	Handrail | Design	Sub-Contractor	0	
13	76	9.0	-9	--/--/--	Area 2	Backing Wall | Design | Details	Senior Designer 1	0	
14	87	9.0	-7	--/--/--	Area 2	Sinusoidal Cladding | Design | Details	Senior Designer 1	0	
15	96	10.0	-6	--/--/--	Area 2	Louvres | Design	Senior Designer 1	0	
16	102	11.0	-5	--/--/--	Area 2	Soffits | Design	Senior Designer 1	0	
17	161	36.0	-3	--/--/--	O & M Manual	Operations & Maintenance Manual	Designer 1 [Cladding]	0	
							Total	0	

Establish Design Budget and Price

- Show percentage of project value.

PC | DESIGN DELIVERABLES					
ID	Area / Drawing Title / Location	Type	Level	No. Drawings	Notes
0.0	Project Value as %	71.0	£ 124,171.06	275	
	£ 40,000,000	General	0 [Adm]		Admin / Co-ordination
5%	£ 2,000,000	GA	0 [Adm]		2D Low Level Design
6%	£ 2,400,000	Spec Drawing	1 [2DL]		2D Medium Level Design
7%	£ 2,800,000	Detail	2 [2DM]		2D High Level Design
8%	£ 3,200,000	Schedule	3 [2DH]		2D+ / 3D Low Level Design
9%	£ 3,600,000	Sundry	4 [3DL]		2D+ / 3D Medium Level Design
10%	£ 4,000,000		5 [3DM]		3D Modelling / Geometry
11%	£ 4,400,000		6 [3DH]		Engineering
12%	£ 4,800,000		7 [Eng]		Document Control

- Allocate time to drawings and assign resources.

Code	Task	Type				Resource				
01.00	**General | Project Start Up**				**0**					
01.01	Information Review / Handover / Technical Review	General	0 [Adm]	0		Design Manager	8.00	8.00	8.00	8.00
02.00	**General | Setting Out & Principle Detailing**				**0**					
02.01	Models / Grids / Building Lines / Levels / Sections	General	3 [2DH]	0		Senior Designer	8.00	8.00	8.00	8.00
03.00	**Design | Roof**	28			**27**					
03.01	Low Level Liner Layout	GA	2 [2DM]	1		Designer [Cladding]	2.00			
03.02	Low Level Top Hat & Clip Layout	GA	2 [2DM]	1		Designer [Cladding]	2.00			
03.03	Low Level Top Sheet Roof Plan	GA	2 [2DM]	1		Designer [Cladding]	2.00			
03.04	Low Level Gutter Support Layout	GA	2 [2DM]	1		Designer [Cladding]	2.00			
03.05	Low Level Gutter & Outlet Plan	GA	2 [2DM]	1		Designer [Cladding]		2.00		
03.06	High Level Liner Layout	GA	2 [2DM]	1		Designer [Cladding]		2.00		
03.07	High Level Top Hat & Clip Layout	GA	2 [2DM]	1		Designer [Cladding]		2.00		
03.08	High Level Top Sheet Roof Plan	GA	2 [2DM]	1		Designer [Cladding]		2.00		
03.09	High Level Gutter & Outlet Plan	GA	2 [2DM]	1		Designer [Cladding]			2.00	
03.10	High Level Gutter & Outlet Plan	GA	2 [2DM]	1		Designer [Cladding]			2.00	
03.11	Specification Sheet	Spec Drawing	2 [2DM]	1		Assistant Designer	2.00			2.00
03.12	Ridge Detail	Detail	2 [2DM]	1		Assistant Designer	2.00			2.00
03.13	Top Sheet Fixed Point Detail	Detail	2 [2DM]	1		Assistant Designer	2.00			2.00
03.14	High Level Eaves Detail [GL A & D]	Detail	2 [2DM]	1		Assistant Designer		2.00		
03.15	Low Level Eaves Detail [GL D]	Detail	2 [2DM]	1		Assistant Designer		2.00		
03.16	Low Level Eaves Detail [GL H]	Detail	2 [2DM]	1		Assistant Designer			2.00	
03.17	High Level Eaves Detail [GL 1 & 14]	Detail	2 [2DM]	1		Assistant Designer			2.00	
03.18	Low Level Eaves Detail [GL 1 & 14]	Detail	2 [2DM]	1		Designer [Cladding]				2.00
03.19	Outlet / RWP Connection Detail	Detail	2 [2DM]	1		Designer [Cladding]				2.00
03.20	Gutter Corner Detail	Detail	2 [2DM]	1		Designer [Cladding]				2.00

- To be costed appropriately to suit the specific rate.

PC | DESIGN DELIVERABLES

Resource	1	2	3	4	5	Total Days	Total Weeks	Weekly Rate	Cost
Design Manager	10.00	10.00	10.00	10.00	10.00	50.00	10.00	£ 1,644.15	£ 16,441.50
Senior Designer	5.00	5.00	5.00	5.00	5.00	25.00	5.00	£ 1,236.45	£ 6,182.25
Senior Designer	2.00	2.00	2.00	2.00	2.00	10.00	2.00	£ 968.70	£ 1,937.40
Senior Designer	2.00	2.00	2.00	2.00	2.00	10.00	2.00	£ 746.85	£ 1,493.70
Designer	5.00	5.00	5.00	5.00	5.00	25.00	5.00	£ 968.70	£ 4,843.50
Designer	3.00	3.00	3.00	3.00	3.00	15.00	3.00	£ 746.85	£ 2,240.55
Assistant Designer	5.00	5.00	5.00	5.00	5.00	25.00	5.00	£ 746.85	£ 3,734.25
Design Trainee	1.00	1.00	1.00	1.00	1.00	5.00	1.00	£ 572.60	£ 572.60
Structural Engineer	1.00	1.00	1.00	1.00	1.00	5.00	1.00	£ 1,644.15	£ 1,644.15
Sub-Contractor	2.00	2.00	2.00	2.00	2.00	10.00	2.00	£ 1,644.15	£ 3,288.30
Document Controller	2.00	2.00	2.00	2.00	2.00	10.00	2.00	£ 572.60	£ 1,145.20

Design budget – Bronze

- Look at historic projects.
- Review scope and take a view.
- Still never use a percentage.

Design budget – Silver

- Establish scope of work.
- Split design into GA – Elevations, GA – Plans, GA – Sections, Details, Construction Issue.
- Split scheduling into Sheet Lengths, 1st Fix Flashings / Materials / Fixings, Finishing Flashings / Materials / Fixings.

Design budget – Gold

- Full list of drawings.
- Establish complexity.
- Assign resources.

• Add costs to 'Sundry' items to build in contingency.

ID	Area / Drawing Title / Location	Type	Level	No. Drawings	Resource	Fix	Sub	Total Days	Total Weeks	Weekly Rate		Cost
	PC | DESIGN DELIVERABLES											
25.00	**Sundry | Design Management**			0								
25.01	Design Management / Meetings / Co-ordination [100%]	Sundry	0 [Adm]		Design Manager	90.00	90.00	90.00	12.00	£ 2,286.25	£	27,435.00
26.00	**Sundry | Contingency**			0								
26.01	Senior Design Manager [50%]	Sundry	0 [Adm]		Design Manager	40.00	40.00	40.00	6.00	£ 2,286.25	£	13,717.50
27.00	**Sundry | Engineering**			0								
27.01	Structural	Sundry	7 [Eng]		Structural Engineer	5.00	5.00					
27.02	Thermal	Sundry	7 [Eng]		Structural Engineer	5.00	5.00					
27.03	Acoustic	Sundry	7 [Eng]		Structural Engineer	5.00	5.00	15.00	3.00	£ 1,644.15	£	4,932.45
28.00	**Sundry | RFI's**			0								
28.01	Raising / Log onto Report / Further Action [2.5%]	Sundry	0 [Adm]		Design Manager	5.00	5.00	5.00	1.00	£ 2,286.25	£	2,286.25
29.00	**Sundry | Scheduling Updates**			0								
29.01	Checking & Reviewing Updates [2.5%]	Sundry	0 [Adm]		Design Manager	5.00	5.00	5.00	1.00	£ 2,286.25	£	2,286.25
30.00	**Sundry | BIM**			0								
30.01	BIM Co-ordination / Clash Detection / 3D Design	Sundry	0 [Adm]		Senior Designer	5.00	5.00	5.00	1.00	£ 1,549.25	£	1,549.25
31.00	**Sundry | Modelling**			0								
31.01	Co-ordination / 3D Design [2.5%]	Sundry	0 [Adm]		Senior Designer	5.00	5.00	5.00	1.00	£ 1,549.25	£	1,549.25
32.00	**Sundry | Administration**			0								
32.01	Internal Co-Ordination Meetings [Manager]	Sundry	0 [Adm]		Design Manager	5.00	5.00					
32.02	Internal Co-Ordination Meetings [Design Staff]	Sundry	0 [Adm]		Design Manager	5.00	5.00					
32.03	External Design Meetings [Manager]	Sundry	0 [Adm]		Design Manager	5.00	5.00					
32.04	External Design Meetings [Design Staff]	Sundry	0 [Adm]		Design Manager	5.00	5.00					
32.05	Design Report / Minutes / General	Sundry	0 [Adm]		Design Manager	5.00	5.00	25.00	5.00	£ 2,286.25	£	11,431.25
33.00	**Sundry | Operations & Maintenance Manual**			0								
33.01	Collating Information / Liaising With Suppliers / Issue	Sundry	2 [2DM]		Assistant Designer	5.00	5.00	5.00	1.00	£ 968.70	£	968.70
34.00	**Sundry | As-Built Drawings**			0								
34.01	Liaising With Site / Red Line Drawings / Issue	Sundry	2 [2DM]		Assistant Designer	5.00	5.00	5.00	1.00	£ 968.70	£	968.70
35.00	**Sundry | Additional Time For Façade Consultant**			0								
35.01	Additional Calculations / General Liaison	Sundry	0 [Adm]		Design Manager	5.00	5.00	5.00	1.00	£ 2,286.25	£	2,286.25
36.00	**Sundry | Additional Time For Design Protocols**			0								
36.01	Additional Documents / Forms / General Liaison	Sundry	0 [Adm]		Design Manager	5.00	5.00	5.00	1.00	£ 2,286.25	£	2,286.25
37.00	**Sundry | Contingency**			0								
37.01	General Contingency	Sundry	3 [2DH]		Designer	20.00	20.00	20.00	4.00	£ 1,236.45	£	4,945.80
38.00	**Sundry | Down Time**			0								
38.01	Inactive Design Time / Waiting Between Projects	Sundry	0 [Adm]		Senior Designer	20.00	20.00	20.00	4.00	£ 1,549.25	£	6,197.00

- Produce simple table showing costs using actual rates.

PC	DESIGN COSTS						
No.	**Name**	**Role**	**Hourly Rate**		**Weekly Cost**	
1	Pete Chandler	Design Director	£	79.15	£	3,166.00
2	Angela Chandler	Senior Designer	£	62.05	£	2,482.00
3	Matthew Chandler	Senior Designer	£	62.05	£	2,482.00
4	xxx	Senior Designer	£	62.05	£	2,482.00
6	xxx	Designer	£	47.72	£	1,908.80
7	xxx	Designer	£	47.72	£	1,908.80
8	xxx	Designer	£	47.72	£	1,908.80
9	xxx	Designer	£	47.72	£	1,908.80
10	xxx	Designer	£	47.72	£	1,908.80
12	xxx	Designer	£	47.72	£	1,908.80
15	xxx	Assistant Designer	£	28.45	£	1,138.00
16	xxx	Assistant Designer	£	28.45	£	1,138.00
15	xxx	Trainee Designer	£	18.96	£	758.40
18	xxx	Document Controller	£	18.17	£	726.80
			£	645.65	£	25,826.00

- Produce simple table showing costs using PC's inflated rates [next level up] to build in contingency.

	PC	DESIGN INFLATED COSTS			
No.	Role	Hourly Rate	Weekly Cost	Weekly Cost	Notes
1	Design Manager	£ 79.15	£ 3,166.00	£ 3,166.00	
4	Senior Designer	£ 62.05	£ 2,482.00	£ 3,166.00	
12	Designer	£ 47.72	£ 1,908.80	£ 2,482.00	
15	Assistant Designer	£ 28.45	£ 1,138.00	£ 1,908.80	
15	Trainee Designer	£ 18.96	£ 758.40	£ 1,138.00	
18	Structural Engineer	£ 18.17	£ 726.80	£ 3,166.00	Use rate as Design Manager
18	Specialist Subcontractor	£ 18.17	£ 726.80	£ 2,482.00	Use rate as Senior Designer
18	Document Controller	£ 18.17	£ 726.80	£ 758.40	
		£ 290.84	£ 11,633.60	£ 726.80	

Specification Review

- To be carried out electronically and worded appropriately for sending to a 3rd party.
- If document is only in PDF, then it must be converted to Word first and track changes.

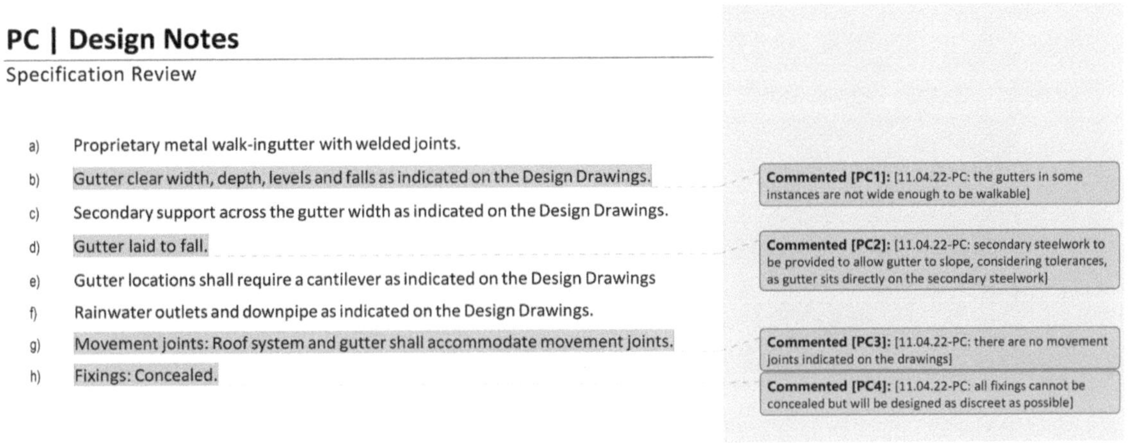

PC | Design Notes

Specification Review

a) Proprietary metal walk-in gutter with welded joints.

b) Gutter clear width, depth, levels and falls as indicated on the Design Drawings.

c) Secondary support across the gutter width as indicated on the Design Drawings.

d) Gutter laid to fall.

e) Gutter locations shall require a cantilever as indicated on the Design Drawings

f) Rainwater outlets and downpipe as indicated on the Design Drawings.

g) Movement joints: Roof system and gutter shall accommodate movement joints.

h) Fixings: Concealed.

Commented [PC1]: [11.04.22-PC: the gutters in some instances are not wide enough to be walkable]

Commented [PC2]: [11.04.22-PC: secondary steelwork to be provided to allow gutter to slope, considering tolerances, as gutter sits directly on the secondary steelwork]

Commented [PC3]: [11.04.22-PC: there are no movement joints indicated on the drawings]

Commented [PC4]: [11.04.22-PC: all fixings cannot be concealed but will be designed as discreet as possible]

- A full Specification and Document Commentary should be produced during the BID process and issued as part of the submittal. This must clearly identify where the business is not compliant.

					PC | DRAWINGS / DOCUMENT COMMENTARY		
ID	Document / Drawing Number	Revision No.	Drawing Status	Risk	Architects Comment	Subcontractor Response	Date

Door Schedule Review

- Ensure a Door Schedule is produced for all doors included in Scope of Works.
- Ensure that the Door Schedule meets exactly what has been priced.

PC | DOOR SCHEDULE

Door Location								General								Levers & Slots					Door rating				Security & Access Control		Ironmongery
Door Reference	Location	Room Function	Door Type	Blast	Interior Exterior	Material	Finishes	Sliding / Hinged	Operation	Clear	Steel Goal Post	Ventilation Grilles	Vision Panel	Push & Kick Plates	DDA Threshold	Configuration of Leaves	Opening	Clear Width	Clear Height	Panic Bar	Thermal Rating	Fire Rating	Acoustic (dB)	SR Rating	Access Control	Presence Detector	Set

Produce Glass Matrix and Summary Sheet

- Ensure photometrics are added.
- Ensure glass technical performance is added.

PC | GLASS SUMMARY SHEET

Glass Supplier										
Type								Notes:		
Description										
Specification	Outer Pane [mm]									
	Cavity [mm]									
	Inner Pane [mm]									

Ref:	Quantity	Location	Width	Height	m²	Ground Edge	Polished Edge	Total Edge Length	Weight kg/sq.m	Glass Unit Weight Kg

Glass Schedule Information

Estimated Area [m²]	G - Value	Light Transmission	U value W/m2K	Acoustic Rating dB	Barrier Load kN	Wind Load kN/m2	Snow Load kN/m2	Walkability	Blast Mitigation	Thermal risk		
										Required	Completed	Passed

Establish Fire Strategy

- Download drawings showing fire strategy, ensuring compartmentation is clearly understood.

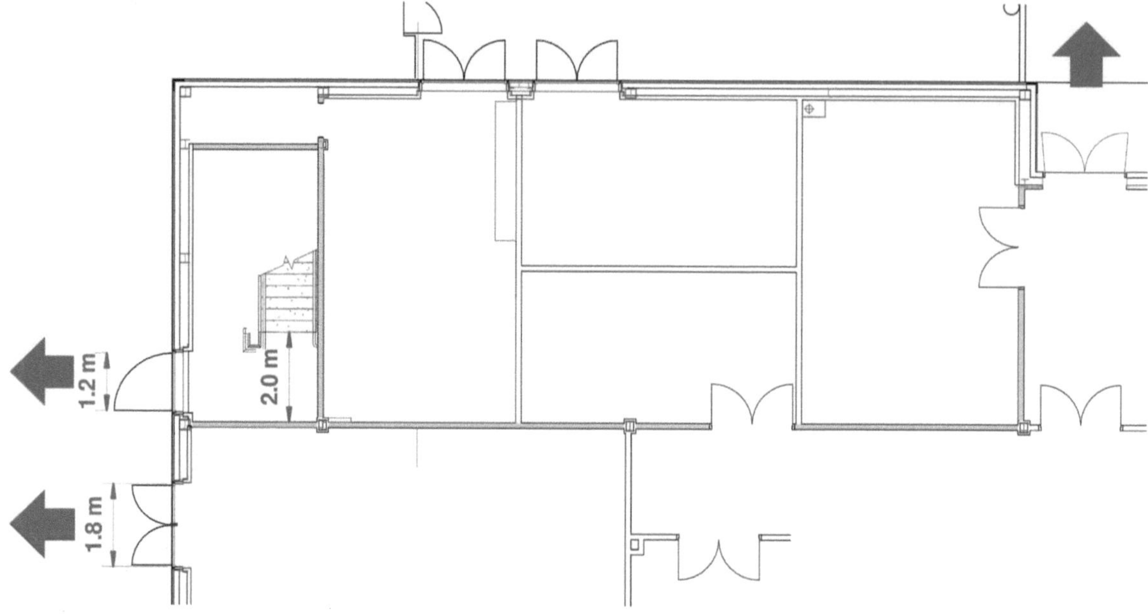

Glass and Panel Replacement Strategy

- An example is shown below:

PC | Design Notes

Ground Floor Curtain Walling [Externally Glazed]

All of the Curtain Walling areas are of the 'Capped' systems requiring feature cap and pressure plate removal. It is essential that the replacement unit is fully checked for quality and size before commencement.

The sequence of operation is as follows:

01   Make sure the area is safe and exclusion zones are in place in accordance with the approved Risk Assessments and Method Statements.

02   Remove any loose materials such as toughened glass granules.

03   Remove caps to transoms and mullions around the unit in question and set aside for reuse.

04   Remove mullion pressure plate screws and pressure plates sequentially and remove sealing tape, secure vertical sides of unit with temporary 'stitch' plates and place pressure plates and caps in a safe location for re-use.

05   Remove transom pressure plates as above ensuring stitch plates are in position.

06   Attach suitable electro-pneumatic lifting apparatus in accordance with agreed Risk Assessments and Method Statements to unit and 'pinch' up to take weight.

07   Remove perimeter 'stitch' plates to jams and head only with base plates eased off.

08   Allow top of unit to lean out at head past frame line.

09   Carefully lift unit out of glazing rebate to safe location and dispose of in accordance with the agreed Environmental Policy.

10   Check the frame for debris and/or damage particularly to in-situ grid gaskets and rectify if required.

11   Ensure glazing rebates are clear and glass setting block in position to receive replacement unit.

12   Insert replacement unit into rebate [ensuring orientation is correct] and onto setting blocks.

13   Ensure unit is fully back within rebate and setting blocks are not caught or gaskets nipped or folded.

14   Apply stitch plates round perimeter of unit and fully secure prior to removal of suckers.

15   Ensure unit is centralised within glazing rebate and sides parallel with mullions.

16   Apply new sealing tape to transoms and mullions ensuring correct lapping sequence [vertical over horizontal] and that holes are cut over drainage/ventilation mouldings.

17   Re-fix pressure plates sequentially removing stitch plates as you progress, pressure plate screws should be greased prior to insertion through tape to maintain weathering integrity.

18   Re-fit feature caps over pressure plates.

19   Remove any glass labels and clean down.

Produce and Issue Materials, Finishes & Testing Schedule

- An example is shown below:

No	Item	Speciation / Clause	Supplier	Product	Location	Material	Finish	Colour	Gloss Level	Fire Rating	Acoustic	U-value W/m2K	Barrier Loads	Impact	Warranty	Service life	Testing Requirements	Samples Required	Sample Issued	Signed Off

PC | MATERIALS, FINISHES & TESTING SCHEDULE

Establish Approval Process and Timescales

- The design approvals will typically be identified in the Contract documents. Some projects require two approval workflows.

PC | DESIGN & APPROVAL PROCESS

No.	Design Activity	Design Responsibility	–	–	–	–	–	–	1	2	3	4	5	6	7	8	9	–	–	–	–
1	Design GA's & Details	PC				Design Duration [varies]			P01 Issue												
2	Client Approval	Main Contractor							2 Weeks		Consultant Approval		Note: Status C's go to start of week 3								
3	Drawing Updates & Resubmission	PC									1 Week	Resubmission [P02]									
4	Client Approval	Main Contractor										2 Weeks		Consultant Approval							
5	Scheduling	PC										2 Weeks									
6	Client Approval	Client												2 Weeks		Client Approval [A & B Status Only]					
7	Update & Issue For Construction	PC														1 Week	Resubmission [C01]				
8	Final Client Approval	Main Contractor															1 Week	Final Approval			
9	Design Complete	–																★ Complete			

PC | DESIGN & APPROVAL PROCESS

No.	Design Activity	Design Responsibility	1	2	3	4	5	6	7	8	9	10	11	12	13	14	15	16	17	18	19	20	–
1	Review of Information	PC	1 Week																				
2	Initial Design	PC		Design Duration [varies]																			
3	Issue For Approval	PC										★											
4	Initial Client Approval / Design Workshop	Main Contractor											2 Weeks										
5	Initial Material Scheduling	PC											2 Weeks										
6	Receipt of Comments	Main Contractor												★									
7	Reservation of Key Materials	PC					10 Weeks																
8	Update Drawings	PC													2 Weeks								
9	Final Approval	Main Contractor															2 Week						
10	Scheduling	PC															2 Weeks						
11	Update Drawings For Construction	PC																	2 Weeks				
12	Issue For Construction	PC																	★				
13	Procurement	PC															6 Weeks						
14	Start on Site	PC																				★	

CDM Assessment

- It is the designer's responsibility to carry out a Design Assessment and CDM Assessment of the works. This should follow a strict process.

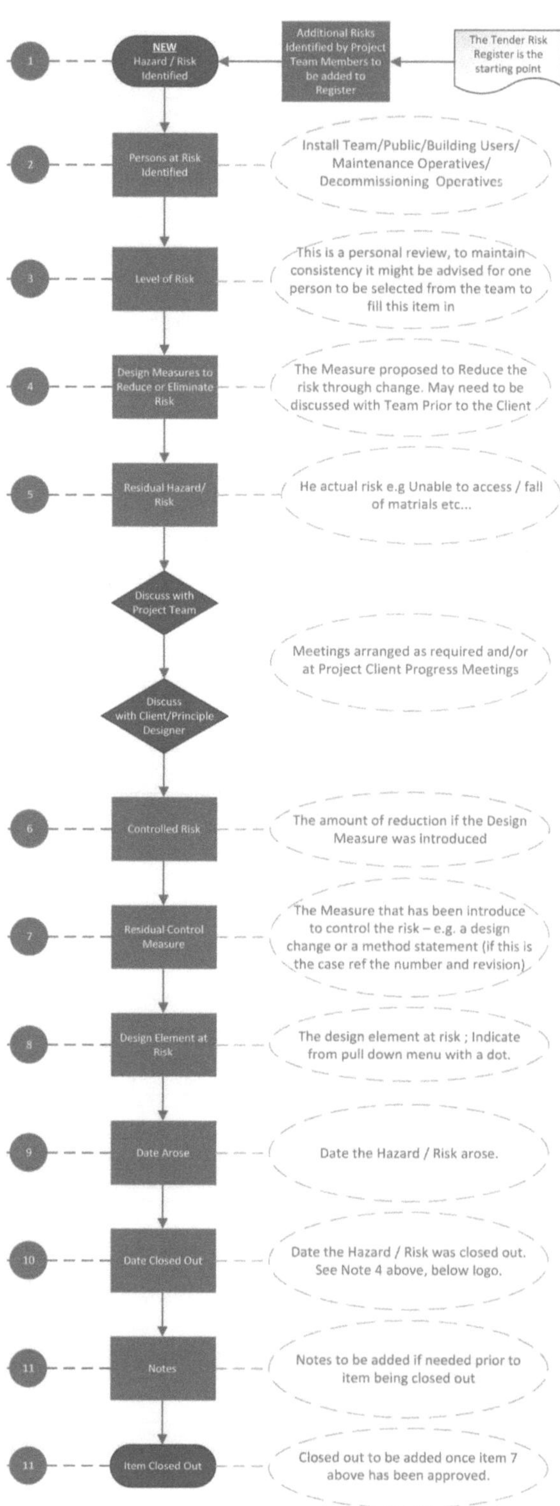

Identify In-House Manufacture

- An example is shown below:

ID	Item	Status	Anticipated On-Site	0.7-1.6mm Plain Galv	2.0-3.0mm Plain Galv	0.7mm Pre-Coated Coloured Steel	0.9-1.6mm Mill Finish Aluminium	2.0-3.0mm Mill Finish Aluminium	0.9mm Pre-Coated Coloured Aluminium	Mill Finish Aluminium Welded Bracket	PPC Finished Aluminium Welded units

PC | POTENTIAL IN HOUSE MANUFACTURE

3D Models

- 'Running track' around building for access.
- Hard standing for installation.
- Containers / site offices.
- Grid lines.
- North, East, South, West.
- Storage area / compound.

Risk Register

- A full Risk Register should be produced during the BID process and issued as part of the submittal. This must clearly identify where the business is not compliant with any documents and identify the risks through all disciplines.
- The Risk Register should be reviewed and updated during the progress of the project.

PC | RISK REGISTER

ID	Item	Location	Measured Risk	Risk Owner	Proposed Action	Open / Closed	Risk Implication [Cost / Programme]	Estimated Risk Value / Programme Implication

Marked-up Drawings

- A full set of scope drawings should be produced during the BID process and issued as part of the submittal.
- Where there are significant deviations on scope, setting out or sight lines, these should be identified.

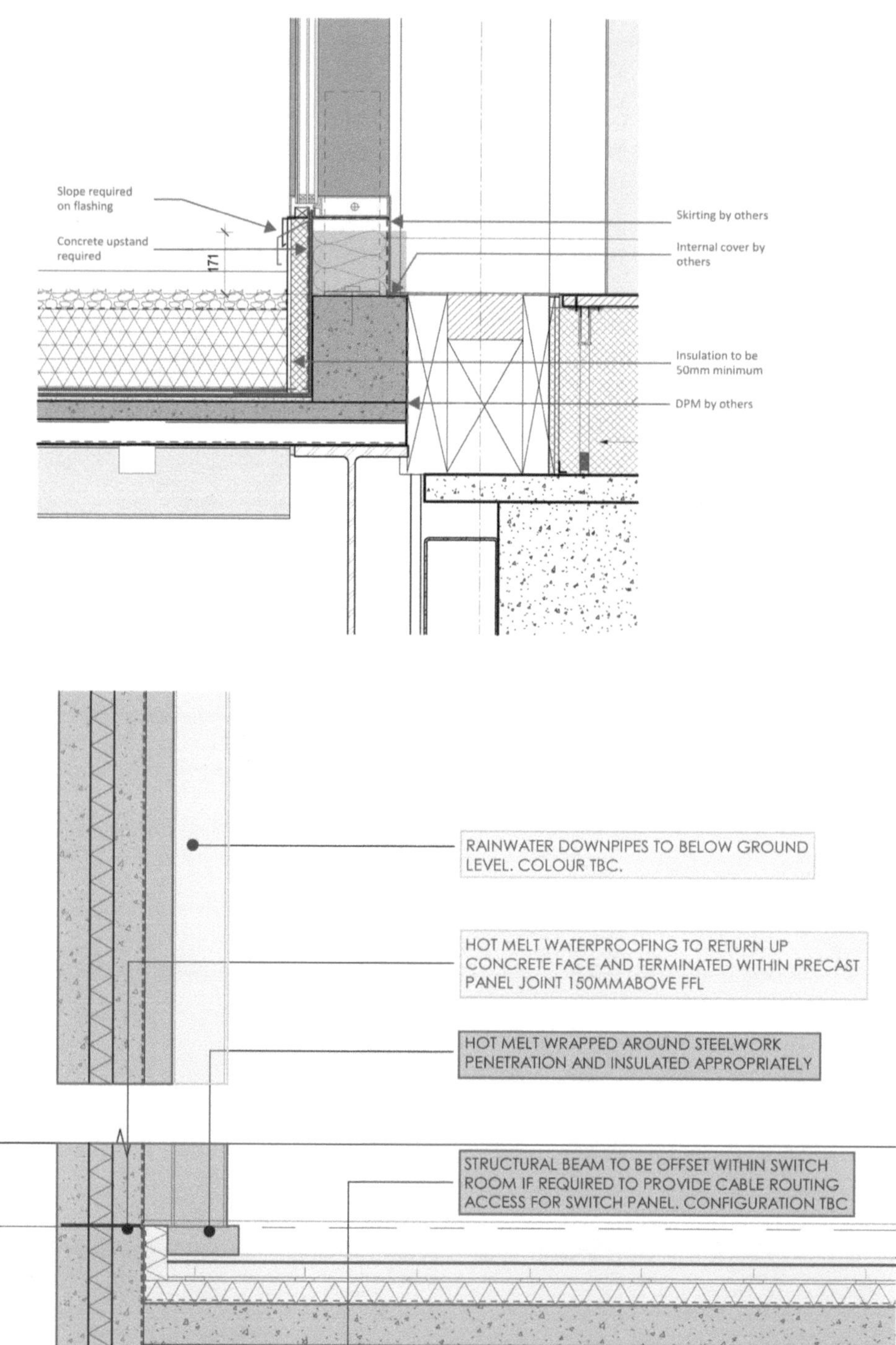

Technical Queries

- Technical queries [TQs] are to be used at Pre-Construction stage.

<table>
<tr><td colspan="5" align="center">PC | TECHNICAL QUERY</td></tr>
<tr><td align="center">Contract No.</td><td align="center">Area</td><td align="center">No.</td><td colspan="2" align="center">Revision</td></tr>
<tr><td></td><td></td><td></td><td colspan="2"></td></tr>
<tr><td colspan="3" align="center">Project Name</td><td colspan="2"></td></tr>
<tr><td colspan="3"></td><td colspan="2"></td></tr>
<tr><td colspan="1.5" align="center">Originator</td><td align="center">Issue Date</td><td colspan="2" align="center">Response Required By</td></tr>
<tr><td></td><td></td><td colspan="2"></td></tr>
<tr><td colspan="2" align="center">Issued To</td><td colspan="3" align="center">Copied To</td></tr>
<tr><td colspan="2"></td><td colspan="3"></td></tr>
</table>

Query

Should the request information not be received by the date indicated, the following may be incurred:

☐ Programme Implications   ☐ Cost Implications

Client Response

From [Name]	Company	Position	Signature	Date

STEELWORK REVIEW

Introduction

- Steelwork design is a critical interface with our works; it is a critical interface that needs to be addressed as soon as possible, typically during an ECI, PCSA or Early Works Order. More often than not we are involved with both the MEP contractor and steelworker at this early stage of a project.

- The steelwork design is a critical interface with the building envelope works and needs to be addressed as soon as possible. The collaboration between us will ensure that key aspects of the interfacing elements are carefully considered, and the steelwork is designed to accommodate the building envelope.

- We will endeavour to identify all missing steelwork by working with the engineer in respect of the building envelope, however, this is a much more efficient and successful process with the steelworker who is on board to deliver the works.

- The steelwork will be reviewed on the basis of the Tender Information available. Whilst we will endeavour to identify all missing steelwork required in respect of the building envelope, we cannot be held responsible for any additional elements that have been missed or found to be required.

- Engaging with a steelwork subcontractor brings a wealth of experience from other projects and will mitigate the risk of missing elements, potentially rationalise the steelwork requirements and develop off-site opportunities.

Primary / Secondary / Tertiary Steelwork

- Primary Steel – everything without which the building will not stand up. Typically this means columns, rafters and bracing in steel construction.

- Secondary Steel – everything that holds something up [provides "structure"] but is not crucial to the building's structural integrity. Typically this means side rails, purlins, cleader angles, ledger angles to hold roofing, cladding and facades. It is also various structural steel that holds up secondary elements like canopies.

- Tertiary Steel – has no significant influence on the integrity of the structure. Typically this means stairs, floor grating, line and level. The Tertiary steelwork comprises of light gauge material typically 2.0mm to 4.0mm thick galvanised steel or aluminium. It is often top hats, back-to-back angles or channels to allow for line and level of the external façade system.

SECONDARY STEEL

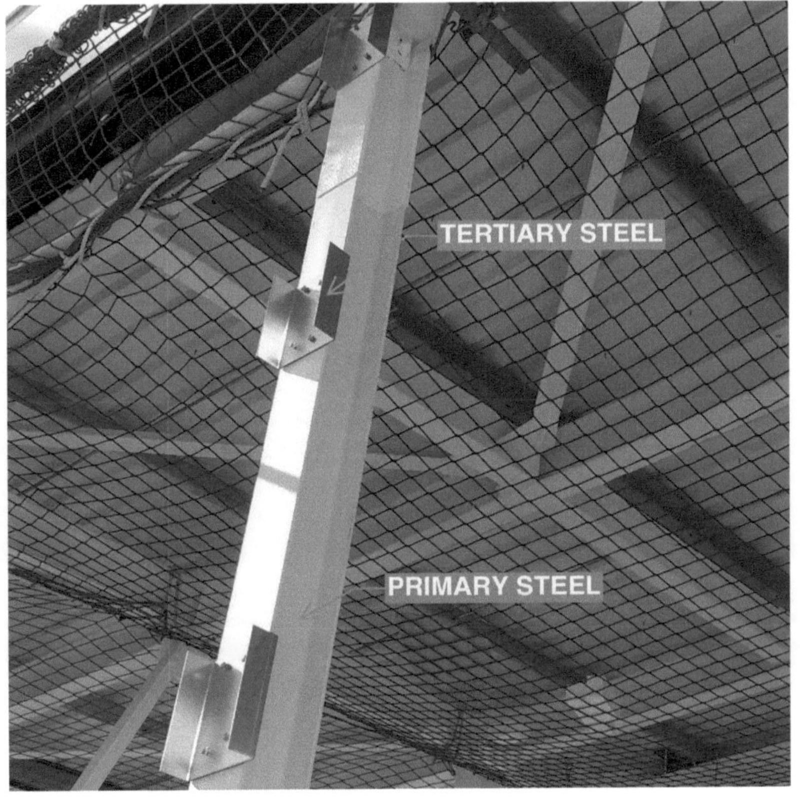

TERTIARY STEEL
PRIMARY STEEL

High Level Setting Out

- Prior to the commencement of any steelwork review it is critical that modules, setting out, corners and zones are established for ALL elements of the façade.

- Steelwork member sizes, dead loads, imposed loads, wind loads, live loads will be determined by the Clients' Structural Engineer.

- Minimum face sizes, bearing requirements, orientation, SHS / RHS or PFC can be identified by us.

Method of Review

- 01 – Mark up of Architectural elevations [can also be plans and section drawings].

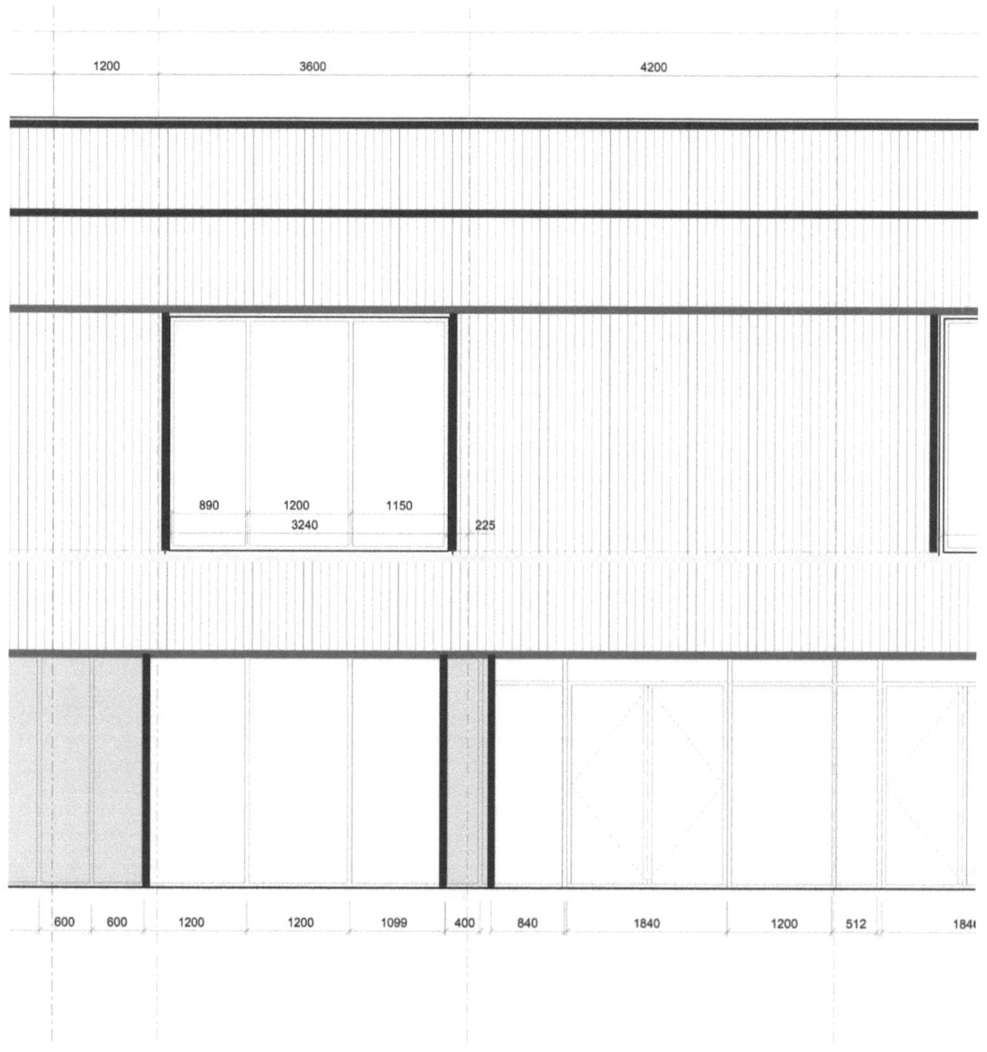

- 02 – Mark up of Engineers elevation [can also be plans, sections and detail drawings].

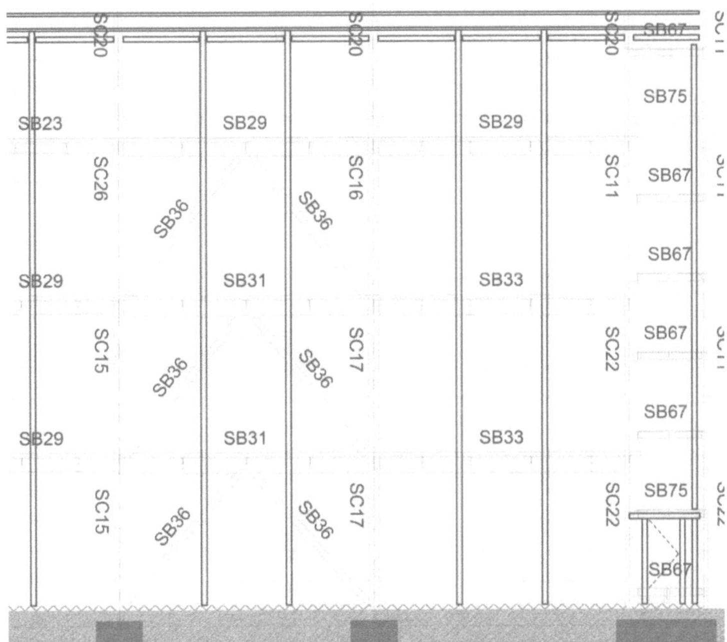

- 03 – Use of 3D software and provide images of all junctions and areas where steel will be required.

PC | Steelwork Review

Project Example

15 | Cladding

- Rails required to form soffit of piers, note columns extend below soffit steels

16 | Cladding

- Steelwork required around freight doors

PROCESSES AND PROCEDURES

Design Process

- Ensure a robust, tried and tested process is in place and that all staff have been trained in use of the systems.

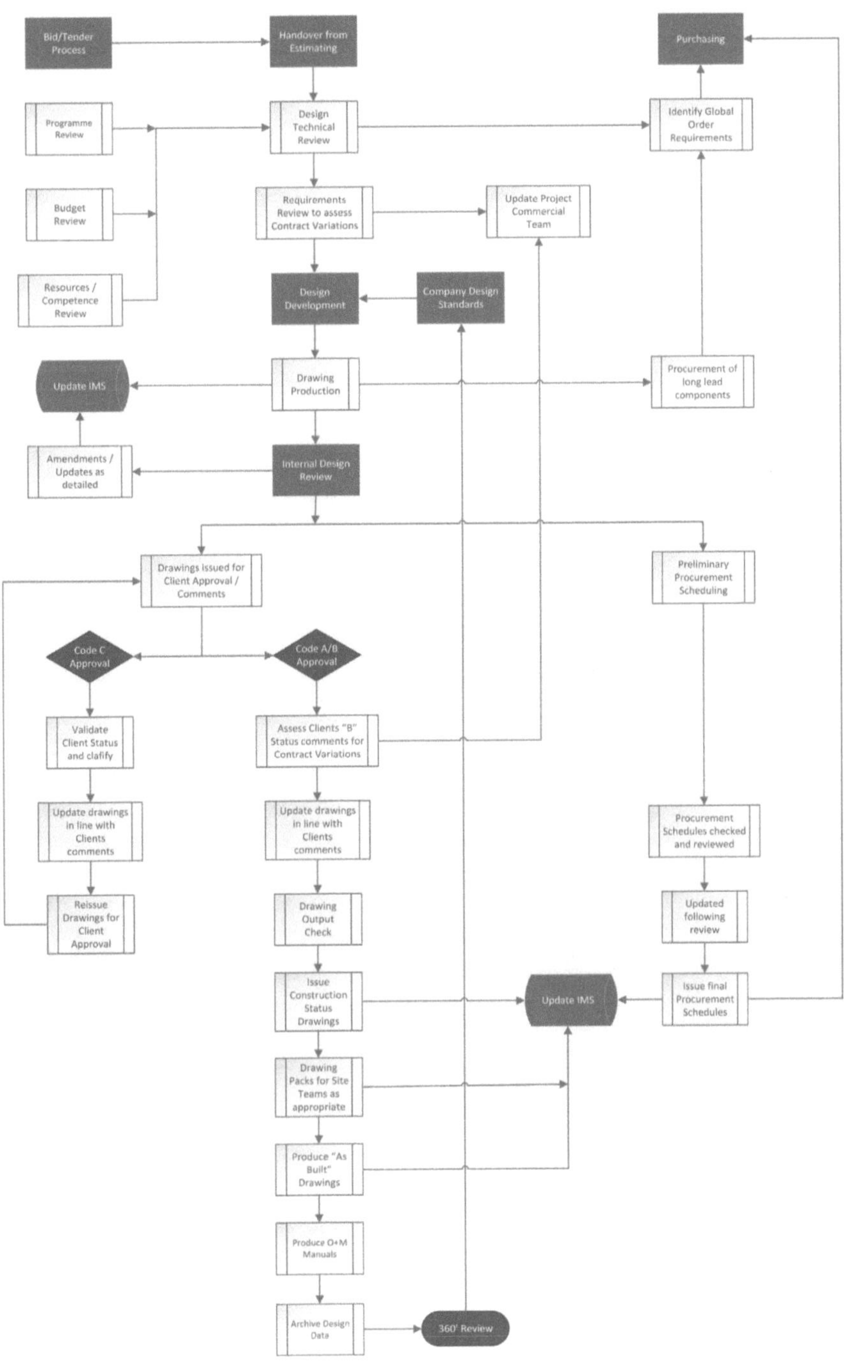

- Cross reference policies, procedures and forms within the Process.

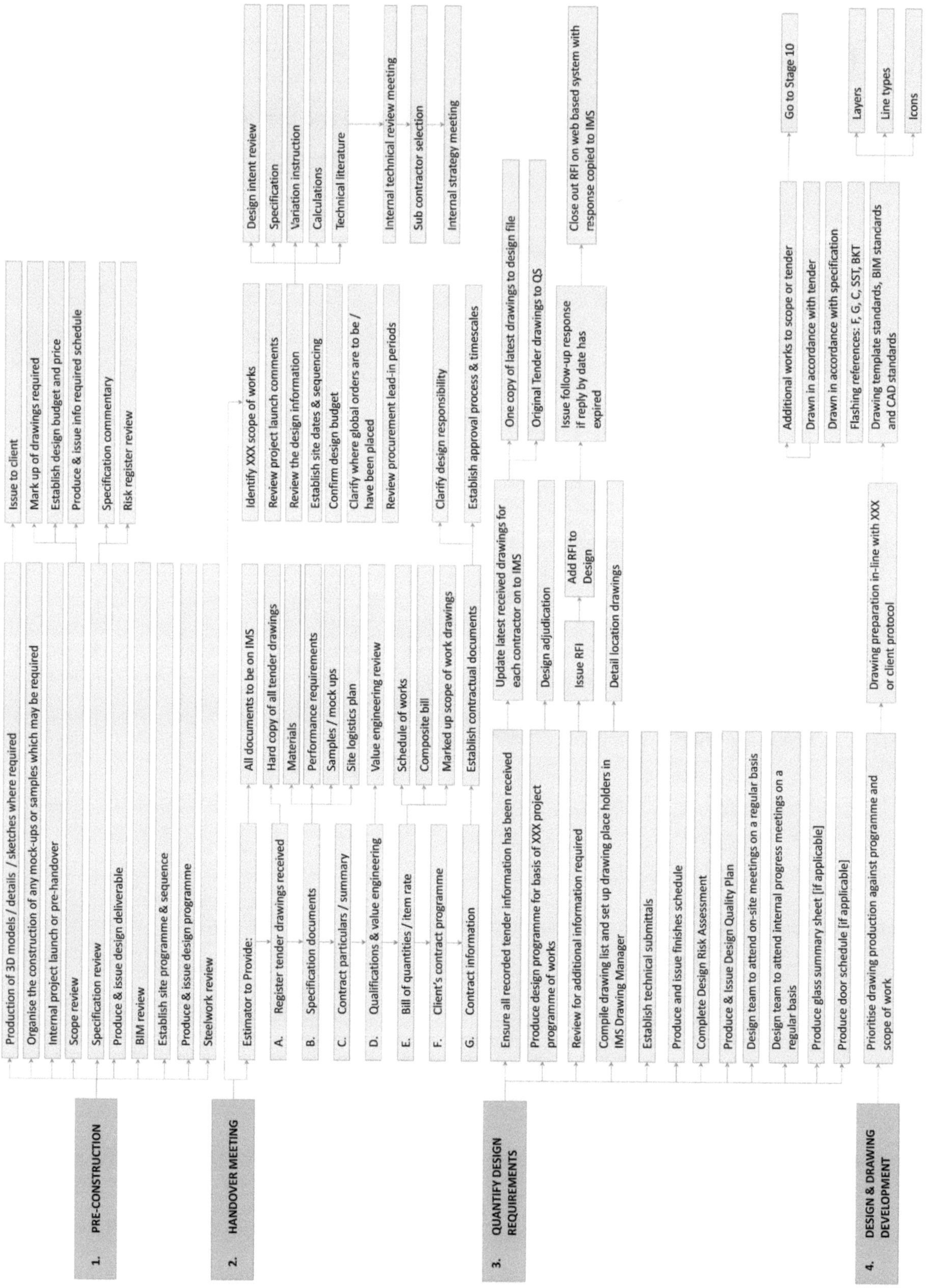

1. PRE-CONSTRUCTION

- Production of 3D models / details / sketches where required
- Organise the construction of any mock-ups or samples which may be required
- Internal project launch or pre-handover
- Scope review
- Specification review
- Produce & issue design deliverable
- BIM review
- Establish site programme & sequence
- Produce & issue design programme
- Steelwork review

  - Issue to client
  - Mark up of drawings required
  - Establish design budget and price
  - Produce & issue info required schedule

  - Specification commentary
  - Risk register review

2. HANDOVER MEETING

- Estimator to Provide:
  - A. Register tender drawings received
  - B. Specification documents
  - C. Contract particulars / summary
  - D. Qualifications & value engineering
  - E. Bill of quantities / item rate
  - F. Client's contract programme
  - G. Contract information

  - All documents to be on IMS
  - Hard copy of all tender drawings
  - Materials
  - Performance requirements
  - Samples / mock ups
  - Site logistics plan
  - Value engineering review
  - Schedule of works
  - Composite bill
  - Marked up scope of work drawings
  - Establish contractual documents

  - Identify XXX scope of works
  - Review project launch comments
  - Review the design information
  - Establish site dates & sequencing
  - Confirm design budget
  - Clarify where global orders are to be / have been placed
  - Review procurement lead-in periods

  - Clarify design responsibility
  - Establish approval process & timescales

  - Design intent review
  - Specification
  - Variation instruction
  - Calculations
  - Technical literature

  - Internal technical review meeting
  - Sub contractor selection
  - Internal strategy meeting

3. QUANTIFY DESIGN REQUIREMENTS

- Ensure all recorded tender information has been received
- Produce design programme for basis of XXX project programme of works
- Review for additional information required
- Compile drawing list and set up drawing place holders in IMS Drawing Manager
- Establish technical submittals
- Produce and issue finishes schedule
- Complete Design Risk Assessment
- Produce & Issue Design Quality Plan
- Design team to attend on-site meetings on a regular basis
- Design team to attend internal progress meetings on a regular basis
- Produce glass summary sheet [if applicable]
- Produce door schedule [if applicable]

  - Update latest received drawings for each contractor on to IMS
  - Design adjudication
  - Issue RFI
  - Detail location drawings

    - Add RFI to Design
    - Issue follow-up response if reply by date has expired

  - One copy of latest drawings to design file
  - Original Tender drawings to QS
  - Close out RFI on web based system with response copied to IMS

4. DESIGN & DRAWING DEVELOPMENT

- Prioritise drawing production against programme and scope of work

  - Drawing preparation in-line with XXX or client protocol

  - Additional works to scope or tender
  - Drawn in accordance with tender
  - Drawn in accordance with specification
  - Flashing references: F, G, C, SST, BKT
  - Drawing template standards, BIM standards and CAD standards

    - Go to Stage 10

    - Layers
    - Line types
    - Icons

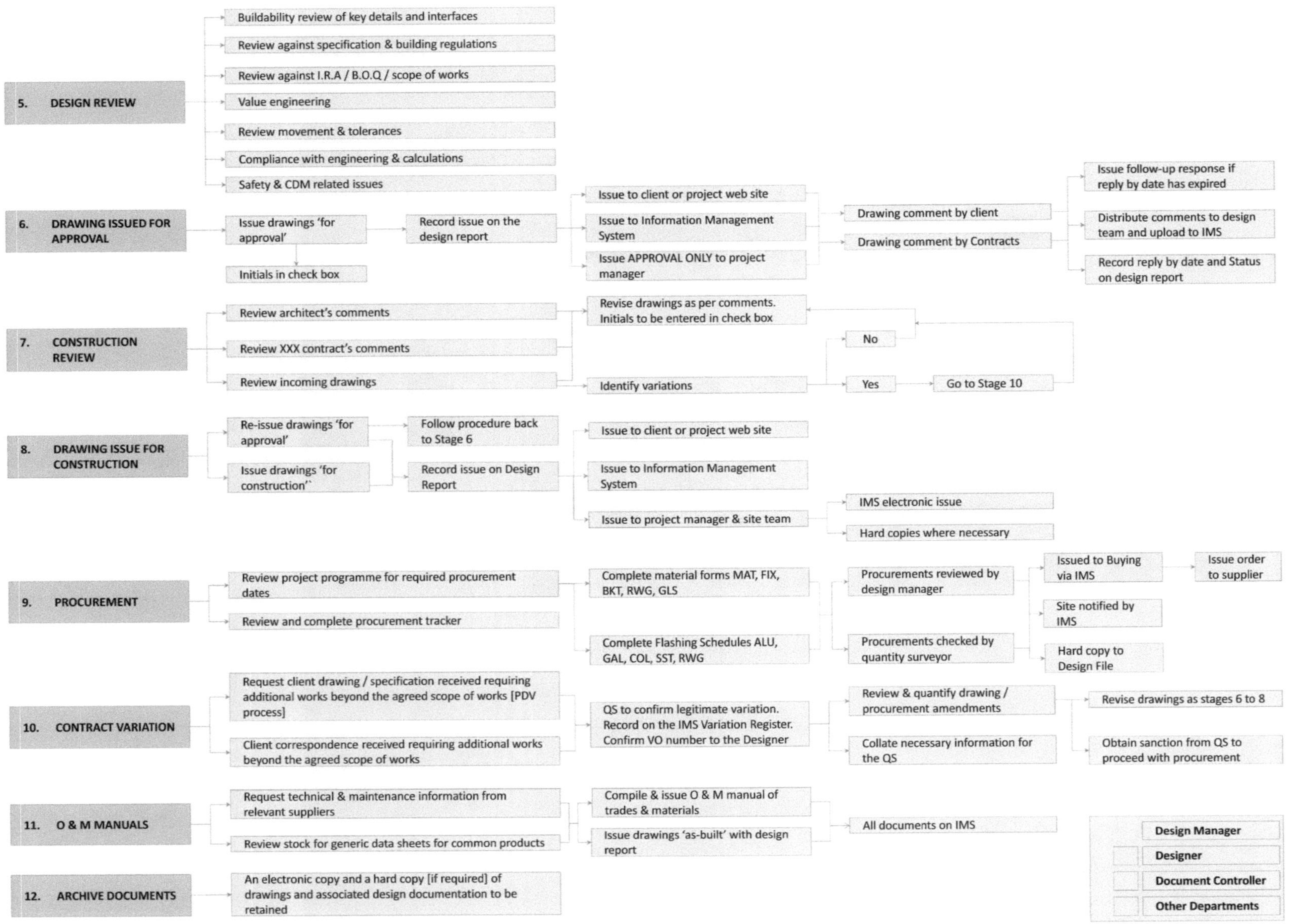

5. DESIGN REVIEW
Buildability review of key details and interfaces
Review against specification & building regulations
Review against I.R.A / B.O.Q / scope of works
Value engineering
Review movement & tolerances
Compliance with engineering & calculations
Safety & CDM related issues

6. DRAWING ISSUED FOR APPROVAL
Issue drawings 'for approval'
Initials in check box
Record issue on the design report
Issue to client or project web site
Issue to Information Management System
Issue APPROVAL ONLY to project manager
Drawing comment by client
Drawing comment by Contracts
Issue follow-up response if reply by date has expired
Distribute comments to design team and upload to IMS
Record reply by date and Status on design report

7. CONSTRUCTION REVIEW
Review architect's comments
Review XXX contract's comments
Review incoming drawings
Revise drawings as per comments. Initials to be entered in check box
Identify variations
No
Yes
Go to Stage 10

8. DRAWING ISSUE FOR CONSTRUCTION
Re-issue drawings 'for approval'
Issue drawings 'for construction''
Follow procedure back to Stage 6
Record issue on Design Report
Issue to client or project web site
Issue to Information Management System
Issue to project manager & site team
IMS electronic issue
Hard copies where necessary

9. PROCUREMENT
Review project programme for required procurement dates
Review and complete procurement tracker
Complete material forms MAT, FIX, BKT, RWG, GLS
Complete Flashing Schedules ALU, GAL, COL, SST, RWG
Procurements reviewed by design manager
Procurements checked by quantity surveyor
Issued to Buying via IMS
Site notified by IMS
Hard copy to Design File
Issue order to supplier

10. CONTRACT VARIATION
Request client drawing / specification received requiring additional works beyond the agreed scope of works [PDV process]
Client correspondence received requiring additional works beyond the agreed scope of works
QS to confirm legitimate variation. Record on the IMS Variation Register. Confirm VO number to the Designer
Review & quantify drawing / procurement amendments
Collate necessary information for the QS
Revise drawings as stages 6 to 8
Obtain sanction from QS to proceed with procurement

11. O & M MANUALS
Request technical & maintenance information from relevant suppliers
Review stock for generic data sheets for common products
Compile & issue O & M manual of trades & materials
Issue drawings 'as-built' with design report
All documents on IMS

12. ARCHIVE DOCUMENTS
An electronic copy and a hard copy [if required] of drawings and associated design documentation to be retained

Design Manager
Designer
Document Controller
Other Departments

Process Mapping

- Ensure robust processes are in place for all systems and process within the Department.

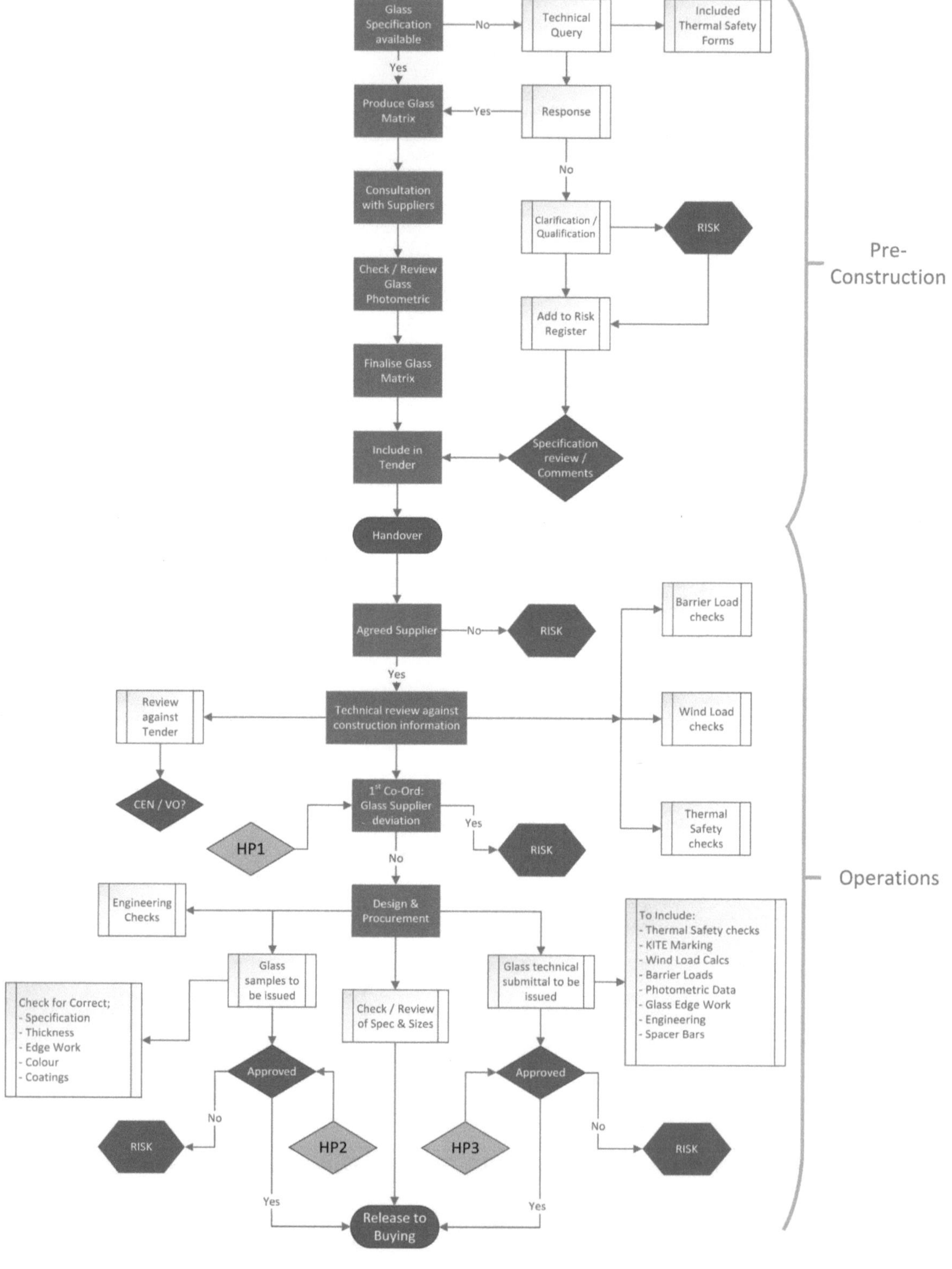

- This should all be part of the overall company ISO documentation and certification.

Mind Mapping

- The use of mind maps is a quick, easy, efficient and professionally looking document to aid in the development of policies, processes and systems.

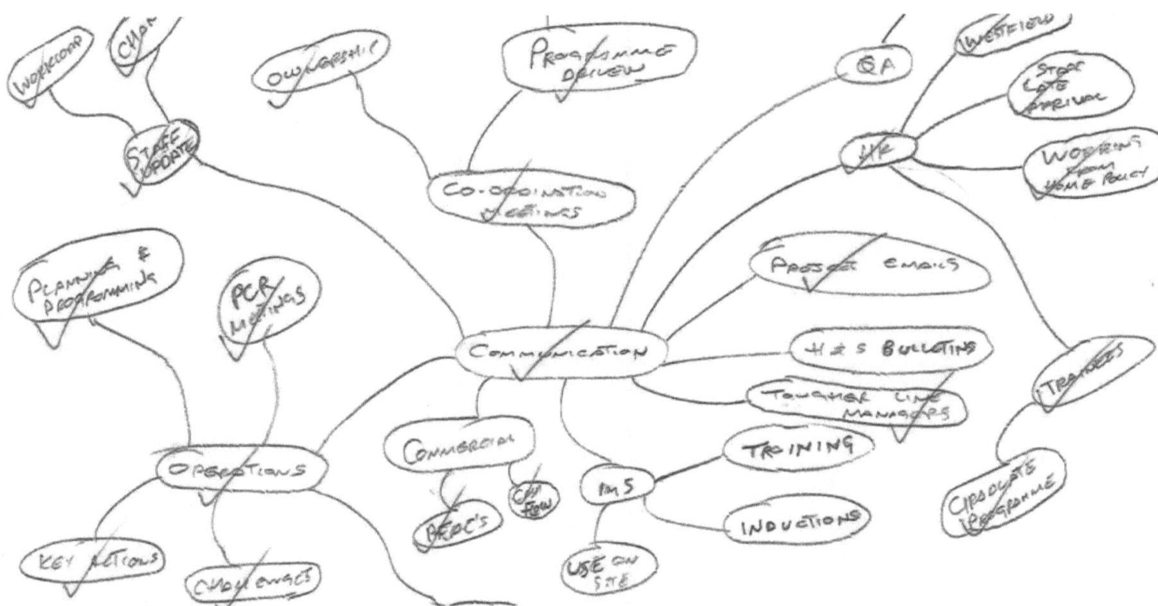

- Hand produced mind maps van be created electronically which allows them to updated easily.

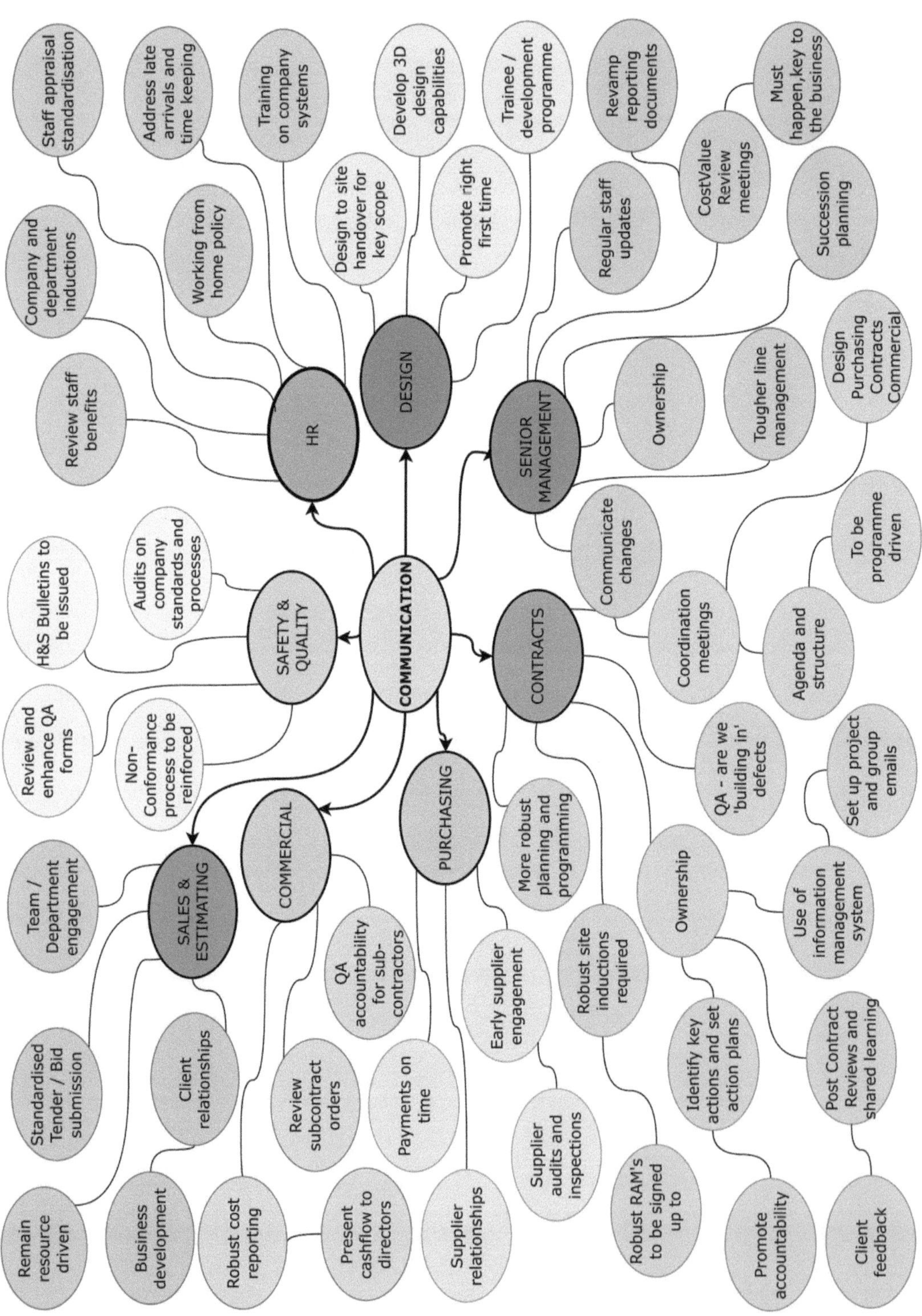

Building Information Modelling [BIM] / 3D Strategy

- Ensure there is a Building Information Modelling [BIM] process.

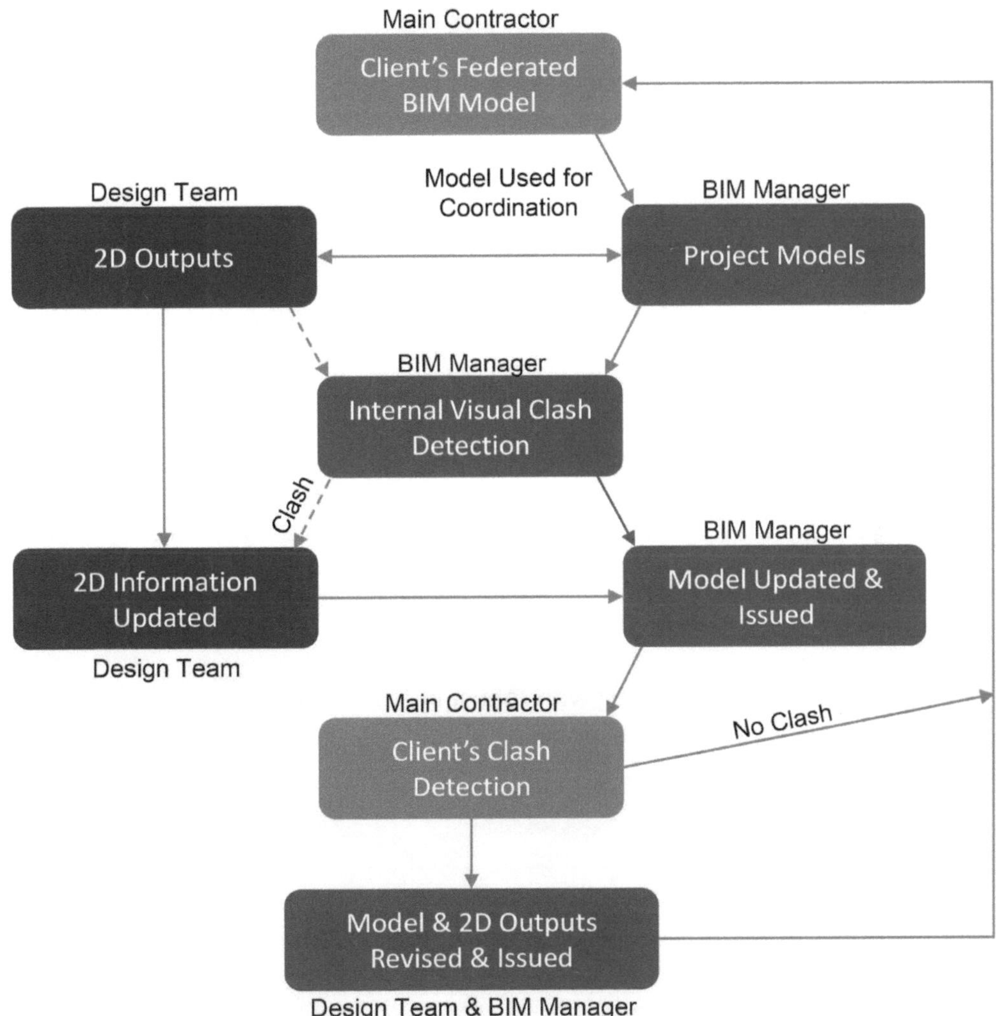

Timesheets

- Ensure timesheets accurately reflect the work being done by the team, with correct time being allocated to the correct projects along with day notes providing additional information.

PC | Design Notes

Timesheets

Notes | Project 1

- Reviewing and updating design report / reviewing and updating programme / reviewing procurement tracker / reviewing and checking of drawings and schedules / project coordination meeting / management of the design team / general correspondence / internal weekly team meeting.

Notes | Project 2

- Liaising with the roof design team / internal roof progress meeting / checking of roof sheet lengths / review design deliverables / review programme / drop line programme / site visit / QA review.

- Time booked to variations, along with robust notes, is critical to future evidence, potential design claims and cost recovery.

PC | TIMESHEET								
User								
Week								
Project	Analysis	Mon	Tue	Wed	Thu	Fri	Sat	
Overtime	Analysis	Mon	Tue	Wed	Thu	Fri	Sat	
Overhead	Analysis	Mon	Tue	Wed	Thu	Fri	Sat	
	Total							

Storage of Information

- Ensure the design information is stored correctly in pre-defined folder set up. This needs to be consistent across all projects.

PC | Design Notes

Folder Structure

01 Tender Information
- 01.01 Tender Marked Up Drawings
- 01.02 Item Rate Analysis / Bill of Quantities
- 01.03 Handover Information
- 01.04 Tender Specification & Commentary
- 01.05 Tender Risk Register
- 01.06 Tender Drawings

02 Programmes
- 02.01 Construction Programme
- 02.02 Design Programme

03 Design Reporting
- 03.01 Design Reports
- 03.02 Design Notes
- 03.03 Design Tracker
- 03.04 Procurement Tracker

04 Drawings
- 04.01 Drawings
- 04.02 Architects Drawings & 3D Models
- 04.03 Engineers Drawings & 3D Models
- 04.04 Steelwork Drawings & 3D Models
- 04.05 M & E Drawings & 3D Models
- 04.06 Transmittals
- 04.07 Client Protocols
- 04.08 BIM

05 Request for Information
- 05.01 Tender TQ's
- 05.02 RFI's Sent
- 05.03 RFI's Received

06 Design QA Documents
- 06.01 Quality Plan - Project Quality Plan
- 06.02 CDM
- 06.03 Material Compliance Records - Technical Submittal
- 06.04 QA Templates
- 06.05 Specification
- 06.06 Fire Strategy

07 Calculations
- 07.01 Calculations issued
- 07.02 Calculation approval - sign off sheets
- 07.03 Engineering Requests

08 Samples
- 08.01 Samples Issued
- 08.02 Sample approval forms

09 Meeting Minutes
- 09.01 Design Meeting Minutes
- 09.02 Co-Ordination Meeting Minutes
- 09.03 Subcontractor Meeting Minutes

10 Photos
In reverse date order i.e. 22.07.06_Site Visit

11 Commercial
- 11.01 Design Potential Variations
- 11.02 Client Instructions
- 11.03 Site Instructions
- 11.04 Early Warning Notices

12 Procurements
- 12.01 ALU – Aluminium Flashings
- 12.02 BKT – Brackets
- 12.03 COL – Coloured Flashings
- 12.04 FIX – Fixing Schedules
- 12.05 GAL – Galvanised Flashings
- 12.06 GLS – Glass Schedules
- 12.07 MAT – Material Schedules
- 12.08 RWG – Rain Water Goods
- 12.09 SST – Stainless Steel Flashings
- 12.10 ASM – Assembly Drawings
- 12.11 SMP – Samples
- 12.12 GLO – Global Orders

13 Technical Information
Split into different products and systems i.e. metal roof, flat roof etc.

14 Operations & Maintenance Manual
- 14.01 Manual
- 14.02 As-Built Drawings

15 Compliance
- 15.01 R & D
- 15.02 NCR's
- 15.03 QA Records

16 Construction
- 16.01 Health & Safety
- 16.02 Meetings
- 16.03 Programmes
- 16.04 Progress Reporting
- 16.05 Labour
- 16.06 Plant
- 16.07 Quality
- 16.08 Correspondence
- 16.09 Project Closedown

Drawing Process

- Ensure CAD standards and drawing processes are in place. Create Company specific blocks and design information. The drawing process, and sometimes CAD standards, need to be in accordance with the Clients' own systems.

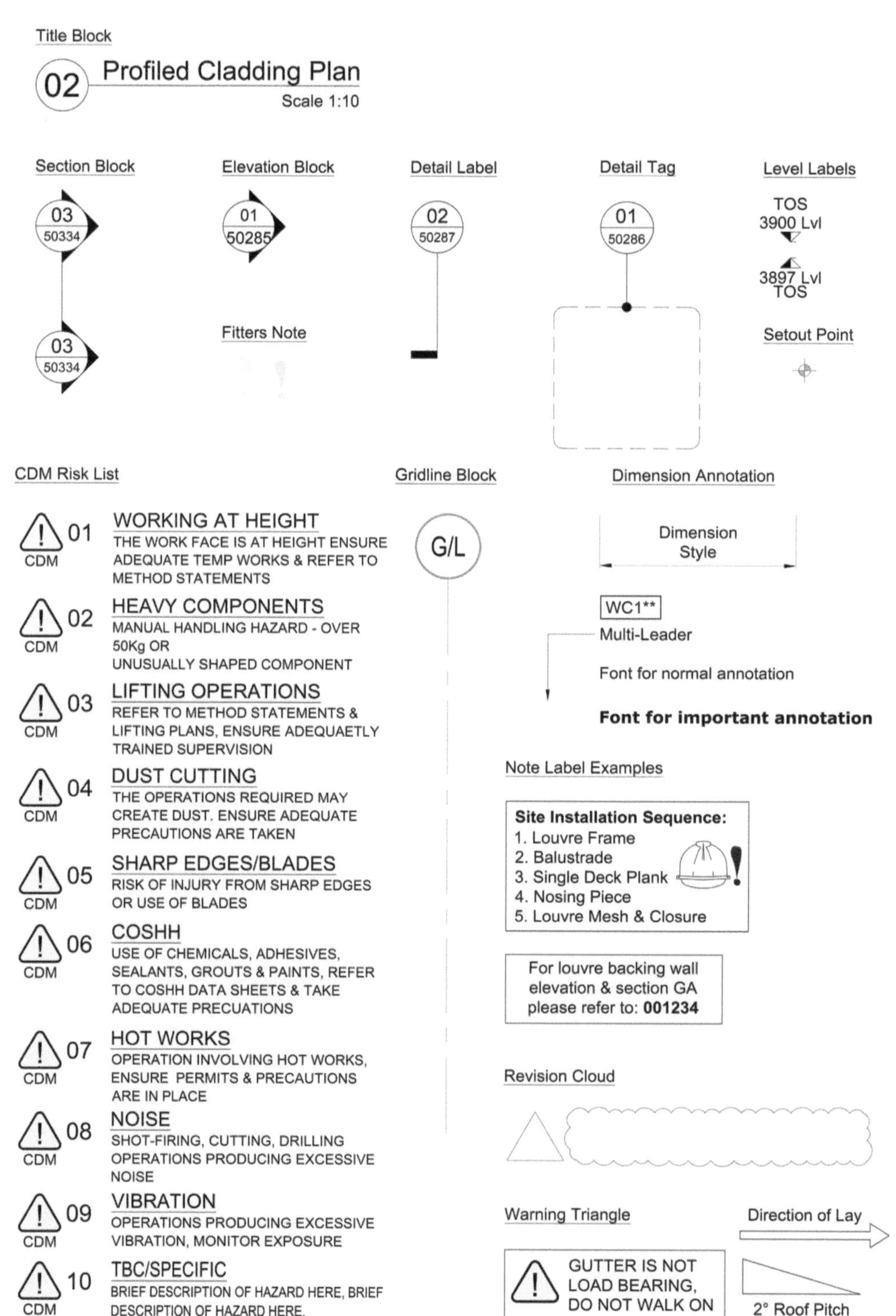

Engineering

- Ensure there is a robust engineering process.

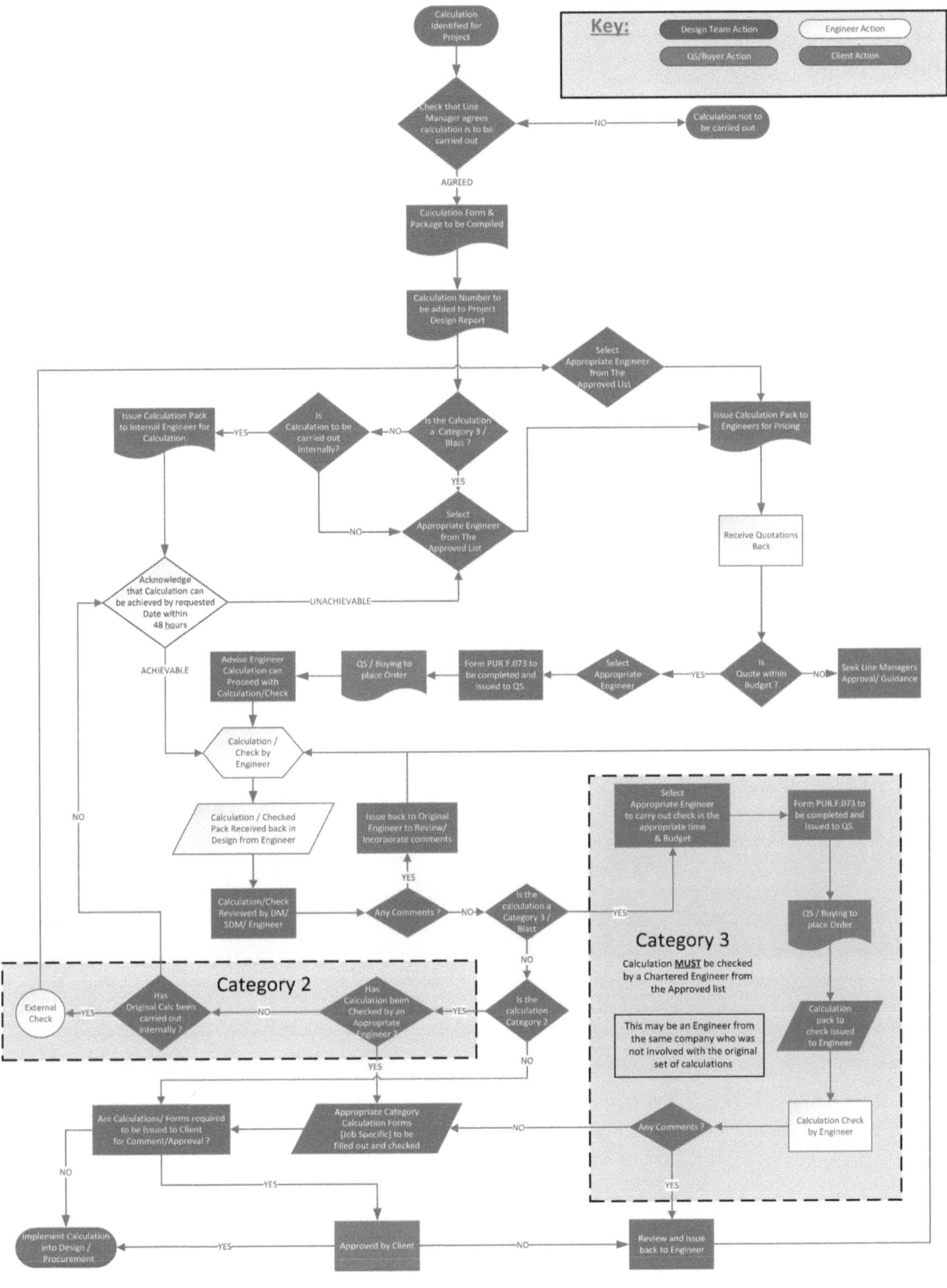

- Ensure an engineering brief is used on all projects.

PC | Design Notes

Engineering Brief

Brief / Scope

- Structural engineering is required for a stainless-steel door cowl within the glazed façade.

Information Provided

- Drawings 1001, 1002, 1003, 2001 and 2002.

Key Information

- There are two door cowls but both are exactly the same in respect of design. They are however, on different elevations so the appropriate wind loads must be considered.

- Cowls are formed from 15mm mild steel, grade to be confirmed by the engineer. All joints are to be fully welded, with either a 6mm fillet weld, or part penetration butt weld, or a combination of both.

- The cowls are base loaded and cantilevered from the Level 5 slab. The cowls are not fixed to the glazed barrier due to movement and are to be self-supporting.

- Note: the full calculation is to be provided with a summary of the final design. All fixing specifications, types and frequencies must be provided using drawing extracts from the information provided as visual confirmation.

- If you don't clearly identify the engineering requirements, then don't expect to get the results you need!

PROJECT SET UP

Resource Forecast

- Overall resourcing is key to the design office.
- The resource forecast allows accurate weekly planning with automated cost awareness.

PC | DESIGN RESOURCE FORECAST

No.	Name	Role	Project	Scope	Design Resource Cost [Week]	No. of Design Weeks	Total Design Cost
1	Pete Chandler	Design Director	Pre-Construction	Management	£ -	0.0	£ -
1	Pete Chandler	Design Director	Project 1	Management	£ -	0.0	£ -
1	Pete Chandler	Design Director	Project 2	Management	£ -	0.0	£ -
2	Matthew Chandler	Senior Designer	Project 1	Roof	£ -	0.0	£ -
2	Matthew Chandler	Senior Designer	Project 2	Soffit	£ -	0.0	£ -
3	Angela Chandler	Designer	Project 1	Walls	£ -	0.0	£ -
3	Angela Chandler	Designer	Project 2	Balconies	£ -	0.0	£ -
4	Designer 1	Designer	Project 1	Roof	£ -	0.0	£ -
4	Designer 1	Designer	Project 2	Cladding	£ -	0.0	£ -
5	Designer 2	Designer	Project 1	Glazing	£ -	0.0	£ -
5	Designer 2	Designer	Project 2	Glazing	£ -	0.0	£ -
				Total Resource Allocation	£ -	0.00	£ -

Weekly forecast calendar (week number / week-commencing date):

June 2023	23 (05/06/2023), 24 (12/06/2023), 25 (19/06/2023), 26 (26/06/2023)
July 2023	27 (03/07/2023), 28 (10/07/2023), 29 (17/07/2023), 30 (24/07/2023), 31 (31/07/2023)
August 2023	32 (07/08/2023), 33 (14/08/2023), 34 (21/08/2023), 35 (28/08/2023)
September 2023	36 (04/09/2023), 37 (11/09/2023), 38 (18/09/2023), 39 (25/09/2023)
October 2023	40 (02/10/2023), 41 (09/10/2023), 42 (16/10/2023), 43 (23/10/2023), 44 (30/10/2023)
November 2023	45 (06/11/2023), 46 (13/11/2023), 47 (20/11/2023), 48 (27/11/2023)
December 2023	49 (04/12/2023), 50 (11/12/2023), 51 (18/12/2023), 52 (25/12/2023)

Resource Organogram

- Overall departmental organograms.

Design Office Organogram

Overall

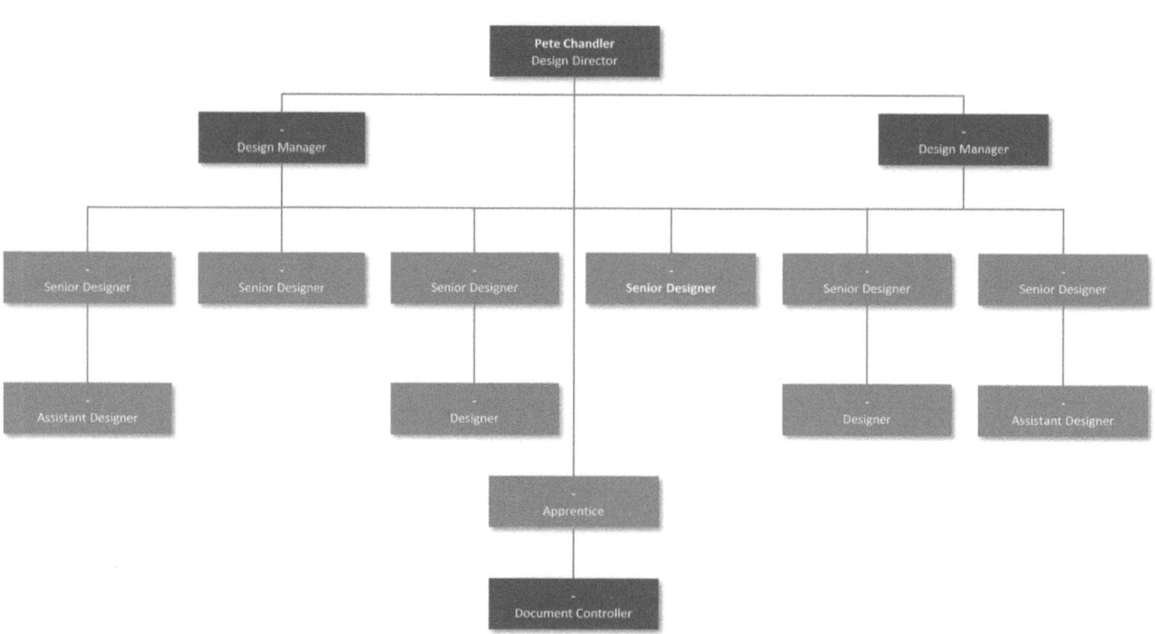

- These should be produced at project level to ensure the suitable level of the individual resource, and with the right skill set, is allocated accordingly.

Design Office Organogram

Project 1

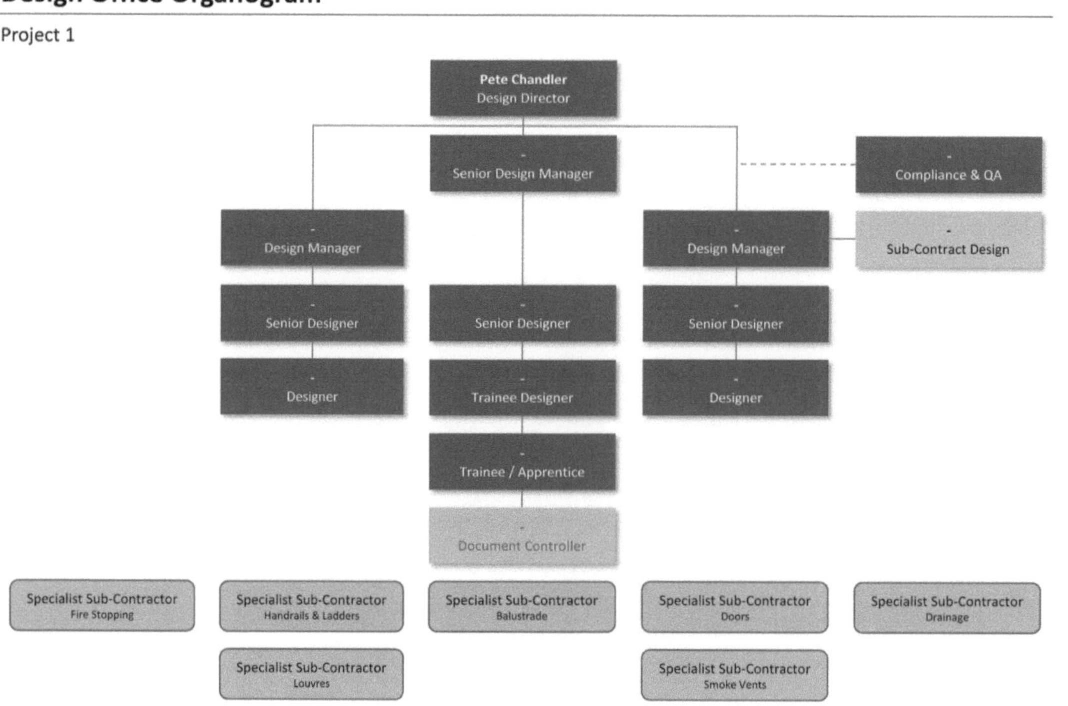

Technical Handover

- Ensure a full technical handover is carried out on all projects so everyone in the team understands what has been included in the BID.

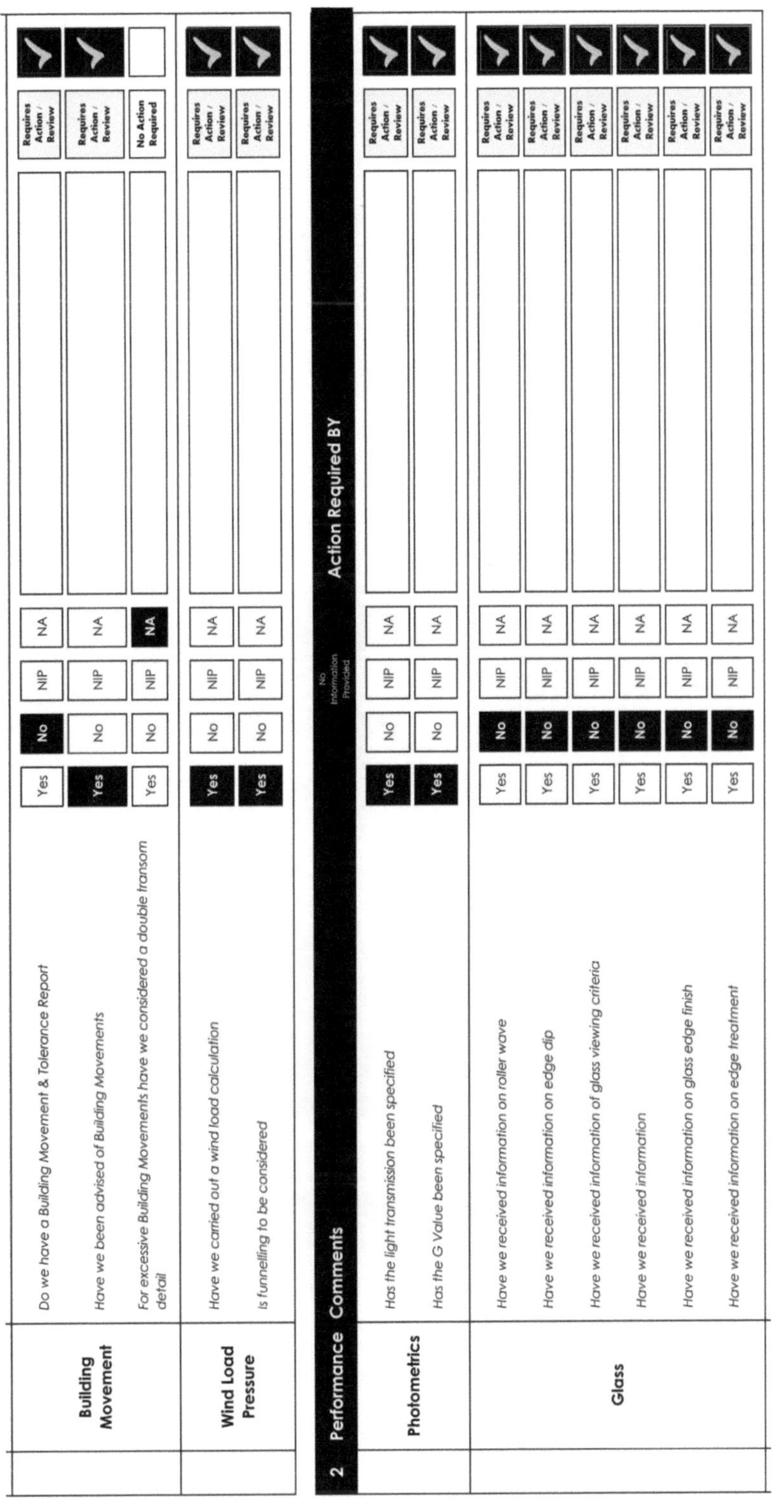

		Yes	No	NIP (No Information Provided)	NA	Action Required BY	Status
Building Movement	Do we have a Building Movement & Tolerance Report	Yes	**No**	NIP	NA		Requires Action / Review ✓
	Have we been advised of Building Movements	**Yes**	No	NIP	NA		Requires Action / Review ✓
	For excessive Building Movements have we considered a double transom detail	Yes	No	NIP	**NA**		No Action Required
Wind Load Pressure	Have we carried out a wind load calculation	**Yes**	No	NIP	NA		Requires Action / Review ✓
	Is funnelling to be considered	**Yes**	No	NIP	NA		Requires Action / Review ✓

2	Performance	Comments	Yes	No	NIP (No Information Provided)	NA	Action Required BY	Status
	Photometrics	Has the light transmission been specified	**Yes**	No	NIP	NA		Requires Action / Review ✓
		Has the G Value been specified	**Yes**	No	NIP	NA		Requires Action / Review ✓
	Glass	Have we received information on roller wave	Yes	**No**	NIP	NA		Requires Action / Review ✓
		Have we received information on edge dip	Yes	**No**	NIP	NA		Requires Action / Review ✓
		Have we received information of glass viewing criteria	Yes	**No**	NIP	NA		Requires Action / Review ✓
		Have we received information	Yes	**No**	NIP	NA		Requires Action / Review ✓
		Have we received information on glass edge finish	Yes	**No**	NIP	NA		Requires Action / Review ✓
		Have we received information on edge treatment	Yes	**No**	NIP	NA		Requires Action / Review ✓

Design Responsibility Matrix

- Ensure the project is split up so managers, design leads and resources can be assigned appropriately.

ID	Element	Sub-Area	Spec / Type	Brief Description	Quant [From Tender]		Approximate Cost		Materials	Design Lead	Internal Design Resource	External Design Resource	Design & Supply Sub-Contractor	Design, Supply & Install Sub-Contractor	Design Budget	
															PC | DESIGN RESPONSIBILTY MATRIX	
01	Roof	Roof	-	Metal roof	5184	m^2	£	-		Designer 1					£	-
02	Roof	Fascia's	-	Aluminium Fascia	456	Lm.	£	-		Designer 1					£	-
03	Main Building	Cladding	-	Aluminium Rainscreen	1880	m^2	£	-		Designer 2					£	-
04	Main Building	Curtain Walling	-	Curtain Walling	276	m^2	£	-		Designer 2					£	-
05	Main Building	Fire Stops	-	Fire Stopping to floor slabs	670	Lm.	£	-		Designer 2					£	-
06	Roof	Doors	-	Steel Doors	9	No.	£	-		Designer 3					£	-
07	Main Building	Doors	-	Glazed Doors	1	Item	£	-		Designer 3					£	-
08	Main Building	GRC	-	Cladding	1194	m^2	£	-		Designer 4					£	-
09	Main Building	GRC	-	Soffit	284	m^2	£	-		Designer 4					£	-
10	Other	3D	-	3D / BIM	-	-	£	-		Designer 5					£	-
11	Engineering	Structural	-	Structural Calculations	-	-	£	-		Other					£	-
12	Engineering	Thermal	-	Thermal Calculations	-	-	£	-		Other					£	-
															£	-

- It is taken to the next level if the design budget can be split into the same packages so the expenditure can be monitored in smaller parts.

- The Design Responsibility Matrix will show the percentage of work allocation.

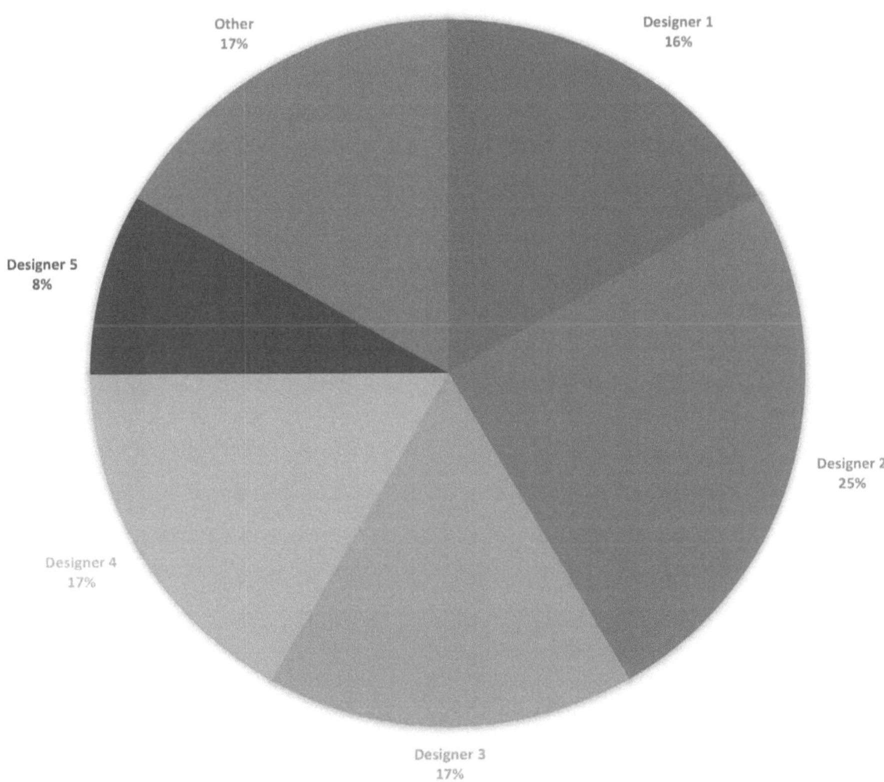

Information Required Schedule [IRS]

- Ensure an Information Required Schedule [IRS] is produced with clearly defined dates.

IRS No	Programme ID	Priority	Information Description	Date Required	Comments	Date Received	Closed Out

PC | INFORMATION REQUIRED SCHEDULE [IRS]

- It is taken to the next level if this is aligned with the project programme.

Key Facts

- Identifying key facts on larger projects helps the design team focus on decisions-making. For example, there may be several kilometers of flashings, which is better in one piece than two.

<table>
<tr><td rowspan="7" style="writing-mode: vertical-rl;">PROJECT 1 | KEY FACTS</td><td>STANDING SEAM ROOF
0.9mm thick | Aluminum Mill Finish</td><td>5500 m²</td></tr>
<tr><td>FLAT ROOFING
Tapered Insulation | Single Ply</td><td>2300 m²</td></tr>
<tr><td>CLADDING
200mm thick | 1000mm module | Silver</td><td>3600 m²</td></tr>
<tr><td>CLADDING
200mm thick | 1000mm module | Grey</td><td>2300 m²</td></tr>
<tr><td>SOFFIT - HORIZONTAL
3.0mm thick | PPC Silver Aluminium</td><td>5000 m²</td></tr>
<tr><td>CURTAIN WALLING
Capped | 25 double glazed units</td><td>1300 m²</td></tr>
<tr><td>WINDOWS
Single Vents | Top Hung Open Out</td><td>110m² [34 No.]</td></tr>
</table>

Activity Schedule

- Generally, an Activity Schedule is used during a Pre-Construction Service Agreement [PCSA], an Early Contractor Involvement [ECI] to identify activities to be carried during the period.

- Activity Schedules are also used to monitor design progress. This is often directly related to costs and payments are typically made upon 100% completion of the design activity.

Item	Description	Scope of Works & Activity Schedule
1	General	Contribute to the development of the detailed design in accordance with the design team definition and the Employer's requirements.
2	General	Undertake procurement activities necessary to formulate the cost plan and programme deliverables and from a supply chain of the requisite skill and capability for a project of this scale and complexity.
3	General	Contractor is to offer advice and guidance how to optimise the design for programme and construction efficiency and to minimise waste.
4	General	Fully integrate the use of BIM for the procurement and construction process and develop the BEP for the construction phase.
5	Design	Produce a package interface schedule, ensuring that all interfaces are identified and design solutions developed such that all works can be efficiently procured and completed by any one of the sub-contractors.
6	Design	Propose a schedule and release of information from relevant members of the Employer's team consistent with the programme for the procurement or market testing of sub-contract packages.
7	Design	Reviewing the specifications and designs for compliance with Site safety requirements and sound construction practice, and reporting regularly to the Employer.
8	Design	Attending such meetings that may be reasonably called by the Employer and promoting additional meetings where it considers the same to be necessary.
9	Design	Leading and developing a construction tolerance document for the project to be co-ordinated with the design team.
10	Design	Appraise the design information and highlight issues of design, cost, programme, value and risk that the Contractor considers will require active management.
11	Design	Investigate and report on the availability and relative suitability of alternative materials and components, methods of working and building systems including the time capital and lifecycle cost implications.
12	Design	Discuss and agree with the design team the engagement of your supply chain in the design development process. In particular this will be required with your specialist materials manufacturers and other specialists.
13	Design	Finalise design and testing proposals in accordance with the programme and demonstrate how this will be achieved.
14	Design Assist Period	Contribute fully and comply with the Employer's protocols in terms of issuing information, commenting upon drawings, calculations, modelling and likewise services.
15	Design Assist Period	Ensure that design engineering considerations include risks to safety of people In the Project and working on it. Provide information about any aspects of design affecting safety.
16	Design Assist Period	Pre-construction programme.
17	Design Assist Period	Logistic Planning & Methodology [including labour & material].
18	Design Assist Period	Select materials and systems in accordance with design intent, drawings and specifications. Provide advice on their durability, performance and any specialist testing requirements. Produce sample schedule.
19	Design Assist Period	DfMA and prefabrication strategy.
20	Design Assist Period	Develop Package Risk register.
21	Design Assist Period	Prepare risk assessments covering the envelope design in respect of current CDM Legislation.
22	Design Assist Period	Review and comment on the Access, Cleaning and Maintenance strategy for the installations, to include feedback on safe and efficient solutions for maintenance, including material replacement for the building.
23	Design Assist Period	Review and comment on the Structural Engineer's Movements and Tolerances Reports with particular emphasis on expansion and contraction implications.
24	Design Assist Period	Review and comment on all related fire performance criteria contained within the Specifications and Reports.
25	Design Assist Period	Review and comment on all supporting specialists reports [e.g. acoustic criteria] contained within the Specifications and Reports, Comment upon/provide advice on documents issued for any services related.
26	Design Assist Period	Assist in producing the Materials Replacement Strategy document in consultation with the Architect and Structural Engineer. Provide Risk Assessments & Method Statements Attend all necessary design meetings.

- Ensure phrases such as assist, advise, help and develop are used.

- Avoid phrases such as design or produce.

Scope Mark Up

- Once design roles and responsibilities are defined, scope mark ups need to be created. This is best carried out using Work Sets within 3D models [i.e. roofing, cladding, doors and glazing].

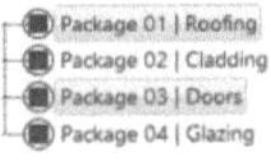

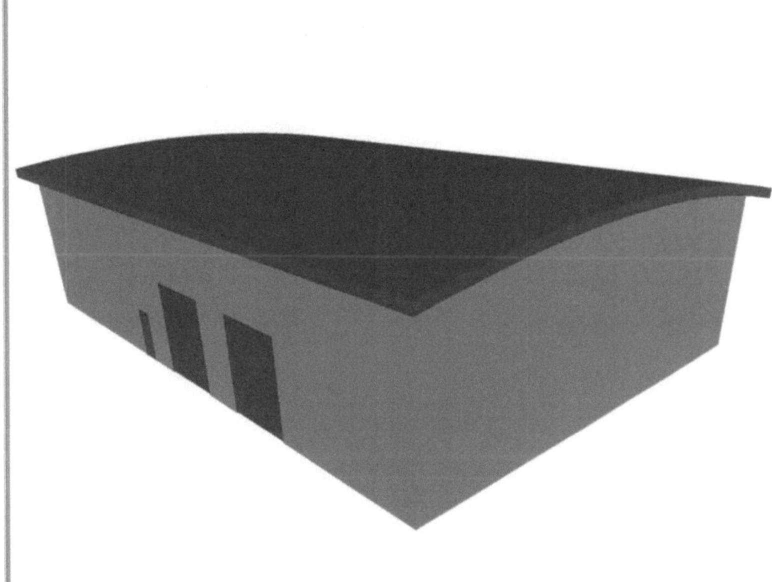

- This should be further developed by creating resource scope mark ups.

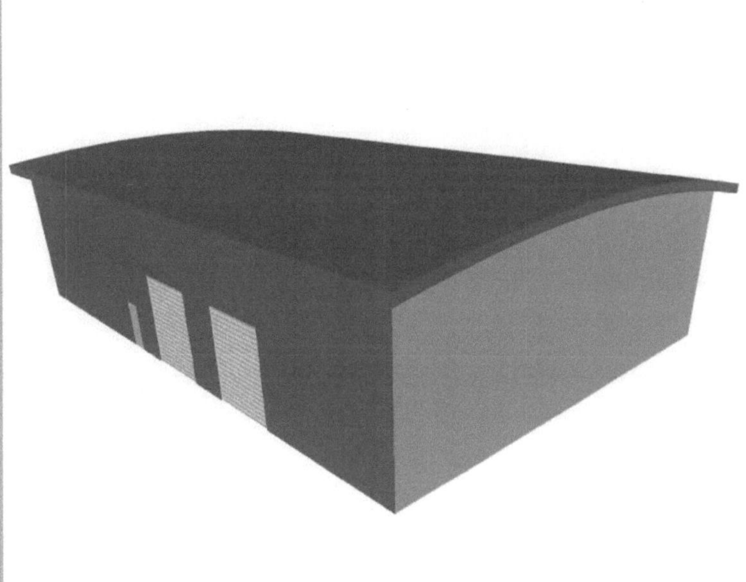

- This will also allow you to highlight specific items by isolating them and hiding everything else [i.e. doors].

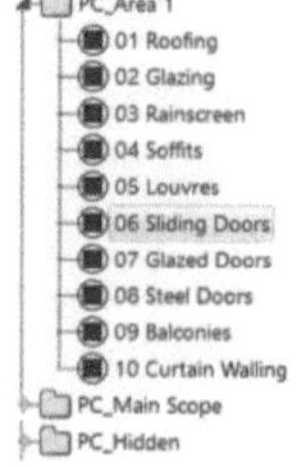

- This will then allow you to do an automated take-off of the items.

PC | WORK BREAKDOWN STRUCTURE & TAKE OFF									
Work Breakdown Structure [WBS]	Item	Object	Width	Width Units	Height	Height Units	Count	Count Units
1	**DRS-210 (KP) - 1810X2260 - Single Swing - Levers**		14.48	m	18.08	m	8	each
1.1	DRS-210 (KP) - 1810X2260 - Single Swing - Levers	Door-01	1.81	m	2.26	m	1	each
1.2	DRS-210 (KP) - 1810X2260 - Single Swing - Levers	Door-02	1.81	m	2.26	m	1	each
1.3	DRS-210 (KP) - 1810X2260 - Single Swing - Levers	Door-03	1.81	m	2.26	m	1	each
1.4	DRS-210 (KP) - 1810X2260 - Single Swing - Levers	Door-04	1.81	m	2.26	m	1	each
1.5	DRS-210 (KP) - 1810X2260 - Single Swing - Levers	Door-05	1.81	m	2.26	m	1	each
1.6	DRS-210 (KP) - 1810X2260 - Single Swing - Levers	Door-06	1.81	m	2.26	m	1	each
1.7	DRS-210 (KP) - 1810X2260 - Single Swing - Levers	Door-07	1.81	m	2.26	m	1	each
1.8	DRS-210 (KP) - 1810X2260 - Single Swing - Levers	Door-08	1.81	m	2.26	m	1	each

BASIC WORK PLANNING

Aims

- To understand basic planning to effectively plan current and future work.

Objectives

- Identify the benefits of planning.
- Create a work breakdown structure.
- Create a project plan [Gantt Chart].
- Understand the importance of Critical Path analysis.
- Risk analysis.
- Identify project constraints.
- Contingency planning.

Benefits of planning [Team Activity]

- What are the benefits of planning and why?
- Provide some examples of benefits in the workplace.

Benefits of planning

- Breaks complex tasks into manageable pieces.
- Sets out the logical sequence of project events.
- Provides an input into processes such as estimating time and resources.
- Provides a framework for continuous assessment of the project progression.
- Provides a communication tool.
- Gives you the ability to monitor and measure and be able to make decisions to effectively execute the plan and deliver on time.

Work Breakdown Structure [WBS]

- In a project or contract, the WBS is developed by starting with the end objective and successively subdividing it into manageable components in terms of size, duration, and responsibility [e.g. systems, sub-systems, components, tasks, sub-tasks and work packages].
- Includes all steps necessary to achieve the objective.

Work Breakdown Structure – Guidelines

- The top level represents the final deliverable or project.
- Sub-deliverables contain work packages that may be assigned to an organisation's department or unit.
- The work package may define the work, duration and costs for the tasks required to produce the sub-deliverable.
- Work packages should be independent of other work packages in the work breakdown structure.
- Work packages are unique and should not be duplicated across the work breakdown structure.

Work Breakdown Structure – Example

- Below is an example of a Work Breakdown Structure for a mountain bike.

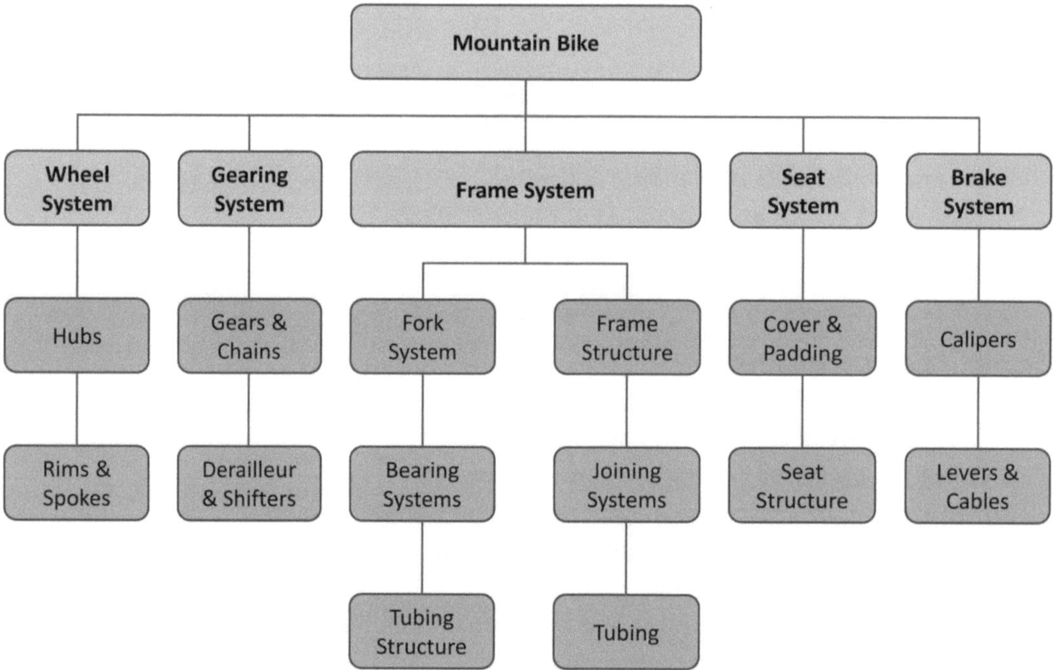

Project Plans – Gantt Charts

- Named after Henry Gantt, a pioneer of scientific work study.
- Represents the project, time taken, activity and resources required at any point in time.
- Used to monitor progress against plan.
- Can be used for individual workloads and total workloads.
- Very useful communication tool.
- Easy to understand.

Project Constraints

- Project constraints are restrictions that affect the project by imposing limitations on the project schedule, such as:
  - Design [late information, late drawing comments].
  - Materials.
  - Equipment.
  - People [numbers, skills, availability].
  - Money.
  - Time.
  - Main Contractor, Sub-contractor.
  - Change.
- Managing and mitigating these constraints is key to meeting project delivery.

Critical Paths

- In Project Management, the Critical Path is the succession of connected tasks that will take the longest to complete. The Critical Path is the longest path to complete the project.
- Therefore, to complete the project on schedule, it is the Critical Path and the tasks that are part of it that must be managed most closely.
- If a task along the Critical Path can be shortened, by assigning more resources, for example, the critical path will be shorter in duration, and the project can be completed in less time.

Risk Analysis

- There are three basic concerns in Project Management:
  - Schedule – will the project go over schedule?
  - Cost – will the project overrun its budget?
  - Performance – will the output satisfy the goal[s] of the project?

Contingency Planning

- What are the types of things you need to consider for contingency plans?
- What would be the likely triggers you would set for implementing contingency plans?

Consider for Contingency

- Change in methods.
- Resources – up and down.
- Type of resource, time, money, people, plant.

Triggers for Implementing Contingency Plans

- Schedule.
- Risk factors.
- Deadlines on delivery.
- Cost overruns.
- Supplier deadlines or cost.
- Budget v planned expenditure.

Work Planner

- Create a work planner and identify key milestones.

PC | PLANNING SHEET

ID	Area / Scope	Task Name	Resource	04-Sep-23					11-Sep-23					18-Sep-23					25-Sep-23					02-Oct-23					09-Oct-23					16-Oct-23					23-Oct-23				
				M	T	W	T	F	M	T	W	T	F	M	T	W	T	F	M	T	W	T	F	M	T	W	T	F	M	T	W	T	F	M	T	W	T	F	M	T	W	T	F
1																																											
2																																										
3																																										
4																																										
5																																										
6																																										
7																																										
8																																										
9																																										
10																																										
11																																										
12																																										
13																																										
14																																										
15																																										
16																																										
17																																										
18																																										
19																																										
20																																										

- Allocate resources, colour code as required and filter to create individual team work plans.

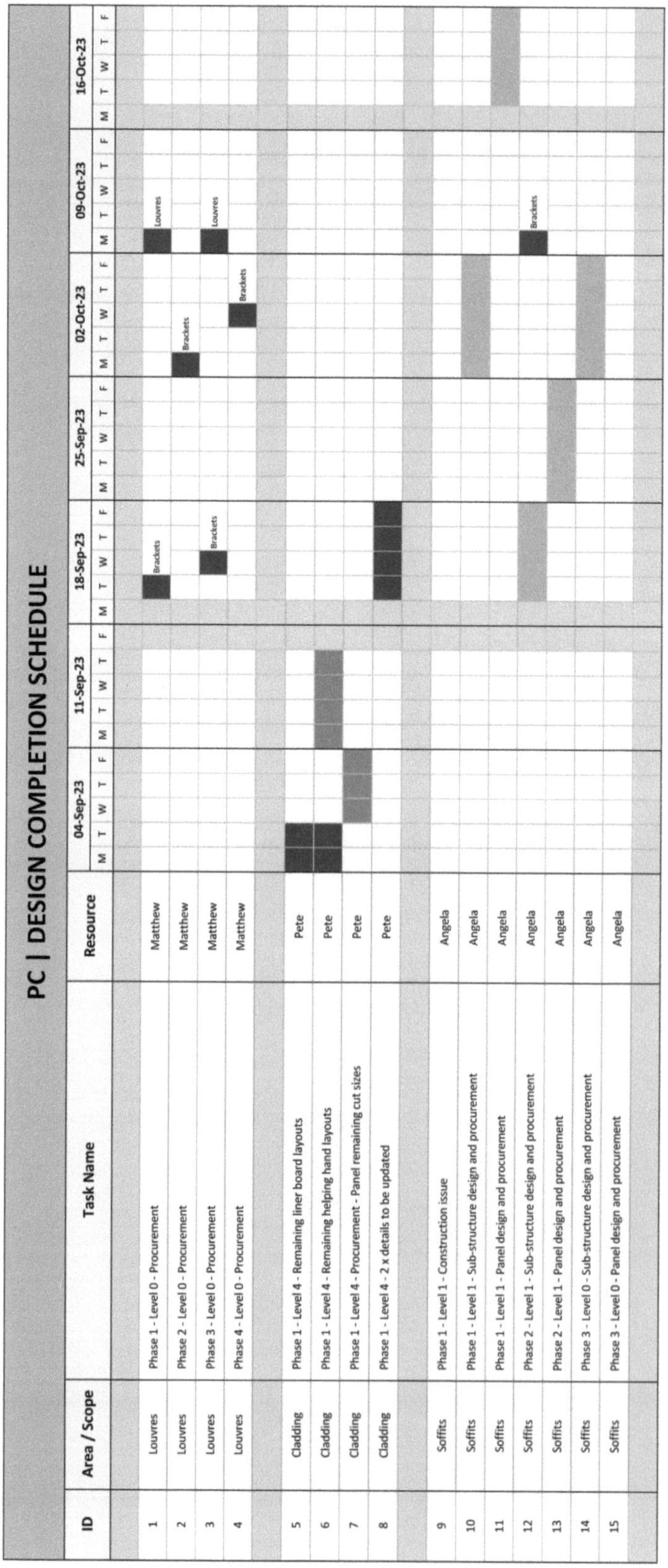

PC | DESIGN COMPLETION SCHEDULE

ID	Area / Scope	Task Name	Resource	04-Sep-23	11-Sep-23	18-Sep-23	25-Sep-23	02-Oct-23	09-Oct-23	16-Oct-23
1	Louvres	Phase 1 - Level 0 - Procurement	Matthew			Brackets			Louvres	
2	Louvres	Phase 2 - Level 0 - Procurement	Matthew					Brackets		
3	Louvres	Phase 3 - Level 0 - Procurement	Matthew			Brackets			Louvres	
4	Louvres	Phase 4 - Level 0 - Procurement	Matthew					Brackets		
5	Cladding	Phase 1 - Level 4 - Remaining liner board layouts	Pete							
6	Cladding	Phase 1 - Level 4 - Remaining helping hand layouts	Pete							
7	Cladding	Phase 1 - Level 4 - Procurement - Panel remaining cut sizes	Pete							
8	Cladding	Phase 1 - Level 4 - 2 x details to be updated	Pete							
9	Soffits	Phase 1 - Level 1 - Construction issue	Angela							
10	Soffits	Phase 1 - Level 1 - Sub-structure design and procurement	Angela							
11	Soffits	Phase 1 - Level 1 - Panel design and procurement	Angela							
12	Soffits	Phase 2 - Level 1 - Sub-structure design and procurement	Angela						Brackets	
13	Soffits	Phase 2 - Level 1 - Panel design and procurement	Angela							
14	Soffits	Phase 3 - Level 0 - Sub-structure design and procurement	Angela							
15	Soffits	Phase 3 - Level 0 - Panel design and procurement	Angela							

DESIGN DELIVERABLES

Introduction

- The following list outlines some of the key design information that is essential to the smooth running of the overall Design process.
- Some of this information is not always available, and our first Technical Queries or Requests for Information we raise ask for these items. The more information from the list below that is available, the more efficient the overall design becomes.

Drawings / Models

- Construction status architect's drawings.
- Construction status steelwork drawings.
- Construction status engineer's drawings.
- 3D architectural models.
- 3D structural models.
- Agreed BIM requirements / strategy.

Specifications

- Construction status specifications.

Commercial Items

- Agreed value engineering schedule.

Drawing Protocol

- Drawing numbering protocol.
- Drawing templates.
- Approval periods.
- Approval procedure / design freeze dates.

Specific Technical Information

- Design wind loadings.
- Specific acoustic requirements.
- Specific thermal requirements.
- Specific fire requirements / fire strategy.
- Barrier loadings.
- Drainage calculations.

Miscellaneous Items

- List of samples / mock ups.
- Colour schedule.
- Agreed tolerances.
- Agreed modules / setting out.
- Door schedule / access requirements.
- Cleaning and maintenance strategy.
- Air sealing principles / responsibilities.
- Meeting Timetable.

Programme

- Agreed programme.
- Agreed sequencing.

DESIGN MANAGEMENT

Programming

- A Gantt chart that follows the Work Breakdown Structure should be used for project planning.

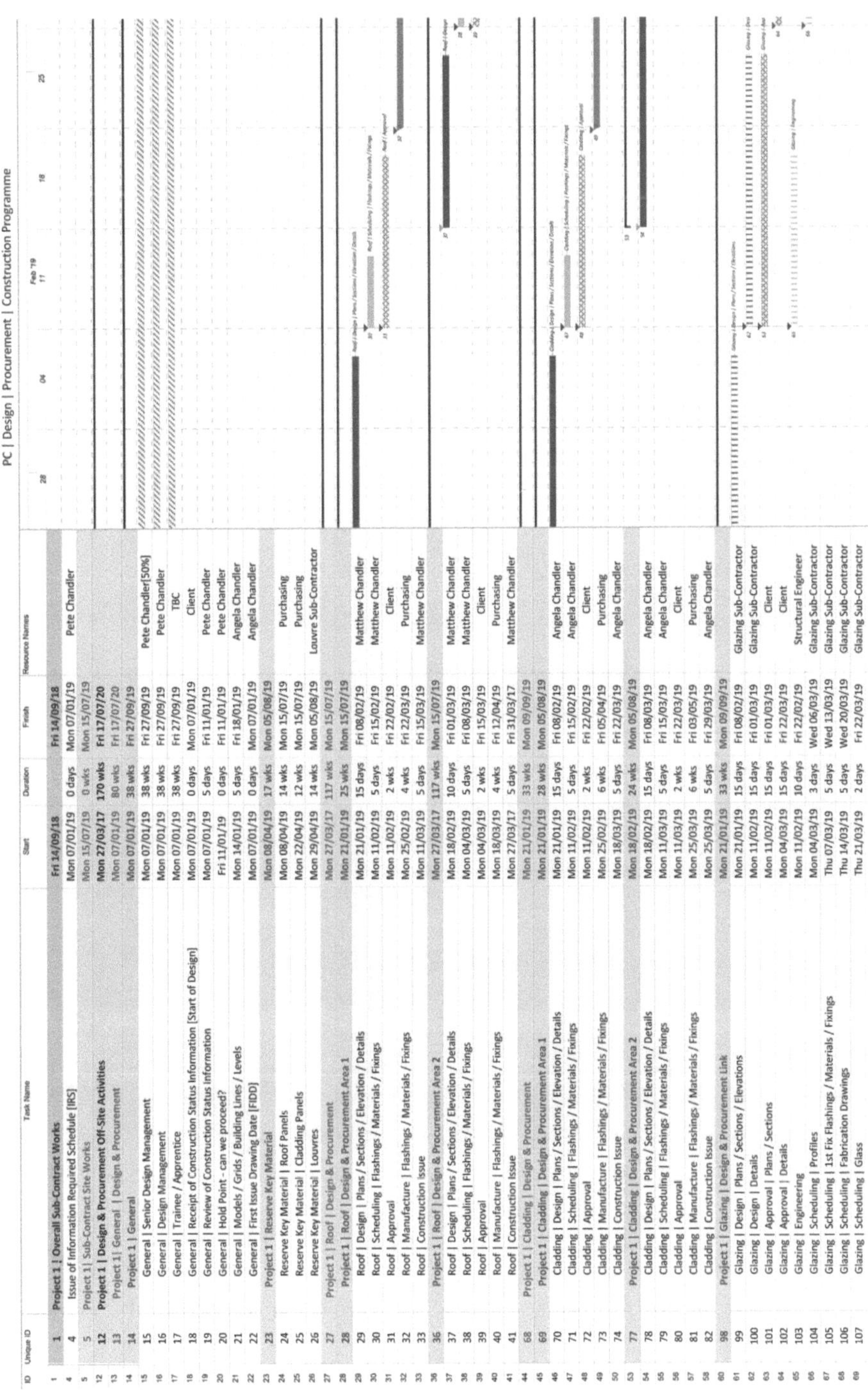

- The programme must be fully resourced, and should there be any changes, it must be kept 'live' and updated accordingly.
- Accurate allocation of resources allows the programme to be filtered, allowing individual people to have their own 'mini programme' and clear work plan.

PC | Target Design & Procurement Programme

ID	Task Name	Start	Duration	Finish	% Complete	Resource Names	Design Activity
1	Area 1 | Design & Procurement Off-Site Activities	Mon 26/07/21	18 wks	Mon 29/11/21	5%		
2	Flat Roofing [Level 04 & 05]	Mon 02/08/21	14.7 wks	Thu 11/11/21	8%		
3	Flat Roofing | Design	Mon 02/08/21	4 wks	Wed 15/09/21	20%	Matthew Chandler	.E | Design
4	Flat Roofing | Approval	Wed 15/09/21	1 wk	Mon 18/10/21	0%	-	.J | Approval
5	Flat Roofing | Scheduling	Wed 15/09/21	1 wk	Mon 18/10/21	0%	Matthew Chandler	.H | Scheduling
6	Flat Roofing | Manufacture	Wed 15/09/21	3 wks	Mon 25/10/21	0%	-	.K | Procuremen
7	Flat Roofing | Construction Issue	Mon 18/10/21	1 wk	Thu 11/11/21	0%	Matthew Chandler	.E | Design
8	Flat Roofing | Earliest Start On Site	Mon 27/09/21	0 wks	Mon 27/09/21	0%	-	.N | Constructic
9	Glazed Balustrade [Level 04 & 05]	Mon 26/07/21	18 wks	Mon 29/11/21	3%		
10	Glazed Balustrade | Design	Mon 26/07/21	3 wks	Fri 13/08/21	20%	Matthew Chandler	.E | Design
11	Glazed Balustrade | Approval	Mon 16/08/21	2 wks	Tue 07/09/21	0%	-	.J | Approval
12	Glazed Balustrade | Scheduling - 1st Fix	Mon 16/08/21	1 wk	Fri 20/08/21	0%	Matthew Chandler	.H | Scheduling
13	Glazed Balustrade | Manufacture - 1st Fix	Mon 23/08/21	4 wks	Fri 17/09/21	0%	-	.K | Procuremen
14	Glazed Balustrade | Scheduling - Glass / Flash / Mat / Fix	Mon 23/08/21	1 wk	Tue 07/09/21	0%	Matthew Chandler	.H | Scheduling
15	Glazed Balustrade | Manufacture - Glass / Flash / Mat / Fix	Wed 08/09/21	6 wks	Tue 19/10/21	0%	-	.K | Procuremen

Drop Line

- As the work progresses, the percentages should be updated to reflect a true and accurate, non-subjective position.

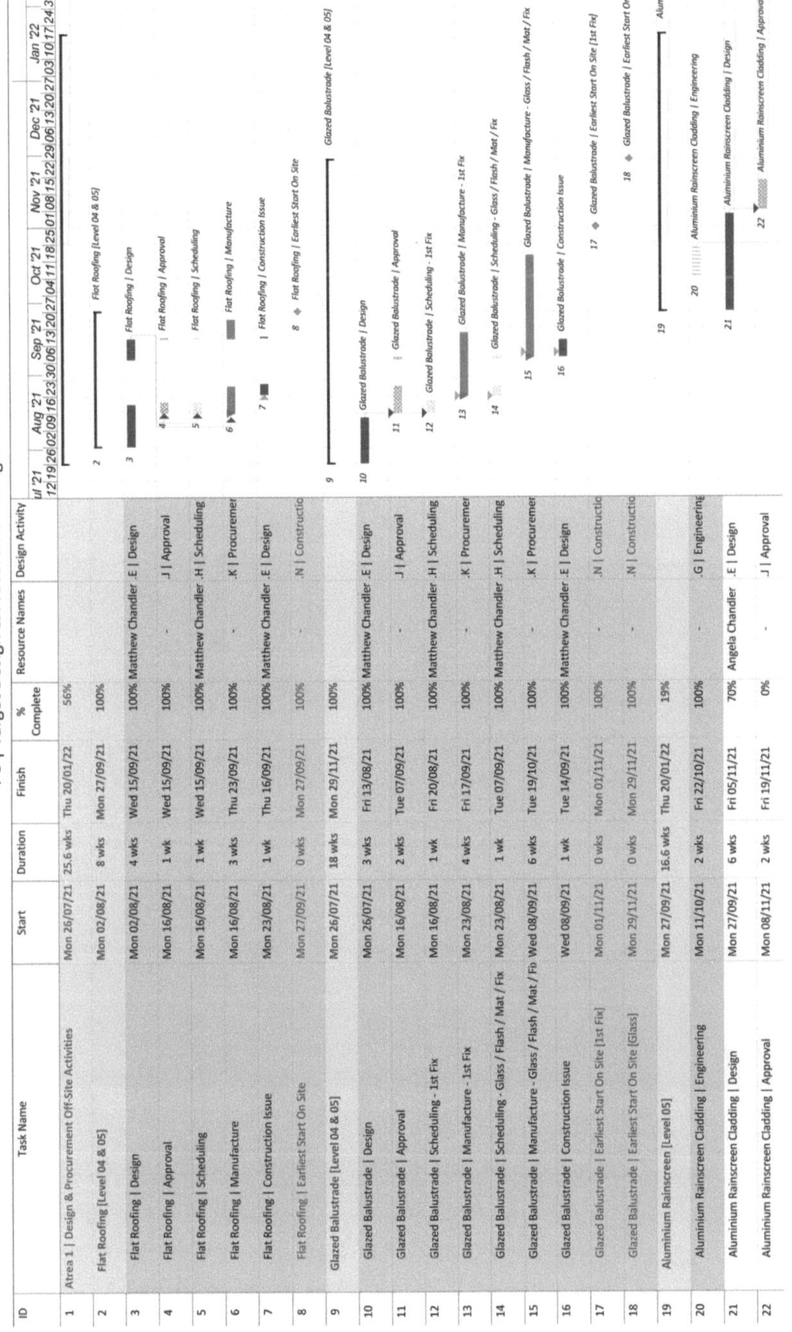

PC | Target Design & Procurement Programme

ID	Task Name	Start	Duration	Finish	% Complete	Resource Names	Design Activity
1	Atrea 1	Design & Procurement Off-Site Activities	Mon 26/07/21	25.6 wks	Thu 20/01/22	56%		
2	Flat Roofing [Level 04 & 05]	Mon 02/08/21	8 wks	Mon 27/09/21	100%		
3	Flat Roofing	Design	Mon 02/08/21	4 wks	Wed 15/09/21	100%	Matthew Chandler	.E	Design
4	Flat Roofing	Approval	Mon 16/08/21	1 wk	Wed 15/09/21	100%	-	.J	Approval
5	Flat Roofing	Scheduling	Mon 16/08/21	1 wk	Wed 15/09/21	100%	Matthew Chandler	.H	Scheduling
6	Flat Roofing	Manufacture	Mon 16/08/21	3 wks	Thu 23/09/21	100%	-	.K	Procurement
7	Flat Roofing	Construction Issue	Mon 23/08/21	1 wk	Thu 16/09/21	100%	Matthew Chandler	.E	Design
8	Flat Roofing	Earliest Start On Site	Mon 27/09/21	0 wks	Mon 27/09/21	100%	-	.N	Construction
9	Glazed Balustrade [Level 04 & 05]	Mon 26/07/21	18 wks	Mon 29/11/21	100%		
10	Glazed Balustrade	Design	Mon 26/07/21	3 wks	Fri 13/08/21	100%	Matthew Chandler	.E	Design
11	Glazed Balustrade	Approval	Mon 16/08/21	2 wks	Tue 07/09/21	100%	-	.J	Approval
12	Glazed Balustrade	Scheduling - 1st Fix	Mon 16/08/21	1 wk	Fri 20/08/21	100%	Matthew Chandler	.H	Scheduling
13	Glazed Balustrade	Manufacture - 1st Fix	Mon 23/08/21	4 wks	Fri 17/09/21	100%	-	.K	Procurement
14	Glazed Balustrade	Scheduling - Glass / Flash / Mat / Fix	Mon 23/08/21	1 wk	Tue 07/09/21	100%	Matthew Chandler	.H	Scheduling
15	Glazed Balustrade	Manufacture - Glass / Flash / Mat / Fix	Wed 08/09/21	6 wks	Tue 19/10/21	100%	-	.K	Procurement
16	Glazed Balustrade	Construction Issue	Wed 08/09/21	1 wk	Tue 14/09/21	100%	Matthew Chandler	.E	Design
17	Glazed Balustrade	Earliest Start On Site [1st Fix]	Mon 01/11/21	0 wks	Mon 01/11/21	100%	-	.N	Construction
18	Glazed Balustrade	Earliest Start On Site [Glass]	Mon 29/11/21	0 wks	Mon 29/11/21	100%	-	.N	Construction
19	Aluminium Rainscreen [Level 05]	Mon 27/09/21	16.6 wks	Thu 20/01/22	19%		
20	Aluminium Rainscreen Cladding	Engineering	Mon 11/10/21	2 wks	Fri 22/10/21	100%	-	.G	Engineering
21	Aluminium Rainscreen Cladding	Design	Mon 27/09/21	6 wks	Fri 05/11/21	70%	Angela Chandler	.E	Design
22	Aluminium Rainscreen Cladding	Approval	Mon 08/11/21	2 wks	Fri 19/11/21	0%	-	.J	Approval
23	Aluminium Rainscreen Cladding	Scheduling - 1st Fix	Mon 25/10/21	1 wk	Fri 29/10/21	0%	Angela Chandler	.H	Scheduling
24	Aluminium Rainscreen Cladding	Manufacture - 1st Fix	Mon 01/11/21	5 wks	Fri 03/12/21	0%	-	.K	Procurement
25	Aluminium Rainscreen Cladding	Scheduling - Panels / Acc	Mon 08/11/21	2 wks	Fri 19/11/21	0%	Angela Chandler	.H	Scheduling

Timeline header: 2022 — Apr '22, May '22, Jun '22, Jul '22, Aug '22, Sep '22, Oct '22, Nov '22, Dec

PC | Target Design & Procurement Programme

ID	Task Name	Start	Duration	Finish	% Complete	Resource Names	Design Activity
26	Aluminium Rainscreen Cladding	Manufacture - Panels / Acc	Mon 22/11/21	6 wks	Fri 31/12/21	0%	-	.K	Procurement
27	Aluminium Rainscreen Cladding	Scheduling - Flash / Mat	Mon 22/11/21	2 wks	Fri 03/12/21	0%	Angela Chandler	.H	Scheduling
28	Aluminium Rainscreen Cladding	Manufacture - Flash / Mat	Mon 29/11/21	5 wks	Fri 31/12/21	0%	-	.K	Procurement
29	Aluminium Rainscreen Cladding	Construction Issue	Mon 06/12/21	2 wks	Fri 17/12/21	0%	Angela Chandler	.E	Design
30	Aluminium Rainscreen Cladding	Earliest Start On Site [1st Fix]	Mon 22/11/21	0 wks	Mon 22/11/21	0%	-	.N	Construction
31	Aluminium Rainscreen Cladding	Earliest Start On Site [1st Fix]	Mon 06/12/21	0 wks	Mon 06/12/21	0%	-	.N	Construction
32	Aluminium Rainscreen Cladding	Earliest Start On Site [Panels]	Thu 20/01/22	0 wks	Thu 20/01/22	0%	-	.N	Construction

Timeline header: 2022 — Apr '22, May '22, Jun '22, Jul '22, Aug '22, Sep '22, Oct '22, Nov '22, Dec

- The drop line should be set with an automated date for ease of use.
- As activities are completed, and reach a true 100% completion, they should be 'greyed out'.
- As activities are completed they can be 'rolled up' so the programme only shows line information and work in progress.

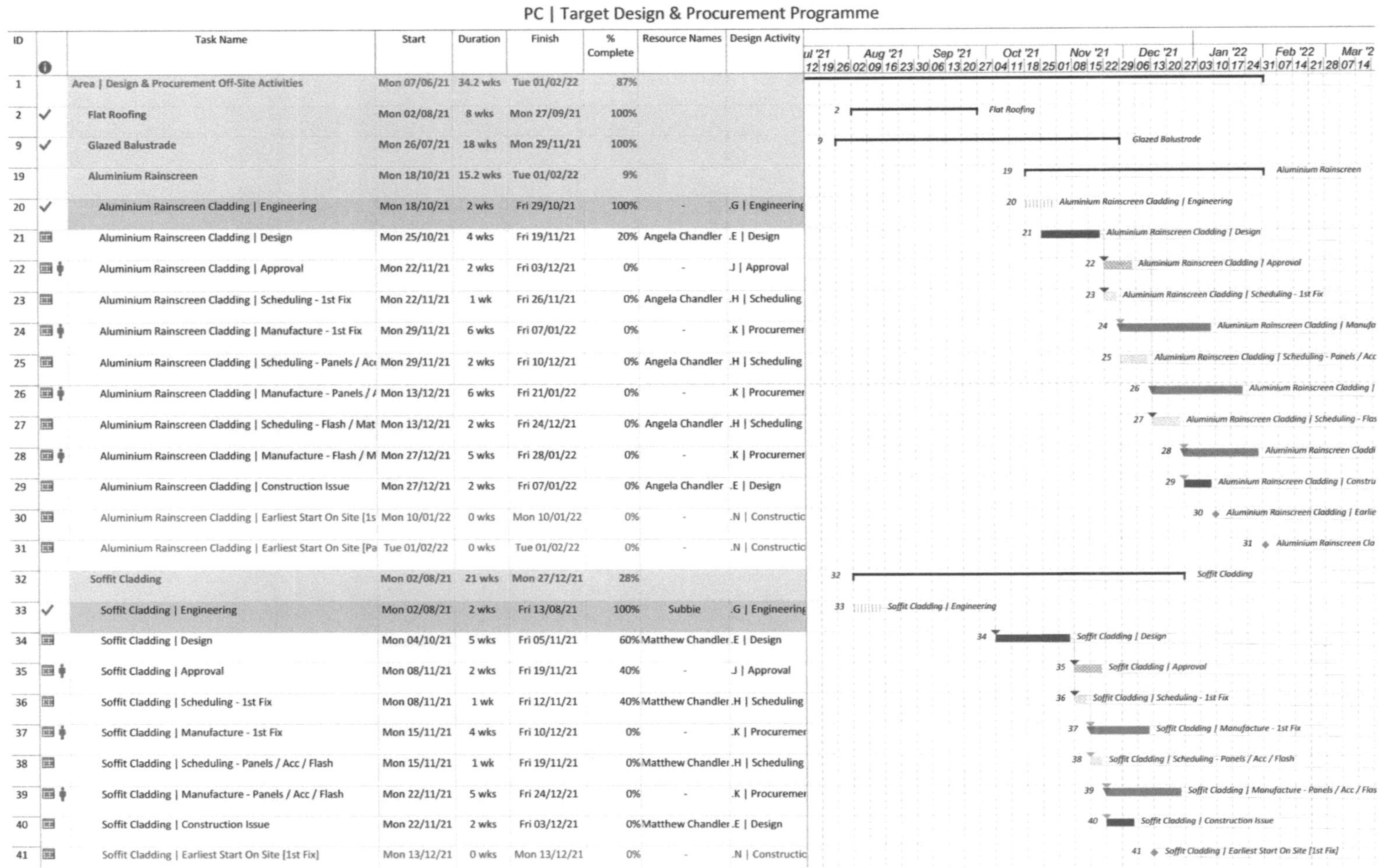

PC | Target Design & Procurement Programme

ID		Task Name	Start	Duration	Finish	% Complete	Resource Names	Design Activity
1		Area	Design & Procurement Off-Site Activities	Mon 07/06/21	34.2 wks	Tue 01/02/22	87%		
2		Flat Roofing	Mon 02/08/21	8 wks	Mon 27/09/21	100%		
9		Glazed Balustrade	Mon 26/07/21	18 wks	Mon 29/11/21	100%		
19		Aluminium Rainscreen	Mon 18/10/21	15.2 wks	Tue 01/02/22	9%		
20		Aluminium Rainscreen Cladding	Engineering	Mon 18/10/21	2 wks	Fri 29/10/21	100%	-	.G	Engineering
21		Aluminium Rainscreen Cladding	Design	Mon 25/10/21	4 wks	Fri 19/11/21	20%	Angela Chandler	.E	Design
22		Aluminium Rainscreen Cladding	Approval	Mon 22/11/21	2 wks	Fri 03/12/21	0%	-	.J	Approval
23		Aluminium Rainscreen Cladding	Scheduling - 1st Fix	Mon 22/11/21	1 wk	Fri 26/11/21	0%	Angela Chandler	.H	Scheduling
24		Aluminium Rainscreen Cladding	Manufacture - 1st Fix	Mon 29/11/21	6 wks	Fri 07/01/22	0%	-	.K	Procuremer
25		Aluminium Rainscreen Cladding	Scheduling - Panels / Acc	Mon 29/11/21	2 wks	Fri 10/12/21	0%	Angela Chandler	.H	Scheduling
26		Aluminium Rainscreen Cladding	Manufacture - Panels / A	Mon 13/12/21	6 wks	Fri 21/01/22	0%	-	.K	Procuremer
27		Aluminium Rainscreen Cladding	Scheduling - Flash / Mat	Mon 13/12/21	2 wks	Fri 24/12/21	0%	Angela Chandler	.H	Scheduling
28		Aluminium Rainscreen Cladding	Manufacture - Flash / M	Mon 27/12/21	5 wks	Fri 28/01/22	0%	-	.K	Procuremer
29		Aluminium Rainscreen Cladding	Construction Issue	Mon 27/12/21	2 wks	Fri 07/01/22	0%	Angela Chandler	.E	Design
30		Aluminium Rainscreen Cladding	Earliest Start On Site [1s	Mon 10/01/22	0 wks	Mon 10/01/22	0%	-	.N	Constructic
31		Aluminium Rainscreen Cladding	Earliest Start On Site [Pa	Tue 01/02/22	0 wks	Tue 01/02/22	0%	-	.N	Constructic
32		Soffit Cladding	Mon 02/08/21	21 wks	Mon 27/12/21	28%		
33		Soffit Cladding	Engineering	Mon 02/08/21	2 wks	Fri 13/08/21	100%	Subbie	.G	Engineering
34		Soffit Cladding	Design	Mon 04/10/21	5 wks	Fri 05/11/21	60%	Matthew Chandler	.E	Design
35		Soffit Cladding	Approval	Mon 08/11/21	2 wks	Fri 19/11/21	40%	-	.J	Approval
36		Soffit Cladding	Scheduling - 1st Fix	Mon 08/11/21	1 wk	Fri 12/11/21	40%	Matthew Chandler	.H	Scheduling
37		Soffit Cladding	Manufacture - 1st Fix	Mon 15/11/21	4 wks	Fri 10/12/21	0%	-	.K	Procuremer
38		Soffit Cladding	Scheduling - Panels / Acc / Flash	Mon 15/11/21	1 wk	Fri 19/11/21	0%	Matthew Chandler	.H	Scheduling
39		Soffit Cladding	Manufacture - Panels / Acc / Flash	Mon 22/11/21	5 wks	Fri 24/12/21	0%	-	.K	Procuremer
40		Soffit Cladding	Construction Issue	Mon 22/11/21	2 wks	Fri 03/12/21	0%	Matthew Chandler	.E	Design
41		Soffit Cladding	Earliest Start On Site [1st Fix]	Mon 13/12/21	0 wks	Mon 13/12/21	0%	-	.N	Constructic

Look Ahead

- The programme should be set up with an automated 4-week look ahead as this will allow activities due in that period to be easily highlighted.

PC | Target Design & Procurement Programme

ID	Task Name	Start	Duration	Finish	% Complete	Resource Names	Design Activity
1	Area 1 | Design & Procurement Off-Site Activities	Thu 29/12/22	96.6 wks	Mon 04/11/24	0%		
2	Aluminium Rainscreen	Mon 20/03/23	85.2 wks	Mon 04/11/24	0%		
3	Aluminium Rainscreen Cladding | Engineering	Thu 10/10/24	2 wks	Wed 23/10/24	0%	-	.G | Engineering
4	Aluminium Rainscreen Cladding | Design	Mon 20/03/23	4 wks	Fri 14/04/23	0%	Angela Chandler	.E | Design
5	Aluminium Rainscreen Cladding | Approval	Mon 17/04/23	2 wks	Fri 28/04/23	0%	-	.J | Approval
6	Aluminium Rainscreen Cladding | Scheduling - 1st Fix	Mon 17/04/23	1 wk	Fri 21/04/23	0%	Angela Chandler	.H | Scheduling
7	Aluminium Rainscreen Cladding | Manufacture - 1st Fix	Mon 24/04/23	6 wks	Fri 02/06/23	0%	-	.K | Procurement
8	Aluminium Rainscreen Cladding | Scheduling - Panels / Acc	Mon 24/04/23	2 wks	Fri 05/05/23	0%	Angela Chandler	.H | Scheduling
9	Aluminium Rainscreen Cladding | Manufacture - Panels / A	Mon 08/05/23	6 wks	Fri 16/06/23	0%	-	.K | Procurement
10	Aluminium Rainscreen Cladding | Scheduling - Flash / Mat	Tue 17/09/24	2 wks	Mon 30/09/24	0%	Angela Chandler	.H | Scheduling
11	Aluminium Rainscreen Cladding | Manufacture - Flash / M	Tue 01/10/24	5 wks	Mon 04/11/24	0%	-	.K | Procurement
12	Aluminium Rainscreen Cladding | Construction Issue	Tue 01/10/24	2 wks	Mon 14/10/24	0%	Angela Chandler	.E | Design
13	Aluminium Rainscreen Cladding | Earliest Start On Site [1s	Mon 05/06/23	0 wks	Mon 05/06/23	0%	-	.N | Construction
14	Aluminium Rainscreen Cladding | Earliest Start On Site [Pa	Tue 27/06/23	0 wks	Tue 27/06/23	0%	-	.N | Construction
15	Soffit Cladding	Thu 29/12/22	93.4 wks	Fri 11/10/24	0%		
16	Soffit Cladding | Engineering	Thu 29/12/22	2 wks	Wed 11/01/23	0%	Subbie	.G | Engineering
17	Soffit Cladding | Design	Mon 27/02/23	5 wks	Fri 23/08/24	0%	Matthew Chandler	.E | Design
18	Soffit Cladding | Approval	Mon 26/08/24	2 wks	Fri 06/09/24	0%	-	.J | Approval
19	Soffit Cladding | Scheduling - 1st Fix	Mon 26/08/24	1 wk	Fri 30/08/24	0%	Matthew Chandler	.H | Scheduling

- The programme can also be filtered by those activities due in the 4-week period, allowing tasks to be closely monitored and critical items achieved as required.

PC | Target Design & Procurement Programme

ID	Task Name	Start	Duration	Finish	% Complete	Resource Names	Design Activity
1	Area 1 | Design & Procurement Off-Site Activities	Thu 29/12/22	96.6 wks	Mon 04/11/24	0%		
2	Aluminium Rainscreen	Mon 20/03/23	85.2 wks	Mon 04/11/24	0%		
4	Aluminium Rainscreen Cladding | Design	Mon 20/03/23	4 wks	Fri 14/04/23	0%	Angela Chandler	.E | Design
5	Aluminium Rainscreen Cladding | Approval	Mon 17/04/23	2 wks	Fri 28/04/23	0%	-	.J | Approval
6	Aluminium Rainscreen Cladding | Scheduling - 1st Fix	Mon 17/04/23	1 wk	Fri 21/04/23	0%	Angela Chandler	.H | Scheduling
7	Aluminium Rainscreen Cladding | Manufacture - 1st Fix	Mon 24/04/23	6 wks	Fri 02/06/23	0%	-	.K | Procuremer
8	Aluminium Rainscreen Cladding | Scheduling - Panels / Acc	Mon 24/04/23	2 wks	Fri 05/05/23	0%	Angela Chandler	.H | Scheduling
9	Aluminium Rainscreen Cladding | Manufacture - Panels / A	Mon 08/05/23	6 wks	Fri 16/06/23	0%	-	.K | Procuremer
13	Aluminium Rainscreen Cladding | Earliest Start On Site [1s	Mon 05/06/23	0 wks	Mon 05/06/23	0%	-	.N | Constructic
14	Aluminium Rainscreen Cladding | Earliest Start On Site [Pa	Tue 27/06/23	0 wks	Tue 27/06/23	0%	-	.N | Constructic
15	Soffit Cladding	Thu 29/12/22	93.4 wks	Fri 11/10/24	0%		
16	Soffit Cladding | Engineering	Thu 29/12/22	2 wks	Wed 11/01/23	0%	Subbie	.G | Engineering
17	Soffit Cladding | Design	Mon 27/02/23	5 wks	Fri 23/08/24	0%	Matthew Chandler	.E | Design
24	Soffit Cladding | Earliest Start On Site [1st Fix]	Mon 08/05/23	0 wks	Mon 08/05/23	0%	-	.N | Constructic
25	Soffit Cladding | Earliest Start On Site [Panels]	Mon 22/05/23	0 wks	Mon 22/05/23	0%	-	.N | Constructic

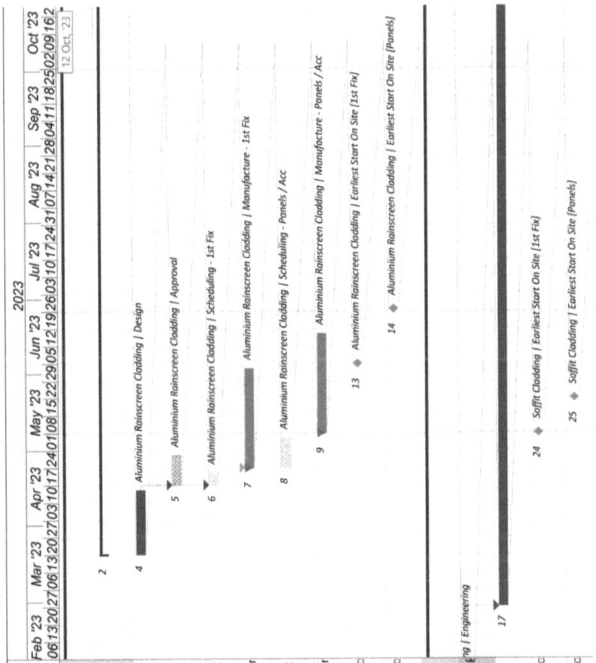

Key Date Matrix

- A key date matrix identifies a short list of key items with a 'week minus' date from when it needs to be completed.

						PC | KEY DESIGN DATE MATRIX			
Matrix No	Programme ID	Deliverables ID	Week Number	Date	Area	Task Name	Responsibility	No. Drawings	Comments
1	19	-	-11	24-Apr-17	Building 1	General | Hold Point - can we proceed?	Senior Design Manager	0	
2	21	-	-10	05-May-17	Building 1	General | First Issue Drawing Date [FIDD]	Senior Designer 1	0	
3	23	-	-14	03-Apr-17	Building 1	Global Orders | Roof Panels [+Flat Sheet]	Purchasing	0	
4	24	-	-14	07-Apr-17	Building 1	Global Orders | Wall Panels [+Flat Sheet]	Purchasing	0	
5	25	-	-14	07-Apr-17	Building 1	Global Orders | Wall Panels [+Flat Sheet]	Purchasing	0	
6	26	-	-11	27-Apr-17	Building 1	Global Orders | Single Skin Sheets [+Flat Sheet]	Purchasing	0	
7	29	3.0	-10	05-May-17	Building 1	Roof | Design | Details	Designer 1 [Cladding]	50	
8	41	4.0	-9	09-May-17	Building 1	Access Hatches | Design	Designer 1 [Cladding]	4	
9	47	5.0	-9	11-May-17	Building 1	Parapet Cladding | Design	Designer 1 [Cladding]	20	
10	55	6.0	-8	16-May-17	Building 1	Parapet Coping | Design	Designer 1 [Cladding]	10	
11	61	7.0	-8	18-May-17	Building 1	Terrace | Design	Designer 1 [Cladding]	14	
12	69	8.0	-8	16-May-17	Building 1	Handrail | Design	Sub-Contractor	10	
13	76	9.0	-9	10-May-17	Building 1	Backing Wall | Design | Details	Senior Designer 1	20	
14	87	9.0	-7	23-May-17	Building 1	Cladding | Design | Details	Senior Designer 1	20	
15	96	10.0	-6	01-Jun-17	Building 1	Louvres | Design	Senior Designer 1	8	
16	102	11.0	-5	06-Jun-17	Building 1	Soffits | Design	Senior Designer 1	18	
17	108	12.0	-3	19-Jun-17	Building 1	Metal Doors | Design	Sub-Contractor	6	
18	115	13.0	-10	05-May-17	Building 1	Glazed Rooflights | Design | Details	Senior Designer 2	8	
19	133	14.0 / 15.0	-7	25-May-17	Building 1	Glazing | Design | Details	Senior Designer 2	32	
							Total	220	

Deliverables / Drawing List

- Ensure a list of drawings is produced so you know how big the task ahead is.

PC | DRAWING LIST					
Drawing Number	Drawing Title	Resource	Drawing Status	Progress	% Complete
Flat Roofing			3		
XXXXXX-XXX-XX-XX-XX-X-XXXXX	Balustrade Interface Details	Pete	08 | Complete	100%	100%
XXXXXX-XXX-XX-XX-XX-X-XXXXX	Facade Interface Details	Pete	08 | Complete	100%	100%
XXXXXX-XXX-XX-XX-XX-X-XXXXX	Waterproofing GA	Pete	05 | Issued For Final Approval	70%	70%
Glazed Balustrade			4		
XXXXXX-XXX-XX-XX-XX-X-XXXXX	Balustrade Setting Out - Support Brackets	Angela	01 | In Progress	30%	30%
XXXXXX-XXX-XX-XX-XX-X-XXXXX	Balustrade Setting Out - Base Channel (& Cutting List) & Glass	Angela	01 | In Progress	30%	30%
XXXXXX-XXX-XX-XX-XX-X-XXXXX	Balustrade Setting Out - Support Brackets	Angela	01 | In Progress	30%	30%
XXXXXX-XXX-XX-XX-XX-X-XXXXX	Balustrade Setting Out - Base Channel (& Cutting List) & Glass	Angela	01 | In Progress	30%	30%
Soffit Cladding			6		
XXXXXX-XXX-XX-XX-XX-X-XXXXX	Soffit substructure layout	Matthew	02 | GA & Details Complete	40%	40%
XXXXXX-XXX-XX-XX-XX-X-XXXXX	Soffit panel layout	Matthew	03 | Issued For Initial Approval	50%	50%
XXXXXX-XXX-XX-XX-XX-X-XXXXX	Soffit steel penetrations	Matthew	04 | Revise Drawings	60%	60%
XXXXXX-XXX-XX-XX-XX-X-XXXXX	Soffit typical sections	Matthew	05 | Issued For Final Approval	70%	70%
XXXXXX-XXX-XX-XX-XX-X-XXXXX	Soffit typical sections 2	Matthew	06 | Revise Drawings	80%	80%
XXXXXX-XXX-XX-XX-XX-X-XXXXX	Soffit typical sections 3	Matthew	07 | Issued For Construction	90%	90%
Check 13		Total	13		
			Cumulative Production		
		Sub-Total [x]	13		

- The drawing list should follow the same order, sequence and Work Breakdown Structure as that of the Programme to maintain consistency.
- Accurate allocation of resources also allows the programme to be filtered, allowing individual people to have their own 'mini programme' and clear work plan.
- Ensure an 'x' is put into the week ending date as it will help you to plan ahead and see the amount of work per individual resource. For example, if a person has to produce 50 number drawings in a particular week, the plan will fail.

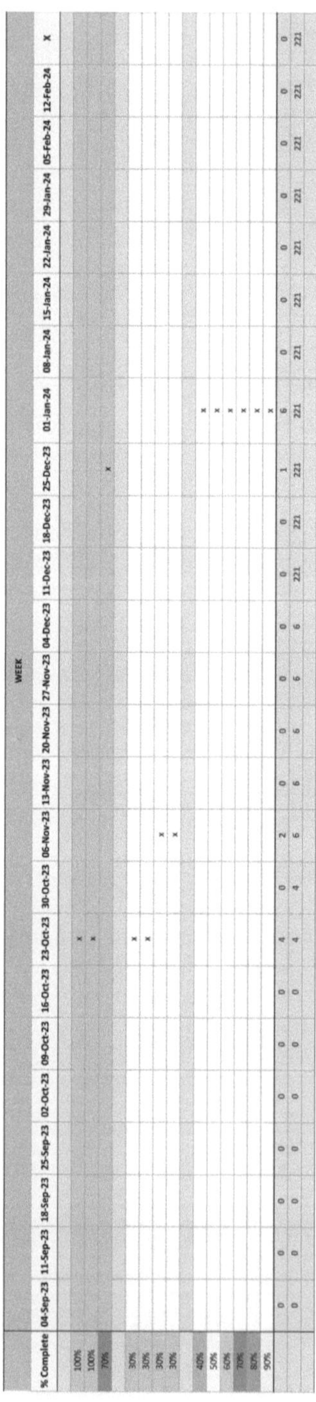

- The drawing list should follow the principle of a 2-stage approval, allowing for the worst case.
- The drawing list should be colour-coded to reflect the 9 different stages.

Drawing Summary		%
01 | In Progress		30%
02 | GA & Details Complete		40%
03 | Issued For Initial Approval		50%
04 | Revise Drawings		60%
05 | Issued For Final Approval		70%
06 | Revise Drawings		80%
07 | Issued For Construction		90%
08 | Complete		100%
09 | As Built		AB

- Using the correct software will allow you to plan and identify drawing stages against the individual resource.

Resource Summary	01 | In Progress	02 | Ready for Issue	03 | Issued For Initial Approval	04 | Revision - Initial	05 | Issued For Final Approval	06 | Revision - Final	07 | Issued For Construction	08 | Complete	09 | As Built
Pete	9	6	2	0	0	0	0	0	0
Designer 1	1	0	4	2	0	0	0	0	0
Designer 2	0	2	0	3	0	0	0	0	0
Designer 3	0	0	0	0	0	0	6	0	0
Designer 4	0	0	0	0	0	0	4	0	0
Designer 5	0	3	5	0	0	0	0	0	0
Designer 6	0	1	2	0	2	0	0	0	0
Designer 7	0	0	5	1	0	0	0	0	0
Designer 8	0	0	4	3	0	0	0	0	0
?	0	0	0	0	0	0	0	0	0
?	0	0	0	0	0	0	0	0	0
?	0	0	0	0	0	0	0	0	0
?	0	0	0	0	0	0	0	0	0
?	0	0	0	0	0	0	0	0	0
?	0	0	0	0	0	0	0	0	0
?	0	0	0	0	0	0	0	0	0
?	0	0	0	0	0	0	0	0	0
?	0	0	0	0	0	0	0	0	0
?	0	0	0	0	0	0	0	0	0
?	0	0	0	0	0	0	0	0	0
65	10	12	22	9	2	0	10	0	0

- With the correct information, you can see the percentage allocation of the workload for each resource.

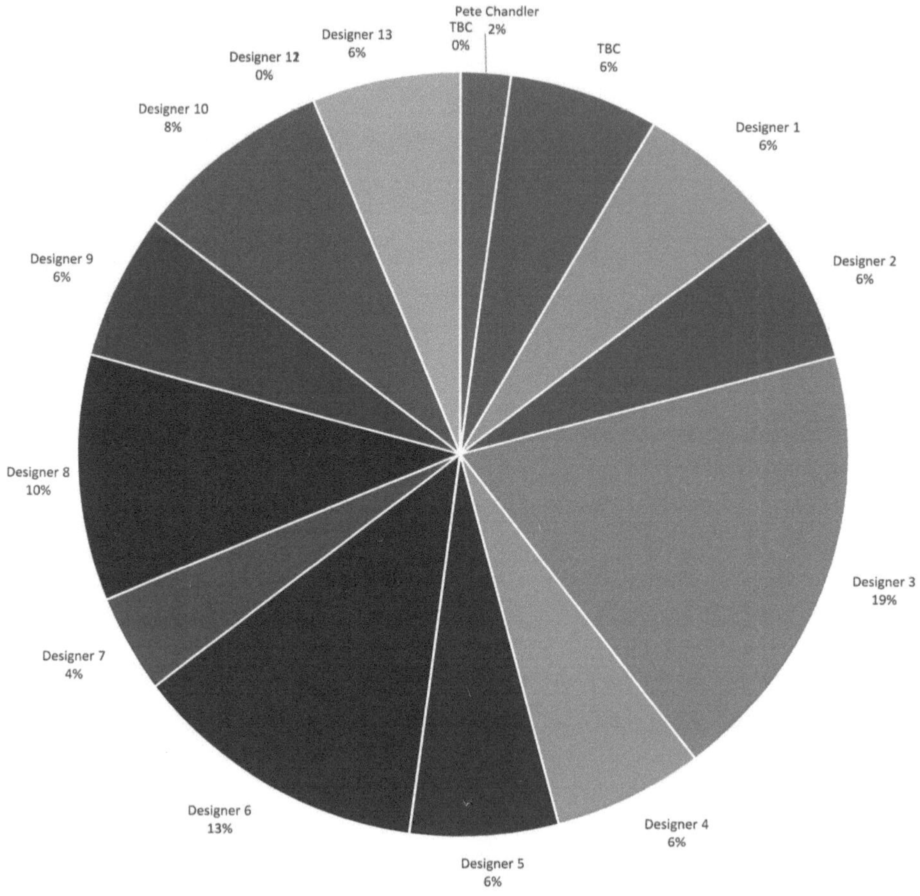

- With the correct information, you can see the total number of drawings through each stage.

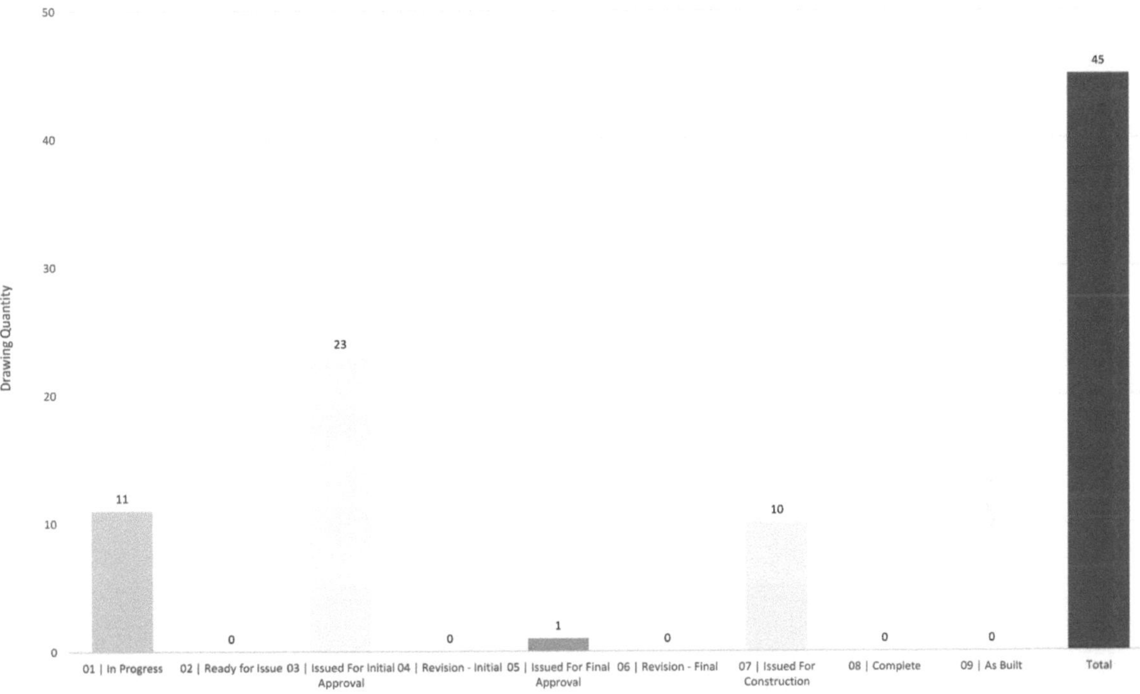

- With the correct information, you can see the total number of drawings through each stage by the individual resource.

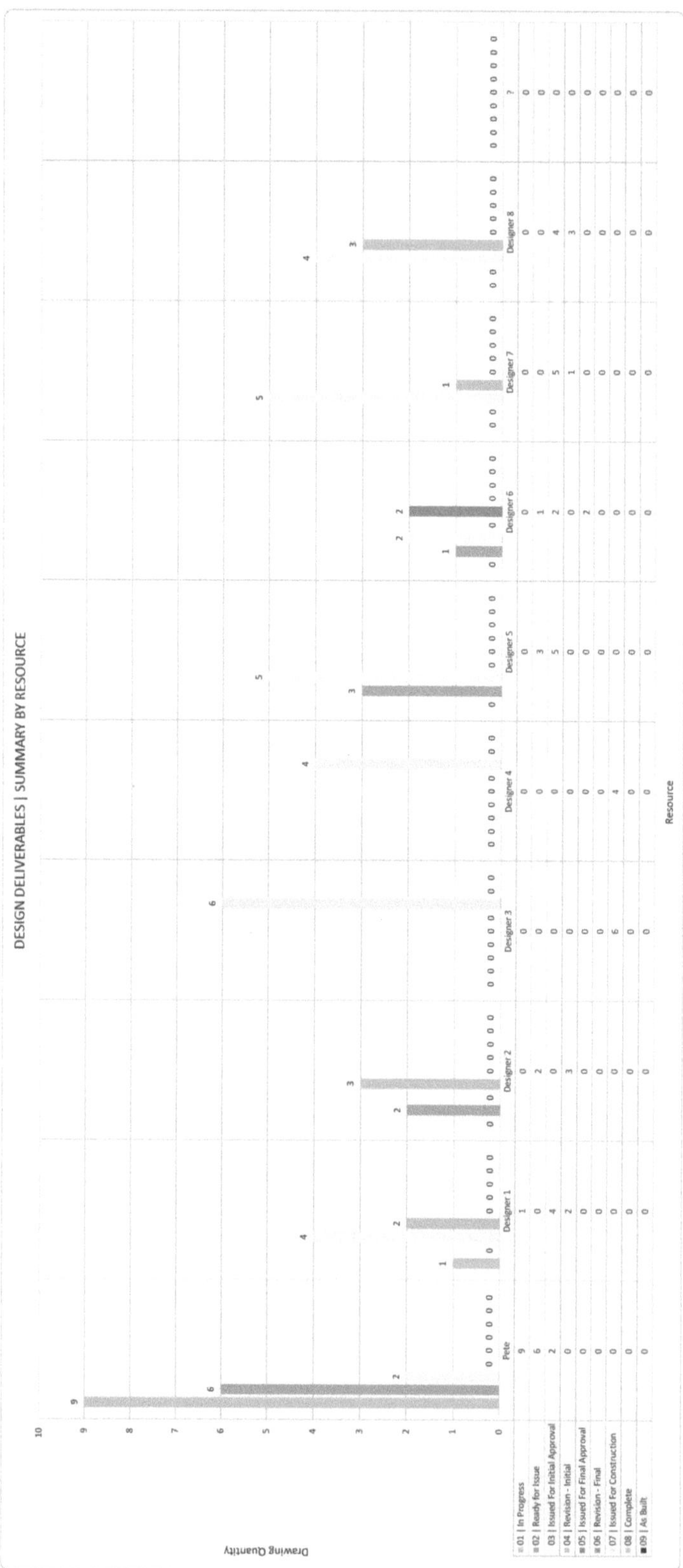

Design Report

- The Design Report is an essential document where the drawing issues, drawing location, total numbers and planned issue dates are stated.

Project Title	PC	Design Report
Project Number	XXXX
Revision	A
Date	17/10/2023
	Not Started
	WIP
	Comments Required
	Approval 1
Colour Key	Approval 2
	Construction Issued
	As Built
	Revised

				Total [unique] Drawings					Total Issued	Total Issued Late
				14					0	14
Program ID Ref	Area [Description]	Area [Code]	Phase / Scope	Drawing Number	Rev	Location	Title	Planned Issue Date	Date Issued	Days Issued Late
1	Project 1	RF-0100 series	Roof	RF-010001	C01	01	Roof	XXXX	29/06/2020	04/07/2020	5
2	Project 1	RF-0200 series	Roof	RF-020001	C02	02	Rooflight	XXXX	19/05/2020	19/05/2020	0
3	Project 1	RF-0300 series	Roof	RF-030001	C02	03	Copings	XXXX	09/11/2020	15/11/2020	6
4	Project 1	RF-0400 series	Roof	RF-040001	C02	04	Plant Wells	XXXX	14/09/2020	20/09/2020	6
5	Project 1	RF-0500 series	Roof	RF-050001	C02	05	Canopy Soffits	XXXX	31/12/2019	01/01/2020	1
6	Project 1	RF-0600 series	Roof	RF-060001	C02	05	Balcony Soffits	XXXX	24/07/2020	26/07/2020	2
7	Project 1	RF-0700 series	Roof	RF-070001	C01	07	Mesh Panels	XXXX	27/10/2020	11/11/2020	15
8	Project 1	RF-0800 series	Roof	RF-080001	C01	08	Flat Roof	XXXX	28/07/2020	01/10/2020	65
9	Project 1	RF-0900 series	Walls	RF-090001	C01	09	Terraces	XXXX	08/09/2020	16/09/2020	8
10	Project 1	WL-1000 Series	Walls	WL-100001	C01	10	Glazing	XXXX	31/12/2019	25/01/2020	25
11	Project 1	WL- 5000 Series	Walls	WL-500001	C03	11	Glazed Doors	XXXX	31/12/2019	02/01/2020	2
12	Project 1	WL- 6000 Series	Walls	WL-600001	C01	12	Glazed Balustrade	XXXX	31/12/2019	30/01/2020	30
13	Project 1	WL- 6200 Series	Walls	WL-620001	C01	13	Glazed Louvres	XXXX	01/09/2020	06/10/2020	35
14	Project 1	WL- 9000 Series	Walls	WL-900001	C01	14	Bespoke Soffits	XXXX	31/12/2019	31/12/2019	0

- The Design Report captures the approval issues, dates in which drawing comments were returned, days late on return of drawings and the Status given during the approval process.

	Total Received	Total Received Or Currently Late				Construction Issued	As Built Issued		
	14	13				14	0		
Date Comments [Final Approval] Required By	Date Comments [Final Approval] Received	Days Comments Received Late	Days Late From Planned Issue Date	Main Contractor Drawing Status [Approval 1]	Client Architect Drawing Status [Approval 2]	Construction Issue Date	As Built	Resource	Status
18/07/2020	28/07/2020	10	29	A		25/05/2021		Pete	Construction Issued
02/06/2020	02/06/2020	0	14	A		25/05/2021		Pete	Construction Issued
29/11/2020	11/12/2020	12	32	B		14/12/2020		Angela	Construction Issued
04/10/2020	16/10/2020	12	32	B		14/12/2020		Angela	Construction Issued
15/01/2020	17/01/2020	2	17	B		14/12/2020		Angela	Construction Issued
09/08/2020	29/08/2020	20	36	C		14/12/2020		Angela	Construction Issued
25/11/2020	09/01/2021	45	74	C		14/12/2020		Angela	Construction Issued
15/10/2020	23/01/2021	100	179	C		14/12/2020		Angela	Construction Issued
30/09/2020	12/10/2020	12	34	C		14/12/2020		Angela	Construction Issued
08/02/2020	11/02/2020	3	42	B		14/12/2020		Sub-Con	Construction Issued
16/01/2020	18/01/2020	2	18	B		14/12/2020		Matthew	Construction Issued
13/02/2020	13/04/2020	60	104	A		14/12/2020		Matthew	Construction Issued
20/10/2020	13/01/2021	85	134	A		02/02/2021		Matthew	Construction Issued
14/01/2020	27/01/2020	13	27	A		02/02/2021		Matthew	Construction Issued

- The Design Report should capture the following:
  - Drawings.
  - Request for Information [RFIs].
  - Potential Variations.
  - Samples.
  - Calculations.
  - Technical Submittals.

Project Title	PC	Design Report
Project Number	XXXX
Revision	A
Date	17/10/2023
	Closed out - No
	Closed out - Yes
Colour Key	Overdue
	Due Within The Next 14 Days
	Complete

			RFI'S - Issued					RFI's - Responses Received	RFI's - Total Received Late			RFI's - Total Closed Out	RFI's - Responses Currently Overdue	
			12					12-Jan-00	8			4	0	
Area Code	RFI Number	Raised By	Date Issued	Rev	Contents	Date Response Required	Date Response Received	Number of Days Late	Remarks	Closed Out	Currently Overdue	Key Blocker
RF	RFI-0001 RF	Pete	22/01/2020	1	PC-RFI-000102 - Roof Drawings	05/02/2020	05/02/2020	0		No	0	Yes
RF	RFI-0002 RF	Pete	22/01/2020	1	PC-RFI-000103 - Balcony Flat Roof Build-Ups.	05/02/2020	01/03/2020	25		No	0	Yes
RF	RFI-0003 RF	Pete	24/02/2020	1	PC-RFI-000115 - Rooflight Specification	02/03/2020	16/03/2020	14		Yes	0	No
RF	RFI-0004 RF	Pete	26/02/2020	1	PC-RFI-000117 - Soffit Colour	04/03/2020	16/03/2020	12		Yes	0	No
RF	RFI-0005 RF	Pete	11/03/2020	1	PC-RFI-000120 - Gutter Category	18/03/2020	12/03/2020	-6		No	0	Yes
RF	RFI-0006 RF	Pete	25/03/2020	1	PC-RFI-000123 - Balcony Floor Details	01/04/2020	25/03/2020	-7		No	0	Yes
RF	RFI-0007 RF	Pete	25/03/2020	1	PC-RFI-000124 - Movement Between Main Structures	01/04/2020	28/04/2020	27		No	0	Yes
RF	RFI-0009 RF	Pete	26/03/2020	1	PC-RFI-000126 - Gutter Design Sketch	02/04/2020	16/04/2020	14		No	0	Yes
RF	RFI-0010 RF	Pete	27/03/2020	1	PC-RFI-000127 - Roof Maintenance Strategy	03/04/2020	23/04/2020	20		Yes	0	No
RF	RFI-0011 RF	Pete	31/03/2020	1	PC-RFI-000130 - Plant Well Door	07/04/2020	06/04/2020	-1		No	0	Yes
RF	RFI-0012 RF	Pete	30/03/2020	1	PC-RFI-000128 - Painting of Steelwork	06/04/2020	04/06/2020	59		No	0	Yes
RF	RFI-0014 RF	Pete	14/04/2020	1	PC-RFI-000135 - Drawings Request for Down Pipe Locations	21/04/2020	21/05/2020	30		Yes	0	Yes

- With the correct information, the Design Report will provide data charts of key information to assist in the overall understanding, awareness and control of the design process.

PC | DRAWING STATUS

Drawing Status	P01	P02	P03	P04	C01	C02	C03	C04	AB01	Totals
SO - Work In Progress	0	0	0	0	0	0	0	0	0	0
A - suitable for construction	0	0	0	0	64	1	1	0	0	66
S1 - Suitable for co-ordination	0	0	0	0	0	0	0	0	0	0
S2 - Suitable for information	17	0	0	0	0	0	0	0	0	17
S3 - Suitable for internal review & comment	252	12	2	0	0	0	0	0	0	266
Totals	269	12	2	0	64	1	1	0	0	349
As A Percentage	77.1	3.4	0.6	0.0	18.3	0.3	0.3	0.0	0.0	100.0

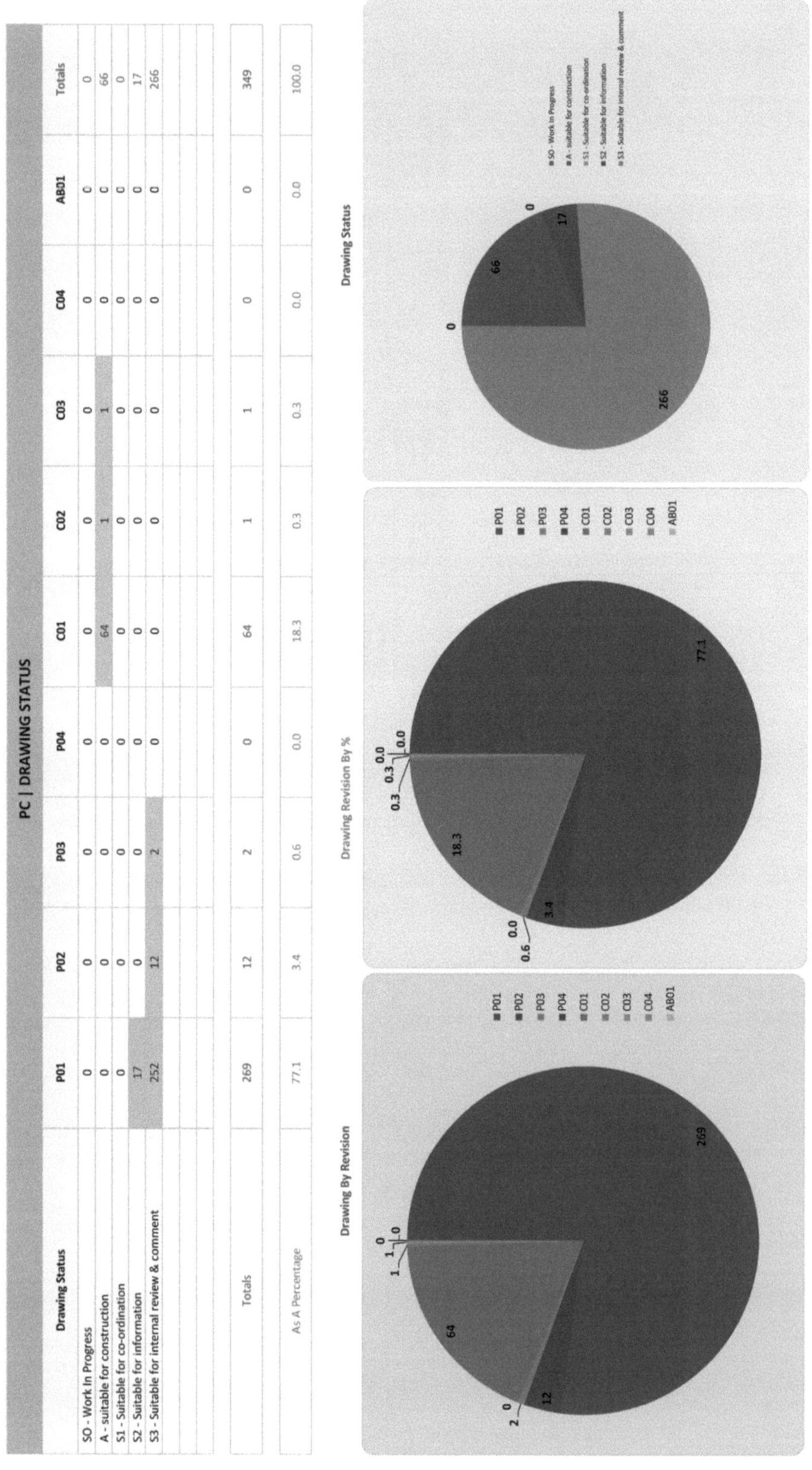

Constraints and Blockers

- Key constraints and blockers should be clearly identified so they can form the agenda of any meetings, and escalation can be carried out where appropriate.

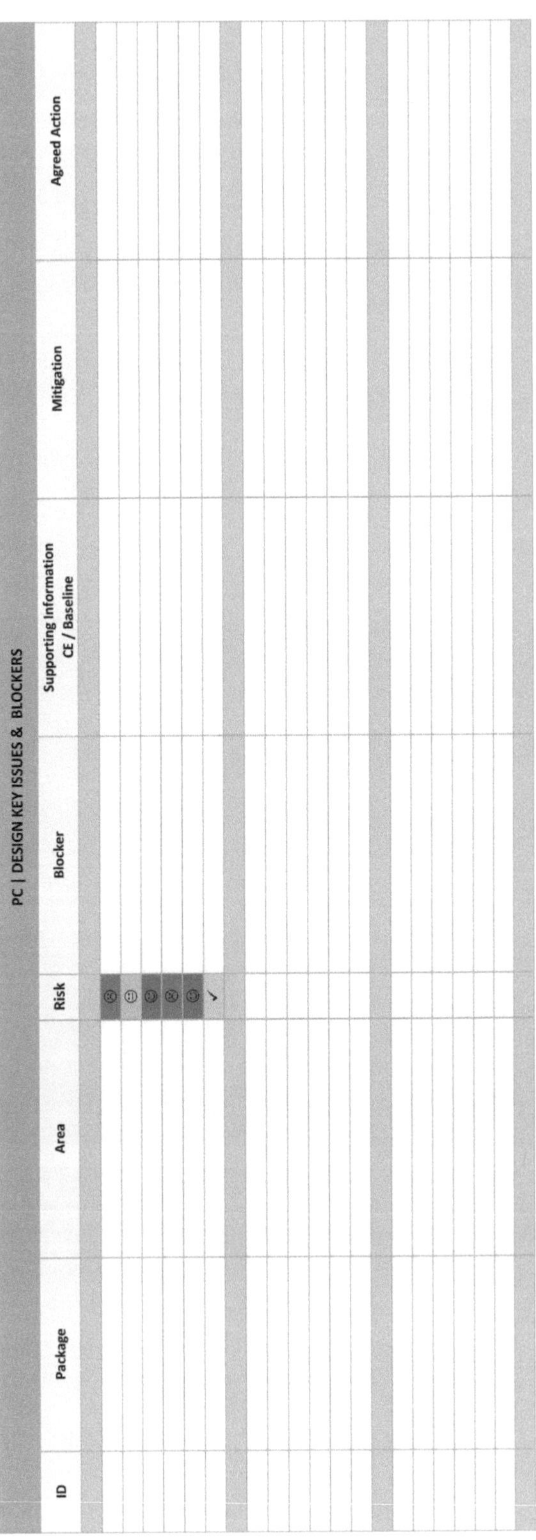

Procurement Tracker

- The Procurement Tracker is an essential document where the procurement issues, location, total numbers and planned issue dates are stated.

Project Name	
Project Number	
Design Manager	
Quantity Surveyor	
Project Manager	
Buyer	

PC | PROCUREMENT TRACKER

Program ID Ref [from the unique program ID]	Procurement Tracking Number	Resource	Area/Phase	Grid Line Ref - Location	Program Activity	Description Of Materials	Due At Logistic Store [If Applicable]	Program Site Start Date	Material Lead-In Period [Days]
ID1	1	Pete	A	11	ONE	Roof Sheeting	15/08/2019	15/08/2019	14
ID2	2	Pete	B	22	TWO	Roof Support Flashings	18/09/2019	18/09/2019	14
ID3	3	Angela	C	33	THREE	Wall Sheeting	30/10/2019	30/10/2019	14
ID4	4	Angela	D	44	FOUR	Wall Fixings	02/12/2019	02/12/2019	7
ID5	5	Matthew	E	55	FIVE	Wall Support Flashings	07/12/2019	07/12/2019	28
ID6	6	Matthew	F	66	SIX	Roof Gutters	19/12/2019	19/12/2019	7

- With the correct information, the Procurement Tracker will provide data charts of key information to assist in the overall understanding, awareness and control of the design process.

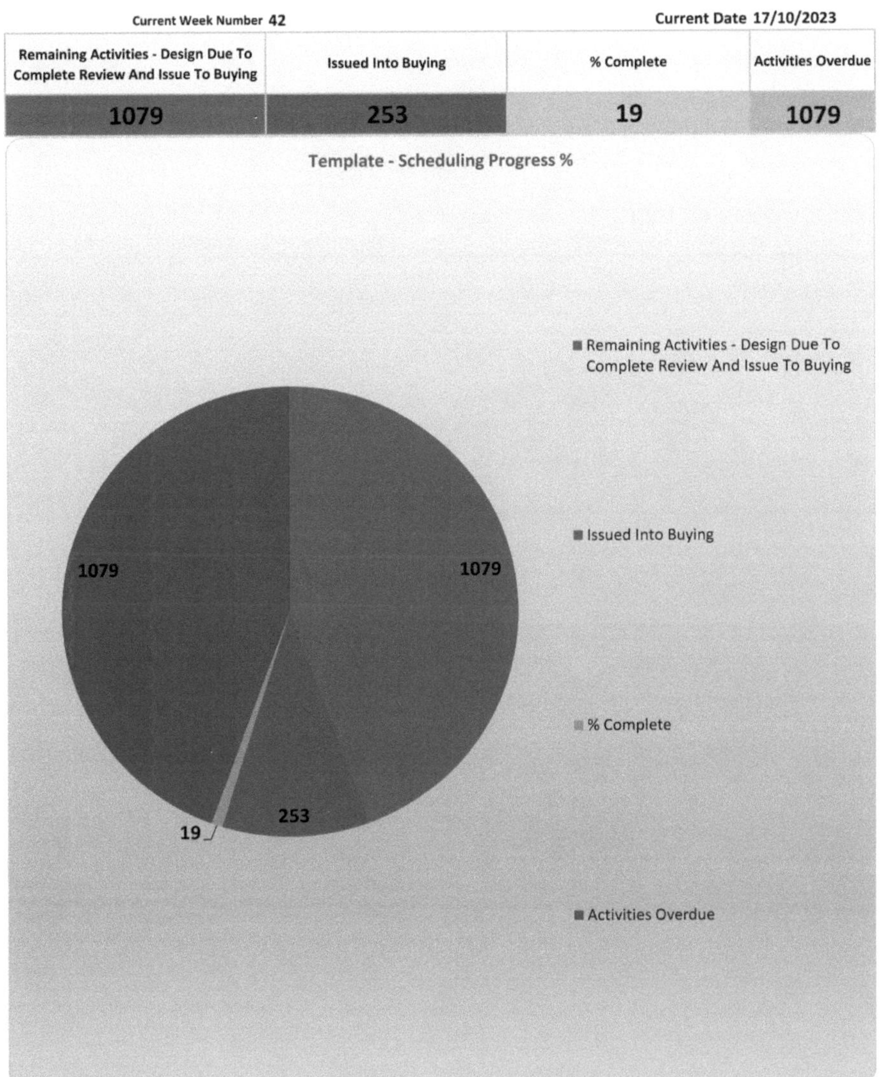

Buying Due To Place Order Date	Order Placed	% Complete	Activities Overdue
1110	222	17	1110

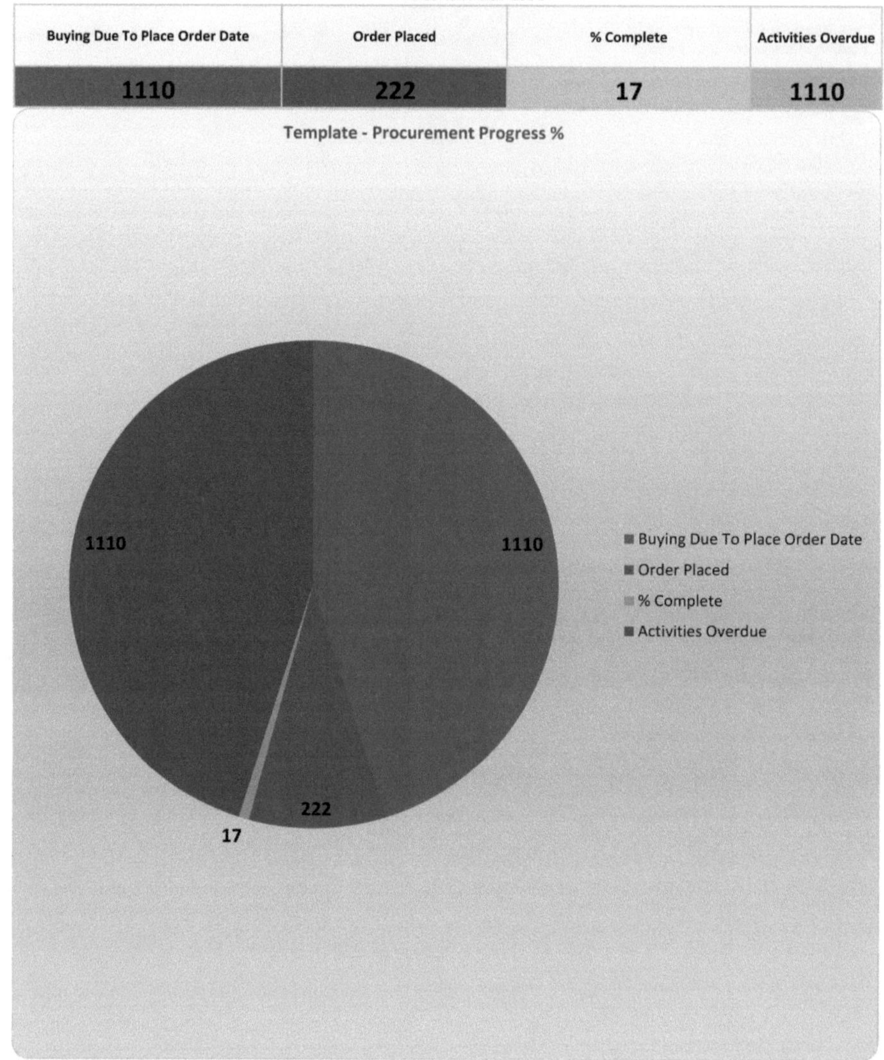

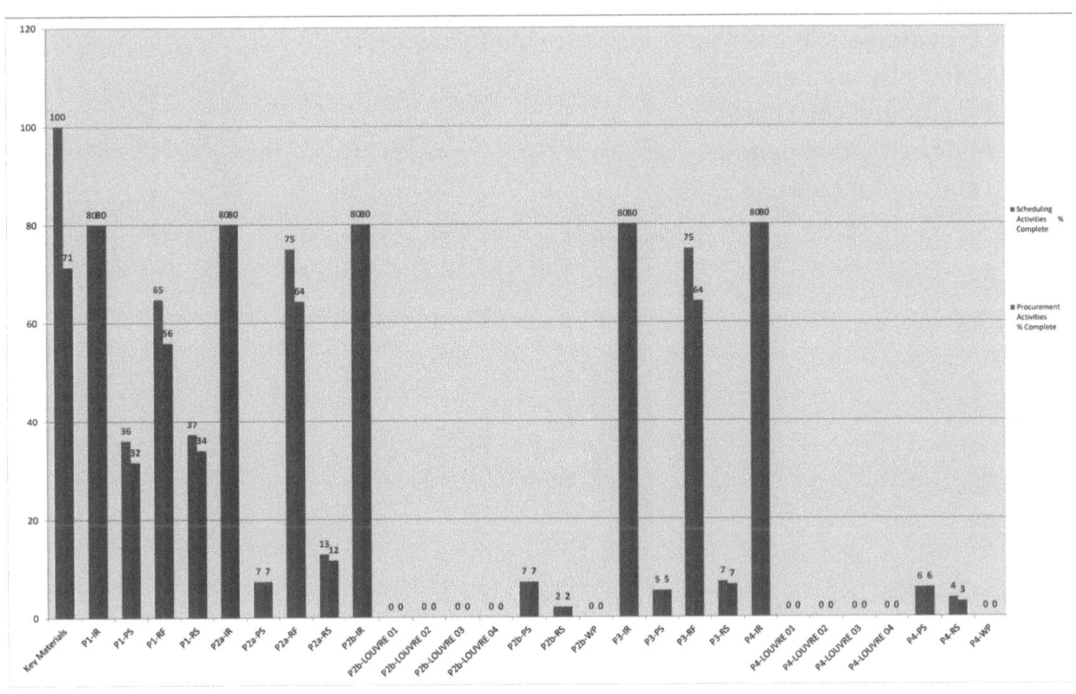

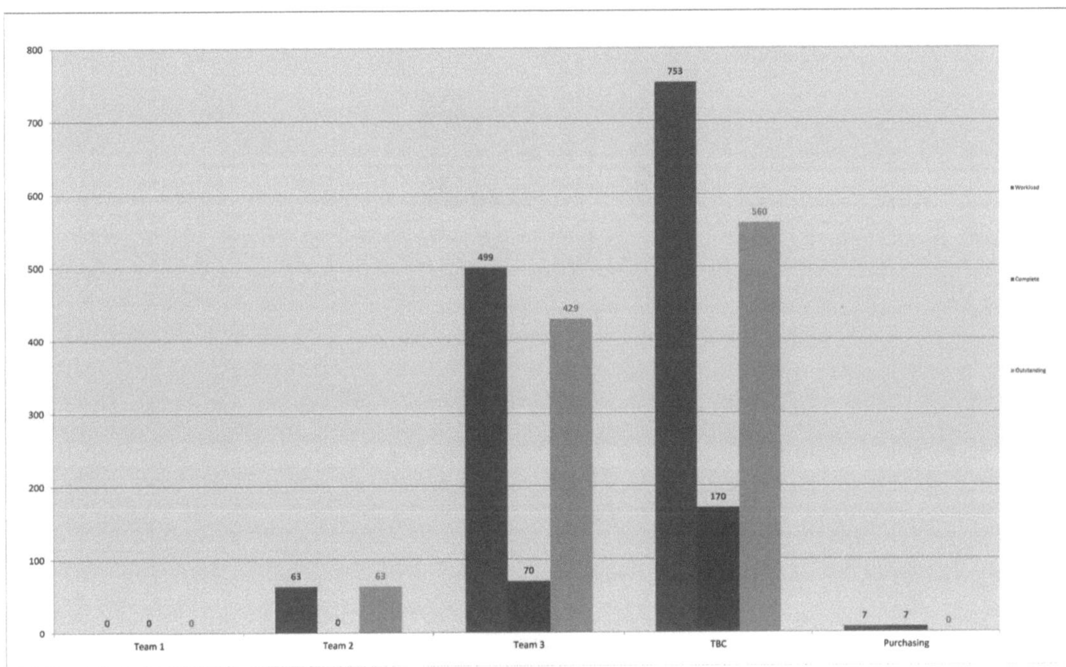

- The Procurement Tracker should capture the following:
  - List of procurements.
  - Programme start dates.
  - Material lead-in periods.
  - Latest order dates.

PC | PROCUREMENT TRACKER											
Design Due To Complete Schedule By Date	Design Due To Complete Review And Issue To Buying	Actual Date -Issued Into Buying Date	Issued To Buying On Time/Late	Document Issue Number	Buying Due To Place Order Date	Date Order Placed	Order Placed On Time/Late	P.O. Reference	Supplier	Estimated Delivery Date	Design Due To Complete Schedule By Date [week No.]
18/07/2019	25/07/2019	25/07/2019	CORRECT	1	01/08/2019						29
21/08/2019	28/08/2019	09/12/2019	LATE	2	04/09/2019						34
02/10/2019	09/10/2019	17/12/2019	LATE	3	16/10/2019						40
11/11/2019	18/11/2019	18/11/2019	CORRECT	4	25/11/2019						46
26/10/2019	02/11/2019	09/12/2019	LATE	5	09/11/2019						43
28/11/2019	05/12/2019	05/12/2019	CORRECT	6	12/12/2019						48

Meetings

- Always set a clear agenda to ensure you maximise time in any meetings, and you get out of them what you need.

PC | Design Notes

Design Meeting Agenda

General Issues

- Progress overview
- Resource cost overview
- Technical challenges
- Engineering
- Testing
- Key blockers / escalation / senior support
- Risks & Opportunities
- Design freeze – status?
- Materials, finishes and testing schedule
- Specifications – conflicting information
- New documents issued – strategy for cost recovery?

Fire Strategy

- Fire stopping
- Fixing to intumescent painted steel

Rooflight

- Choice of system / Supply Chain
- Performance [thermal, acoustic]
- Fragility
- Modularisation / DfMA

- Always take your own meeting minutes and issue them to the Client as a record of what was discussed and agreed upon.
- Ensure you write the notes so they are suitable to be sent externally.

PC	DESIGN MEETING MINUTES	
Project Name		**Project Contract Number**
Date of Meeting		**Location of Meeting**
Attendees		**Distribution**
Apologies		Agenda

No.	Actions Required	Owner	Action by Date

CDM Assessment

- The CDM Assessment should be treated as a live document and be updated as the design progresses. It should be a continuation of the one set up at Pre-Construction stage.
- Any additional work, scope or variations are to be added to CDM Assessment and re-issued as required.
- The same CDM Assessment, if produced during Tender Stage, should be updated.
- It is often best to issue the CDM Assessment by means of an RFI.

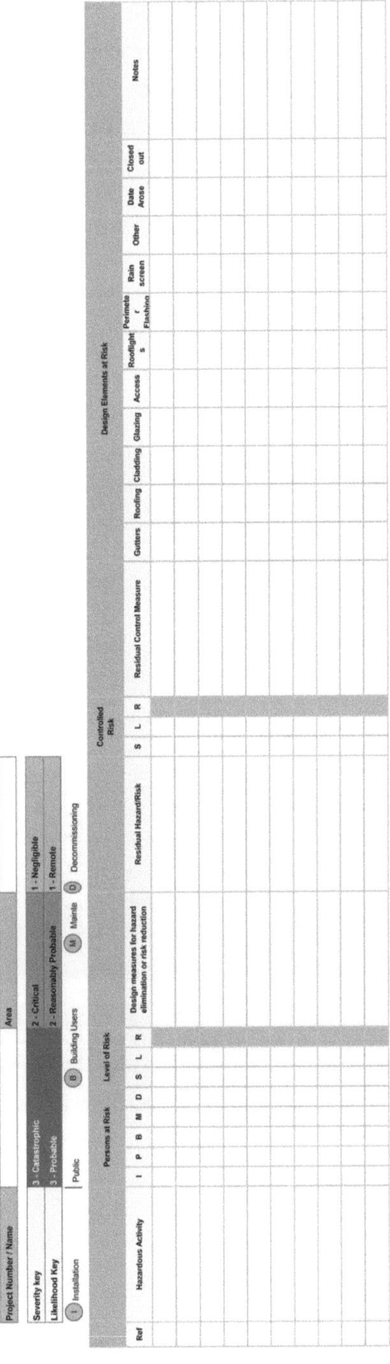

Designing Commercially

- Typically, a percentage of the Contract Sum is used.
- We rarely complete our design work within time or budget.
- It is estimated from Claims recovery stats throughout the Company that we rarely recover more than 20% of our design overspend when compared to the Tender Allowance.
- Reason: design work is done beyond the priced scope, and recovery is not pursued contemporaneously.
- The following is a list of items that may need resolution before final accounts can be agreed or monies paid:
    o 'C' Status calculations may need to be remodelled.
    o Technical queries may need to be resolved.
    o As-Built Drawings required and fully updated to suit 'as-built' conditions.
    o O and M information, including guarantees, re-glazing Methodology, spare parts, etc.
    o Site Water testing certificates.
    o QA issues to be resolved and rectified.
    o Any Other Missing Site Materials.
    o Any Possible Contra Charges.

Design Action List

- Ensure regular team meetings are held; 0900 on a Monday morning works best.
- Keep a Design Action List of the key actions discussed and ensure it follows the red, amber and green [RAG] principle.
- These action lists must have dates and owners to promote ownership and accountability.

ID	Date	Headline	Topic	Comment	Status	Response / Action	Action By	Owner
1.00		Design						
1.01	07-Feb-22	Design	Wind Loads	Review of wind loading criteria in respect of corners - 1.2kPa given but is it the same for the corners.	☺	Check with engineer.	23-Feb-22	Pete
1.02	07-Feb-22	Design	Wall Panels	Top detail to be reviewed at raking wall panels.	☺	PC to review with designer.	23-Feb-22	Pete
1.03	07-Feb-22	Design	Report	Testing report to be issued to Client.	✓	No further action.	-	-
1.04	07-Feb-22	Design	Rails	Drawing for rail height required.	☺	Issued via email on 17 Feb 22 - to be issued onto Information Management System.	23-Feb-22	Matthew
1.05	07-Feb-22	Design	Glazed Rooflight	Glazed rooflight query - check loads on glass roof.	☺	Awaiting engineer.	16-Feb-22	Pete
1.06	07-Feb-22	Design	Wall Panels	Have we been instructed for new cill flashings.	☺	Commercial team to advise.	TBC	Pete
2.00		Purchasing						
2.01	04-Feb-22	Purchasing	Roof Insulation	Roof insulation could be in short supply - to be reviewed with Purchasing.	✓	Site have confirmed there are no issues with insulation.	-	-
2.02	04-Feb-22	Purchasing	Fixings	Fixing changes due to short supply - drawings and calculations to be fully aligned.	☺	Meeting with Purchasing required.	-	Angela
3.00		Contracts						
3.01	07-Feb-22	Contracts	Programme	Road map to be developed and FULL programme of pre-construction activities and site installation to be produced.	☺	PC to discuss with site Project Manager.	TBC	Angela
4.00		Commercial						
4.01	07-Feb-22	Commercial	Cash Flow	Cash flow / expenditure to be reviewed.	✓	PC and Commercial team meeting held.	-	-
4.02	07-Feb-22	Commercial	Supply Chain	How is 'out of manufacturing' tolerance being dealt with Supply Chain - review route of cost recovery.	☹	Purchasing to raise Non Conformance Report.	18-Feb-22	Pete

PC | INTERNAL DESIGN ACTIONS

- With the correct information, the Design Action List will provide data charts of the number of items of each priority to ensure the manager and team are focusing on the right priorities.

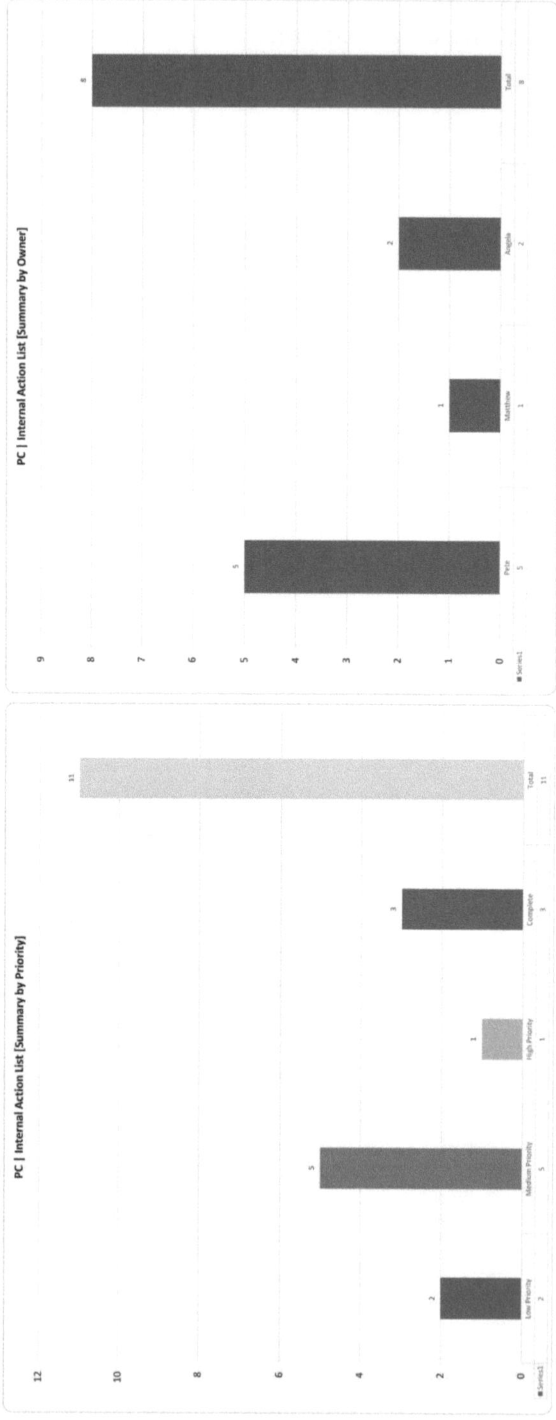

- The Design Action List is an ideal way of closing a project, and will, at some point, overtake the project programme as tasks become hours and days as opposed to weeks.

Drawing Comments Tracker

- The use of a Drawing Comments Tracker will assist in monitoring the comments received on drawings or other documents and the responses.

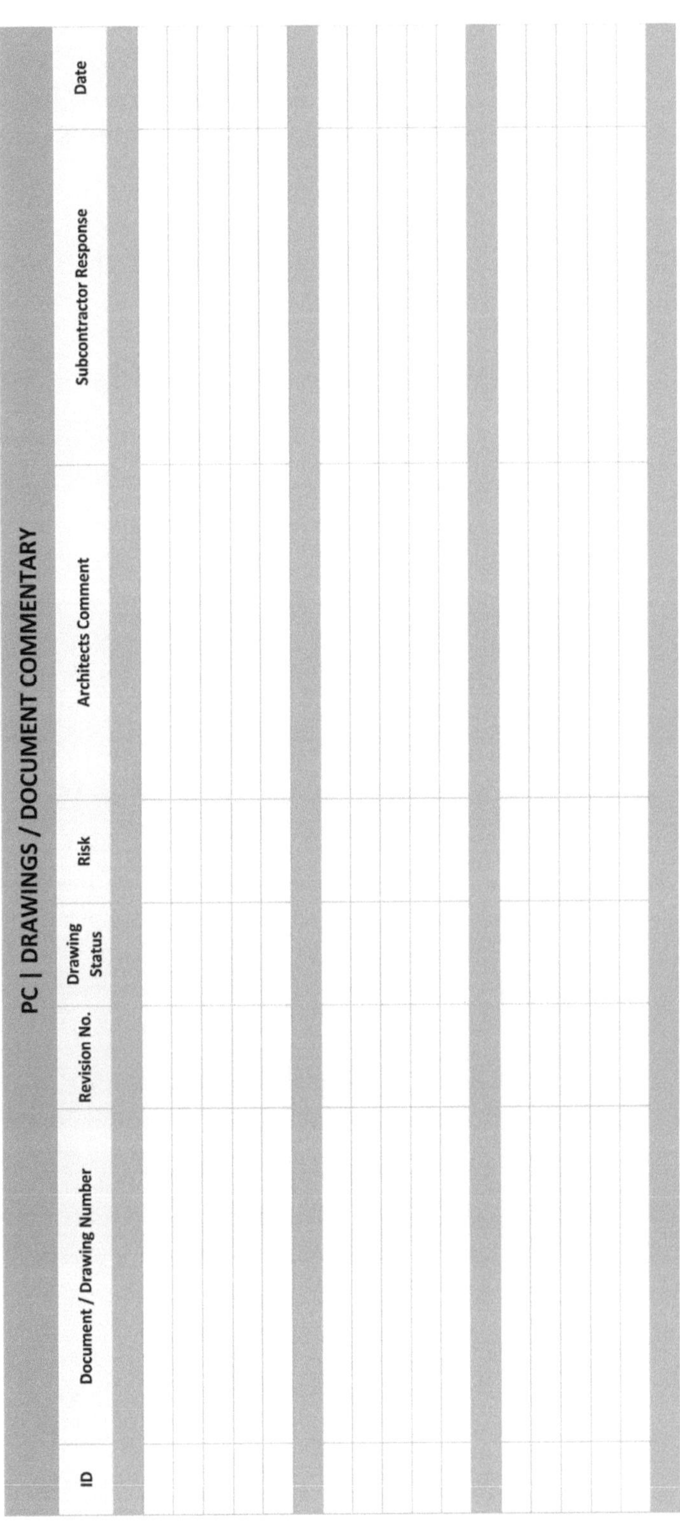

PC | DRAWINGS / DOCUMENT COMMENTARY

ID	Document / Drawing Number	Revision No.	Drawing Status	Risk	Architects Comment	Subcontractor Response	Date

- The Client and their Stakeholders often make comments on 'construction status' drawings, which should not happen unless it is a contractual requirement. A typical response could be:
  - These comments are on construction issue drawings [see attached], all materials have been ordered.
  - All comments made on approval drawings have been addressed or responded to previously.
  - We are unable to incorporate any further comments on construction issue drawings without a specific instruction from The Client to revisit the design.

Design Issue Tracker

- The use of a Design Issue Tracker will assist in monitoring the comments received on drawings or other documents and the responses.

PC | DESIGN ISSUE TRACKER																		
ID	Type	Owner	Document			Client / Main Contractor / Consultant			Priority	Subcontractor / Consultant				Supporting Documents		Further Action	Recorded Action to Close Out	Closed
			Reference	Title	Revision	Comment	Owner	Date		Comment	Owner	Date	Title	Reference	Revision			

- Any design issues that are discussed in meetings, received via email or by other means, should be listed on a Design Issue Tracker.
- As the work progresses, the description is updated along with the status.
- With the correct information, the Design Issue Tracker List will provide data charts of the number of items of each priority to ensure the manager and team are focusing on the right priorities.

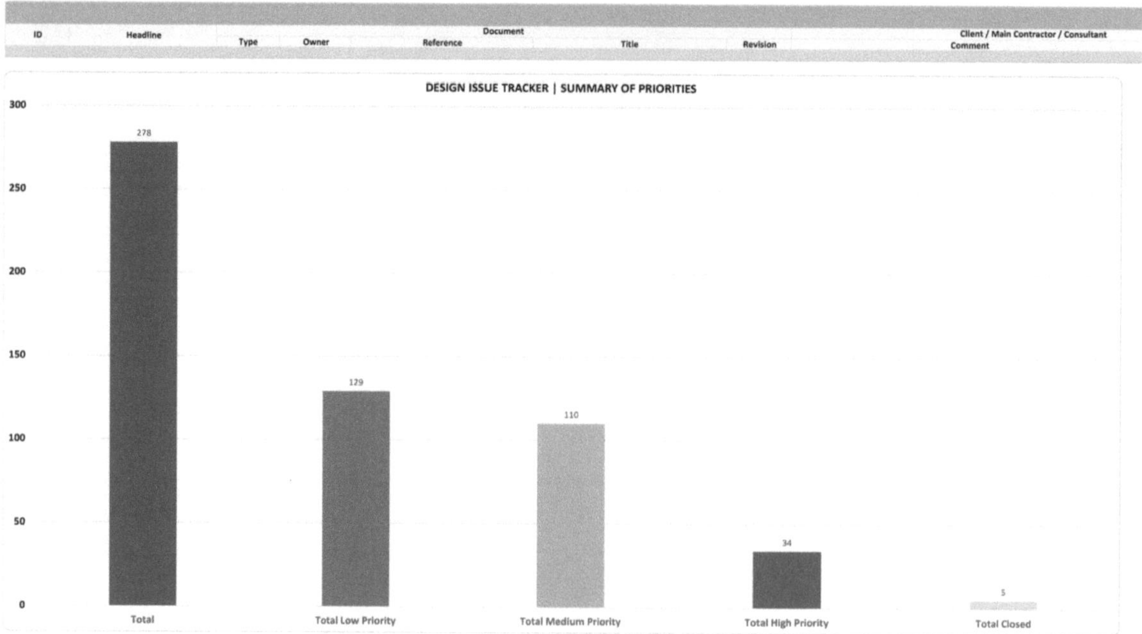

Design Risk and Opportunity Schedule

- A Design Risk and Opportunity Schedule should be maintained throughout the project.
- This is an ideal document to present to Senior Managers so they can understand project and business risks and see how they can support any potential opportunities.

PC | DESIGN RISK & OPPORTUNITY SCHEDULE

ID	Item	Location	Measured Risk	Risk Owner	Proposed Action	Open / Closed	Risk Implication (Cost / Programme)	Estimated Risk Value / Programme Implication

Project Progress Reports

- Project Progress Reports are usually produced by the Project Director or Project Manager, but the Design Manager must contribute to this.
- If the documents, reports and trackers outlined in this Design Managers Handbook are used and kept up to date, they easily form part of the Project Progress Report with minimal extra work.

Programme
Contract Programme
Two Week Lookahead
The following items are due to commence in the next two weeks.
The following items are due to be delivered in the next two weeks.
Progress Photographs
Weather Conditions
Wind speed for the last month
Rainfall for the last month
Temperature for the last month

- For ease of use, the Project Progress Report should have a contents page and be hyper-linked to the relevant section in the document.

<table>
<tr><td colspan="2" align="center">PC | PROJECT PROGRESS REPORT</td></tr>
<tr><td colspan="2" align="center">Contents Page</td></tr>
</table>

Electronic Issuing of Documents

- Below is a brief outline to clarify the responsibilities of the person involved and the order process of issuing electronic procurements to buying and onto site. It briefly suggests how the system needs to operate after the check and review process has happened.
  - The Designer prints all the schedules requiring issue to PDF and hard copy [the Designer must check that the PDF copy file name is correct in accordance with the naming convention stipulated by the project]. The Designer passes the hard copy and emails the PDFs to The Document Controller.
  - The Document Controller processes the PDFs through the electronic procurement system and emails the electronic schedule to buying and site.
  - The Document Controller processes the schedules and Stamps the original copies of schedules with 'document on IMS' and hole-punches the schedules and returns them back to the designer. It is the Document Controller's responsibility to ensure that all schedules have been issued to buying for procurement.
  - The Designer checks he or she has received all the schedules back that they have issued to the Document Controller. He or she should check these against the issue sheet on procurement email received from the Document Controller to ensure that all the schedules have been ordered and none have been missed out.
  - The Designer files original schedule in the procurement file.
- This last part of the process is the only check we have in the system where the designer can ensure that the schedules have been processed and that they have reached buying.
- As with all processes, this should have its own workflow.
- The use of barcodes or QR codes on schedules and materials is a significant benefit in monitoring, control and distribution of materials on site.

Procurement Issue to Document Control

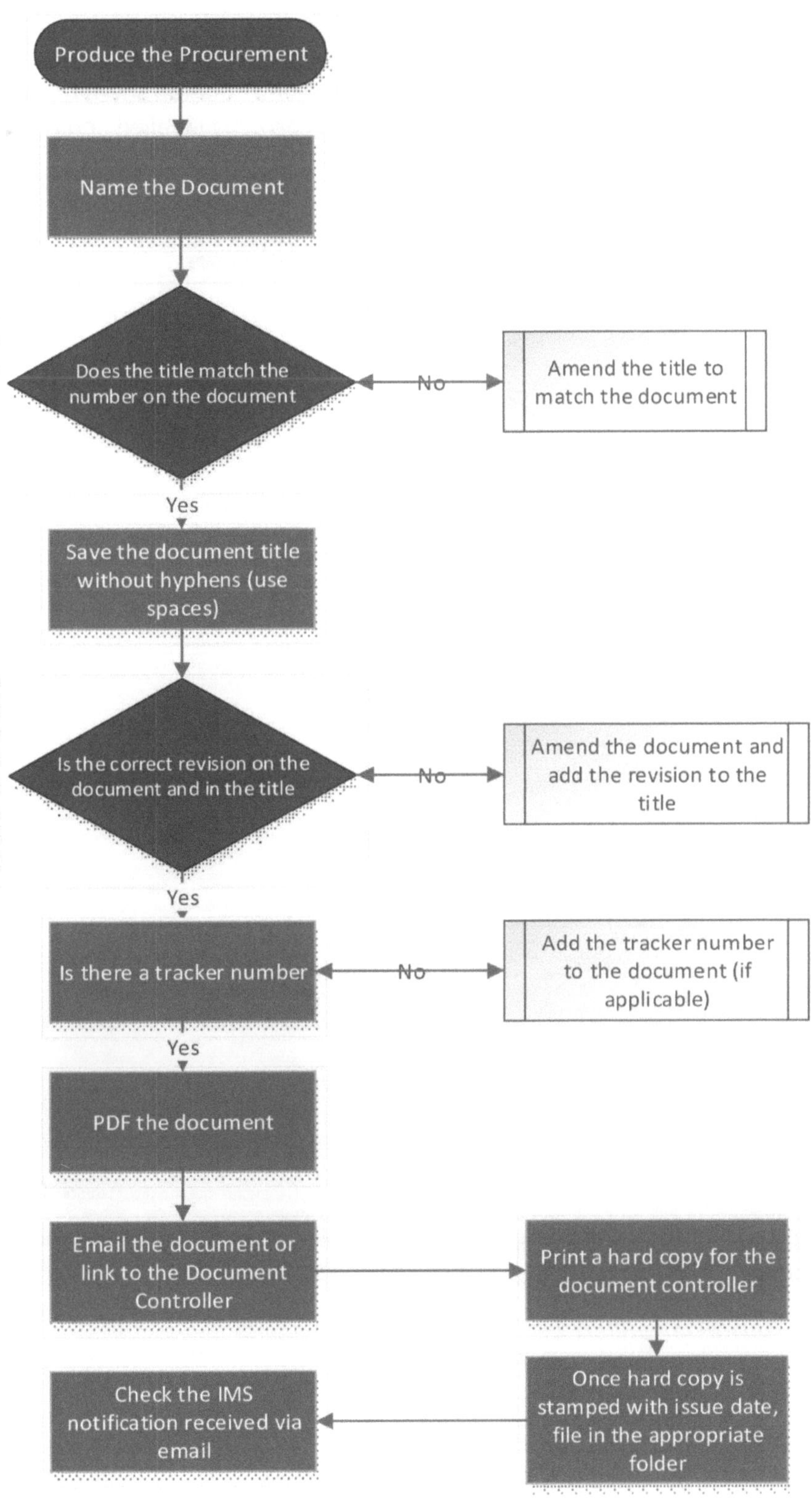

Sample Approval

- Sample approvals are a critical part of the design process, and there is often a defined list in the Contract Specification.
- All samples should be issued with supporting technical information, and any discrepancies from the Client's requirements or contractual information should be clearly identified.
- All samples issued should be photographed, correctly labelled and issued as part of the project protocols.

PC | REQUEST TO APPROVE SAMPLE		
Contract No.	**Sample No.**	**Project Name**

DESIGN		
	Raised By	
	Date of Issue	
	Area of Work	
	Contract Specification	
	Supplier / Manufacturer	
	Batch No [if relevant]	
	Type	☐ Control Sample ☐ Sample ☐ Mock-Up ☐ For Information
	Purpose of Issue	
	Photo Section	
	Technical Literature Attached	☐ Yes ☐ No
	Date Response Required By	

CLIENT		
	Reviewed By	
	Position & Company	
	Acceptance Status	☐ A- Sample is acceptable with the client requirements ☐ B- Sample is acceptable with the client requirements subject to the comments recorded below ☐ C- Sample is not acceptable for the reasons stated below and the actions recorded must be implemented
	Comments	
	Signature	
	Date	

- Samples are never to be delivered directly to the Client.
- Some projects require the use of the Clients' own process, system and forms, but the principle should be maintained.

Approval Form for Samples / Benchmarks / Mock-Ups		
Reference	Revision:	Status:
Owned By		
Date		
Project Name		
Project Reference		

Requests for Information

- Requests for Information [RFIs] are to be used at Post-Construction stage.

PC	REQUEST FOR INFORMATION			
Contract No.	Area	No.		Revision
	Project Name			
Originator		Issue Date		Response Required By
Issued To			Copied To	

Query

Should the request information not be received by the date indicated, the following may be incurred:
☐ Programme Implications   ☐ Cost Implications

Client Response

From [Name]	Company	Position	Signature	Date

- TQs that are not answered during the Pre-Construction stage are to be renumbered and re-issued as RFIs. For example, TQ-012 could become RFI-003.

Calculation Sheets

- Any calculation produced must be issued through the normal approval process and should have a cover sheet so it follows the same protocol as all other design procedures.

PC	CALCULATION SHEET		

Contract No.	Area	No.	Revision

Project Name

Originator	Issue Date	Response Required By

Issued To	Copied To

Calculation

Door Schedule

- A fully concise door schedule should be produced and issued through the approval process.
- This should be produced in conjunction with the door supplier where possible.
- The same door schedule, if produced during Tender Stage, should be updated.

PC | DOOR SCHEDULE

Door Location			General														Leaves & Sizes				Door rating			Security & Access Control			Ironmongery
Door Reference	Location	Room Function	Door Type	Blast	Interior Exterior	Material	Finishes	Sliding / Hinged	Operation	Closer	Steel Goal Post	Ventilation Grilles	Vison Panel	Push & Kick Plates	DDA Threshold	Configuration of Leaves	Opening	Clear Width	Clear Height	Panic Bar	Thermal Rating	Fire Rating	Acoustic (dB)	SR Rating	Access Control	Presence Detector	Set
ED-01	Plant Space	Plant Access	DP-23	No	Exterior	Metal	PPC	Hinged	Manual	Yes	Yes [By Others]	No	No	Yes	No	Single	Inwards	1000	2100	Yes	0	FR-30	0dB	No	No	No	Lever / Lever
ED-02	Façade	Entrance / Fire Exit	DR-26	No	Exterior	Glass	Glass	Hinged	Manual	No	Yes [By Others]	No	No	No	Yes	Double	Outwards	1800	2100	No	2.2	FR-30	0dB	No	No	Yes	Panic Bar Only

Sketch Sheet

- Any sketches carried out during the design process should be put onto a Sketch Sheet and numbered accordingly.

Coordination Meetings / Project Review Meetings

- These are typically set up and chaired by the Project Director or Project Manager, but design contribute significantly to these.
- These meeting should have minutes which identify key actions and dates.

PC	PROJECT COORDINATION MEETING					
Project						
Project Ref			Attendees			
Date						
Meeting Number						
Meeting Location						

Risk Profile				
Health and Safety	Design	Procurement	Installation	Financial

Key Information							
Pre-Construction Programme		Construction Programme		Margin		Cash Position	
Week No.	Status	Week No.	Status	Tender	Current	Planned	Actual

01 | Health, Safety and Environment

Item	Date	Description	Action	Owner	Due Date	Risk	Status

02 | Sales and Estimating

Item	Date	Description	Action	Owner	Due Date	Risk	Status

03 | Programme

Item	Date	Description	Action	Owner	Due Date	Risk	Status

04 | Design

Item	Date	Description	Action	Owner	Due Date	Risk	Status

05 | Procurement

Item	Date	Description	Action	Owner	Due Date	Risk	Status

06 | Installation

Item	Date	Description	Action	Owner	Due Date	Risk	Status

07 | Commercial

Item	Date	Description	Action	Owner	Due Date	Risk	Status

08 | Key Risk and Opportunity

Item	Date	Description	Action	Owner	Due Date	Risk	Status

09 | Quality Management

Item	Date	Description	Action	Owner	Due Date	Risk	Status

10 | Client Satisfaction and Collaboration

Item	Date	Description	Action	Owner	Due Date	Risk	Status

Pre-Order Meetings with Suppliers and Subcontractors

- Meetings with suppliers and subcontractors should be held to ensure scope, programme, key dates, technical issues, specifications, methodology and logistics are clearly understood.
- These meetings should have minutes, and these should form part of the order.

PC | PRE-ORDER MEETING MINUTES

Project Title		Date	
Project Number		Meeting Location	
Approximate order value		Supplier	
Attendees		Quotation Reference	

Minute	Checklist Minutes	Action	Additional Information
	General / Specification		
1.00			
1.01	Have the relevant specification been issued to the supplier?		
1.02	Have we received supplier comments to the specification?		
1.03	Define design responsibility		
1.04	Define 'Design and Service Life' criteria		
1.05	Define Tolerance criteria as laid out in the specification		
1.06	Define Loading and Deflection criteria		
1.07	Define testing criteria as laid out in the specification		
1.08	Do we need to check compatibility with other products?		
1.09	Are samples required?		
1.10	List of drawings included within the quote		
	Programme/Order		
2.00			
2.01	Has the client signed off samples and submittals?		
2.02	Supplier lead in period		
2.03	Phased delivery		
2.04	Notification to deliver to site		
2.05	Anticipated initial delivery due		
2.06	Initial material to be ordered by		
2.07	Are there any products on a long lead in?		
2.08	Does the supplier need to order any components?		
2.09	Does the supplier need to order any components?		
2.10	Are there any special sheet sizes?		
2.11	Are any materials to be manufactured and stored?		
	Delivery		
3.00			
3.01	Site delivery address	As noted on 1st order	
3.02	Who is responsible for off loading?		
3.03	How is this achieved?		
3.04	Any specific packaging requirements for off loading etc.		
3.05	Are there any special handling requirements?		
3.06	Are there any special storage requirements?		
3.07	Are there any delivery charges?		
3.08	Are there minimum order quantities?		
	Financial		
4.00			
4.01	Have we an agreed credit limit?		
4.02	Payment terms?		
4.03	Have we agreed a price for all items on the project?		
	Contacts		
5.00			

Consultancy Agreement

- Work placed with any design subcontractors should have a Consultancy Agreement in place, which should include:
    - Brief.
    - Fees.
    - Agreed additional costs.
    - Payment plan.
    - Design deliverables.
    - Scheduling.
    - Engineering requirements.
    - Programme / key dates.

PC | Design Notes

Consultancy Agreement

Between

Company Name____   [Contractor]
Address   _______________________________________

And

Company Name____   [Consultant]
Address   _______________________________________

The Consultant agrees to provide the Services set out in the Schedule below in return for payment of the Price by *Company Name*.

Contract: Project 1

Scope of Works: Carry out Engineering services as detailed on the schedule below.

Schedule of Services: Fully list out the service requirements.

Programme: State key programme requirements and any key dates.

Price: £xxxx

Other Agreements:
a) Payment of Price – invoices shall be submitted stating the Purchase Order number.
b) Variations – any variation to the Services to be provided that has been instructed in writing shall be valued in accordance with a pre-agreed price.
c) Engineering services – shall be produced in sufficient time to allow the Contractor to meet the site installation programme dates.
d) Disputes – if any dispute or difference arises under this Agreement it shall be dealt with in accordance with the Scheme for Construction Contracts.
e) Etc.

Contacts: List out contacts for both parties.

Progress Mark Ups

- The use of 3D models is essential to identifying design progress. The colours should follow the same principle for the drawing list.

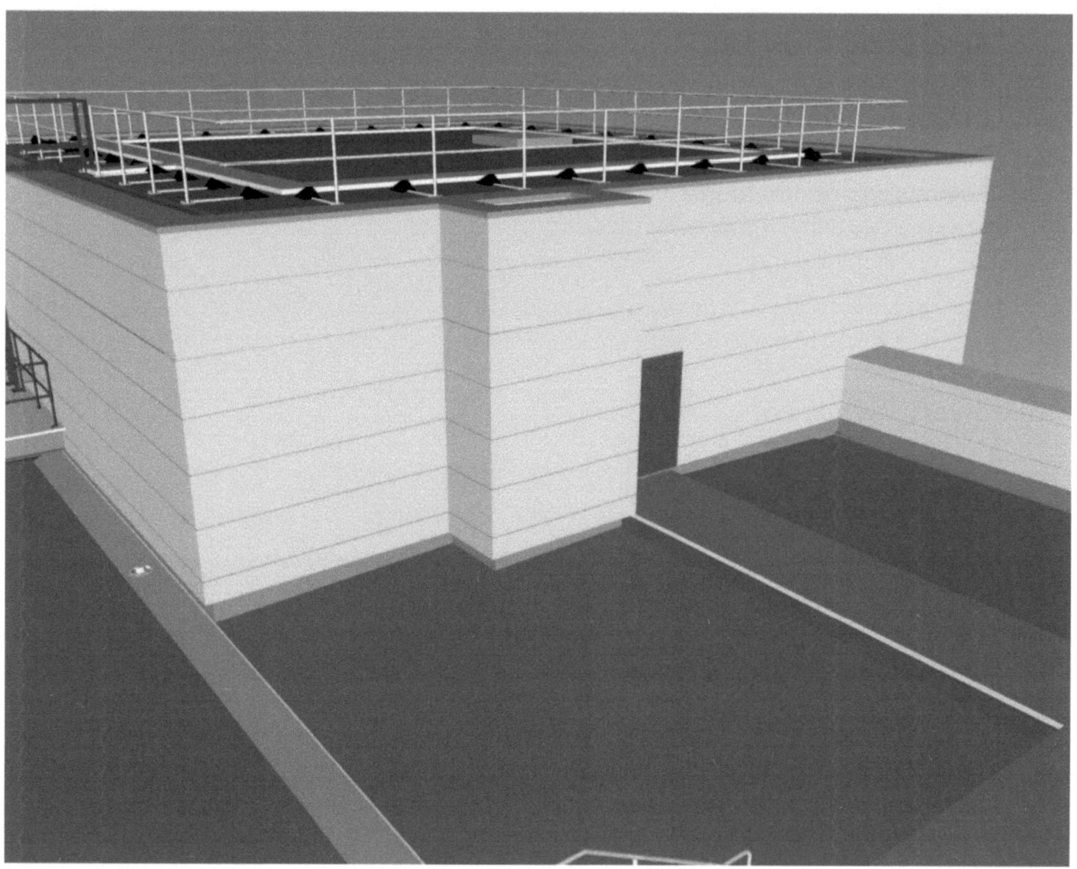

Design Activity	Drawing Summary	%
Design Commenced	01 | In Progress	30%
GA's and Details	02 | GA & Details Complete	40%
Issued For Approval	03 | Issued For Initial Approval	50%
Revise Drawings	04 | Revise Drawings	60%
Final Approval	05 | Issued For Final Approval	70%
Revise Drawings	06 | Revise Drawings	80%
Issue For Construction	07 | Issued For Construction	90%
Materials Scheduled	08 | Complete	100%
Archive	09 | As Built	AB

Coloured 3D models

- The use of 3D models is a good way to identify on-site work and off-site work.

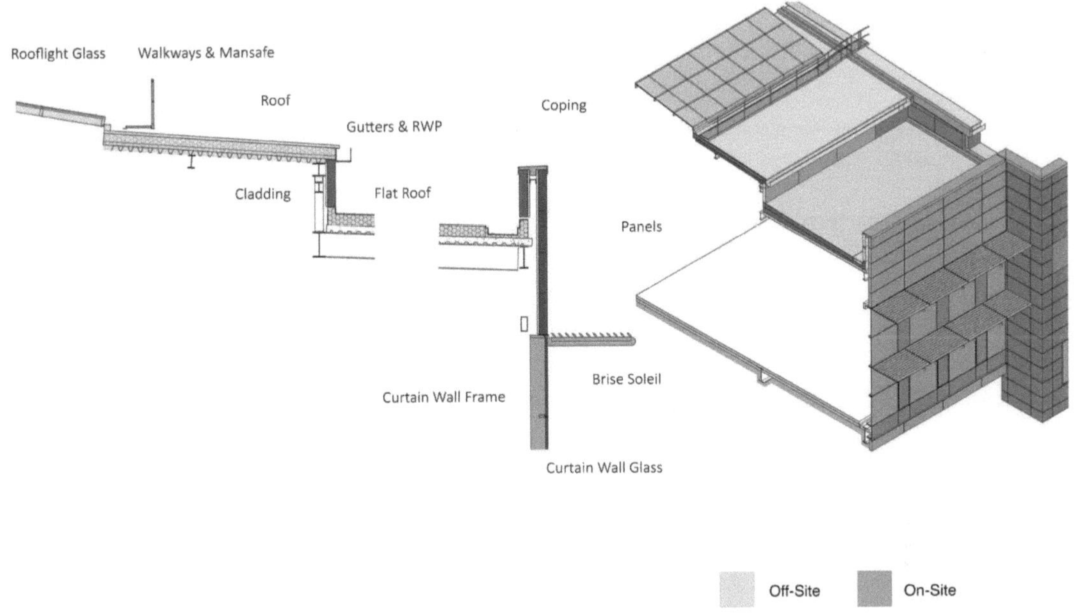

4D Modelling

- The use of 4D modelling allows you to identify where the project should be at an appropriate time as it is linked to a programme.
- This can be for Pre-Construction activities and on-site works.

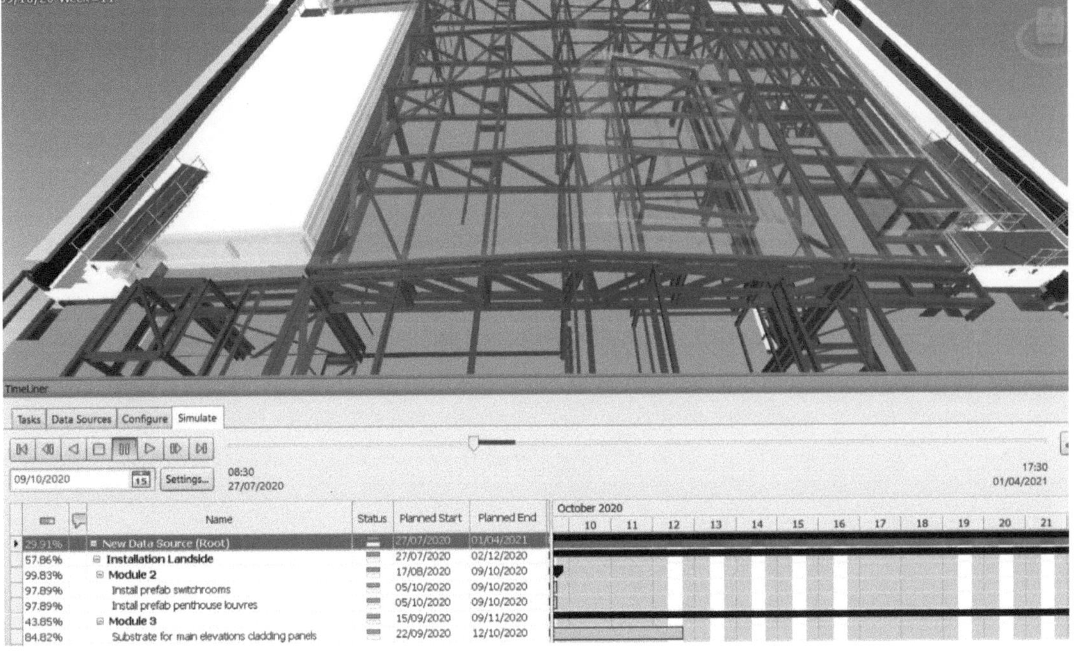

		Name	Status	Planned Start	Planned End	October 2020												
						10	11	12	13	14	15	16	17	18	19	20	21
29.91%	⊞ New Data Source (Root)			27/07/2020	01/04/2021												
57.86%	⊟ Installation Landside			27/07/2020	02/12/2020												
99.83%	⊟ Module 2			17/08/2020	09/10/2020												
97.89%	Install prefab switchrooms			05/10/2020	09/10/2020												
97.89%	Install prefab penthouse louvres			05/10/2020	09/10/2020												
43.85%	⊟ Module 3			15/09/2020	09/11/2020												
84.82%	Substrate for main elevations cladding panels			22/09/2020	12/10/2020												

- The 4D model will show where the construction should be at appropriate times. This can be put into an animation.

DESIGN RESPONSIBILITY

Design Obligation

- The design obligation sets the standard of care required when carrying out design work. There are two different standards:
  1. First, 'reasonable skill and care'.
  2. Second, the much higher standard of 'fit for purpose'.
- To illustrate the difference between the two standards, say, we design a walkable gutter that cannot be used as a walkable gutter once construction is complete.
- If the design standard is 'reasonable skill and care': as long as we can prove that we used reasonable skill in care when preparing our design, we will not be liable regardless of the gutter not being fit for purpose;

As a Business

- As a business, we do not typically accept 'fit for purpose' obligations. The terms of the PI insurance need to be reviewed against this kind of statement.
- We typically only offer to meet the standard of 'reasonable skill and care' when carrying out design work.
- The standard is that of a roofing / cladding / glazing specialist in the "normal course of his working professionalism".

Design Responsibility

- There are three different design responsibilities:
  1. **No design responsibility** – the responsibility is retained by the Contractor [or the Employer], and the specialist sub-contractor [us] simply prepares working drawings.
  2. **Completion of the design** – the usual responsibility is where the Contractor [or the Employer's consultants] prepares the design intent and the specialist sub-contractor completes the design from this design intent. The Contractor/Employer retains responsibility for the intent, and the specialist sub-contractor is responsible for all subsequent design work prepared by him, or on his behalf when completing the design.
  3. **Full design responsibility** – the Contractor passes on all of the design responsibility to the specialist sub-contractor, who is then responsible for meeting the Employer's Requirements.
- We would most likely undertake 'completion of the design'. There is, however, a tendency for the consultant design team to leave gaps in the design intent information,

and we are then expected to fill those gaps, meaning we take on more work and more responsibility / risk than we intended.

- It is therefore important that we establish the exact construction issue information that we require to prepare working drawings or to complete the design. It is only when we receive the required level of information that we can be sure no gaps exist.
- Our default construction issue information requirements are:
    1. Fully coordinated Architects and Structural Engineers drawings.
    2. Fully dimensioned plans, elevations and sections.

If we have NO Design Responsibility

- Prior to design commencement you must be in receipt of:
    1. Large scale, fully dimensioned detailed drawings showing cladding zones, in CAD format.
    2. The relationship of the roofing / cladding / glazing work with the structure and other building elements.
    3. Fully detailed interfaces between all junctions and service penetrations.
    4. Setting out dimensions and datum, including all structural openings to doors, windows, louvres and service penetrations.
    5. Interfaces with other trades.

If we are responsible for Completion of the Design

- Prior to design commencement we must be in receipt of "Construction Status Information" which provides suitable design intent to all areas of installation, allowing us to effectively proceed with the design of workable fixing details, including but not limited to:
    1. Large scale detail drawings showing the intended relationship of the roofing /cladding/ glazing work with the structure and other building elements.
    2. Specifications.
    3. 3D or BIM building models, where available, in a format compatible with the Companies standard software.
    4. We will not produce 3D or BIM models unless agreed as part of the Tender process or Instructed to do so.
    5. Fully resolved material specifications and confirmation of cladding build-up to satisfy where applicable.
    6. Thermal model report, confirming U Values to be achieved.
    7. Acoustic report, confirming criteria to be achieved.
    8. Fire strategy drawings, confirming fire integrity and insulation requirements.
    9. Design life and Warranty / Guarantee requirements.
    10. Full drainage design of all outlet sizes and positions.

- Any other associated documentation deemed necessary to the execution of the design, including where applicable but not limited to:
    1. Notification should the Client approval period of drawings and calculations extend beyond the standard 10 working days.
    2. Agreed scope and any Instructions required for amendment to post Tender information.
    3. Project wind loading values appropriate to the cladding package.
    4. Relevant site survey information, particularly where interfacing with existing structures or conducting renovation works.
    5. Confirmation of structural tolerances to be considered for accommodation within the cladding design.
    6. Confirmation of project wind loading values appropriate to the cladding package.
    7. Indication of structural movement or building movement joints for accommodation within the cladding design where required.
    8. Cladding system test requirements.
    9. Sample and mock-up requirements.
    10. Access strategy for future replacement of cladding.
    11. Health and safety CDM file.

Should this information not be available

- It is likely to affect any agreed programme until such time that sufficient information is received to make effective progress.
- We can provide:
    1. Advice on proposed build-ups and compliance with manufacturer's and system supplier's 'standard details' to achieve the required performance.
    2. Advice on buildability and production issues.
    3. Advice on variation of design works from cost plan.
    4. Advice on supplier's lead-in times and priority of details to suit the programme of works.
    5. Submittal of Requests for Information where it is deemed that further clarification of design is required from the Client's design team.
    6. Attendance at design meetings on a fortnightly basis during the initial stage of design.
    7. Fully dimensioned details and general arrangements to a suitable scale for Client comment review for compliance with the architect's design intent. Design to include system calculations.
    8. Fully dimensioned Construction Status details and general arrangements to a suitable scale which confirm setting out and fixing requirements to a level that allows for the proficient fabrication and site installation of cladding materials.
    9. Scheduling of specification-compliant materials, components and fixings.
    10. Compilation of 'As-Built' drawings and Operations and Maintenance manual.

- Whilst it is our responsibility to ensure that all necessary system calculations are conducted to satisfy that the system is fit for purpose, it is in the client's interest to review these calculations to ensure that the project requirements have been correctly interpreted.

Design Development and Design Change

- Contractors [and consultants] prefer these terms to be interchangeable in order to avoid the cost of any design change within our scope.
- Development of the design intent can often lead to changes within the completion of the design. So what is design development to the contractor is often design change to the specialist sub-contractor.
- This change should not be passed off as design development, and we should be paid for any such change. If design 'development' is being dictated by others, it is likely to be design change.

DESIGN APPROVALS

Allow Enough Time for Design and Drawing Approvals

- Make sure you allow enough time in the Design Programme for drawings and documents to be approved, internally as well as by the Client.
- It is important to keep track of the approval status of these and follow up with people to review and sign them. Drawings are usually issued via web-based extranet sites, which will allow tracking of drawings and documents, but it is essential that the Design Report is used and maintained alongside this.
- It is important to remind people of due approvals, as they often sit on a desk waiting and get buried.

Approval Time Limit

- Make sure that you understand what the contract specifies regarding the length of time allowed for approvals or decisions.
- When drawings or documents are sent to the Client for approval, you need to know [and specify] when they need to be approved in order to attempt to meet programme deadlines.
- Allow for this time in the Design Programme, and make sure the Client knows this is in the plan.
- Ensure that the Design Programme clearly identifies drawing and document approval periods.
- Be sure that the contract specifies what will happen if approvals are delayed beyond the specified time [i.e. can the drawing and document be "issued for construction"?]

Do Not Do Blanket Approvals

- Don't get blanket approvals on drawings or documents without each one being marked as approved by the Client.
- A Client may send documentation stating that the drawings or documents are approved for construction, but unless they mark each drawing as approved and return them to you, you have no proof that they actually did review each of them. Without the marked approval, the Client could deny they saw a particular drawing or design.
- Get each design or drawing individually marked as approved.

Approvals

- The Approval of a particular revision of a drawing or document implies that the Approver takes responsibility for the content of the revision of the document. This responsibility is often shrugged off by the use of alternative terms such as "No Comment". The effect however remains the same, and the arguments about liability remain the same.
- The most common method of approval in the Construction Industry is the "A B C" status, where:
  - "A" is the highest level of Approval – meaning that the Reviewer can find no problems. Proceed with the work as shown on the drawing.
  - "B" is the mid-level of Approval – meaning "Fit for construction or manufacture subject to the notes supplied".
  - "C" is the lowest level of Approval – meaning "Not fit for construction or manufacture". Revise as noted and re-submit for approval. No work shall commence.
- If comments are not incorporated at any stage of the Approval process, it is essential that these are communicated to the Client by means of a comment schedule and agreed upon where possible.
- The expectation is to receive coordinated comments from the Client, preferably by means of one marked-up drawing collating all comments. Where this is unlikely to happen, we must ensure that those individual drawings are returned from different sources [i.e. Client and Architects at the same time].
- If comments are received from multiple sources at various times, this constitutes out-of-sequence comments and affects the efficiency of the design process.

COST CONTROL

Value Engineering / Value Added Options

- Value engineering and different ways of doing things should be looked at as often as possible.
- Value engineering is not always about money; it can be about safety.
- Sometimes you have to spend money in the early phase of a project to bring future benefits. For example, £1 spent in design could save £2 out on site.
- Value engineering should be identified as part of the BID process and should form part of the BID documents.

Design Budget

- A design budget should be produced on every project, ideally at BID stage.
- The design budget will then be reviewed against any new information and reviewed with the Commercial team as necessary.
- A robust and fully resourced programme will allow an automated cost report.

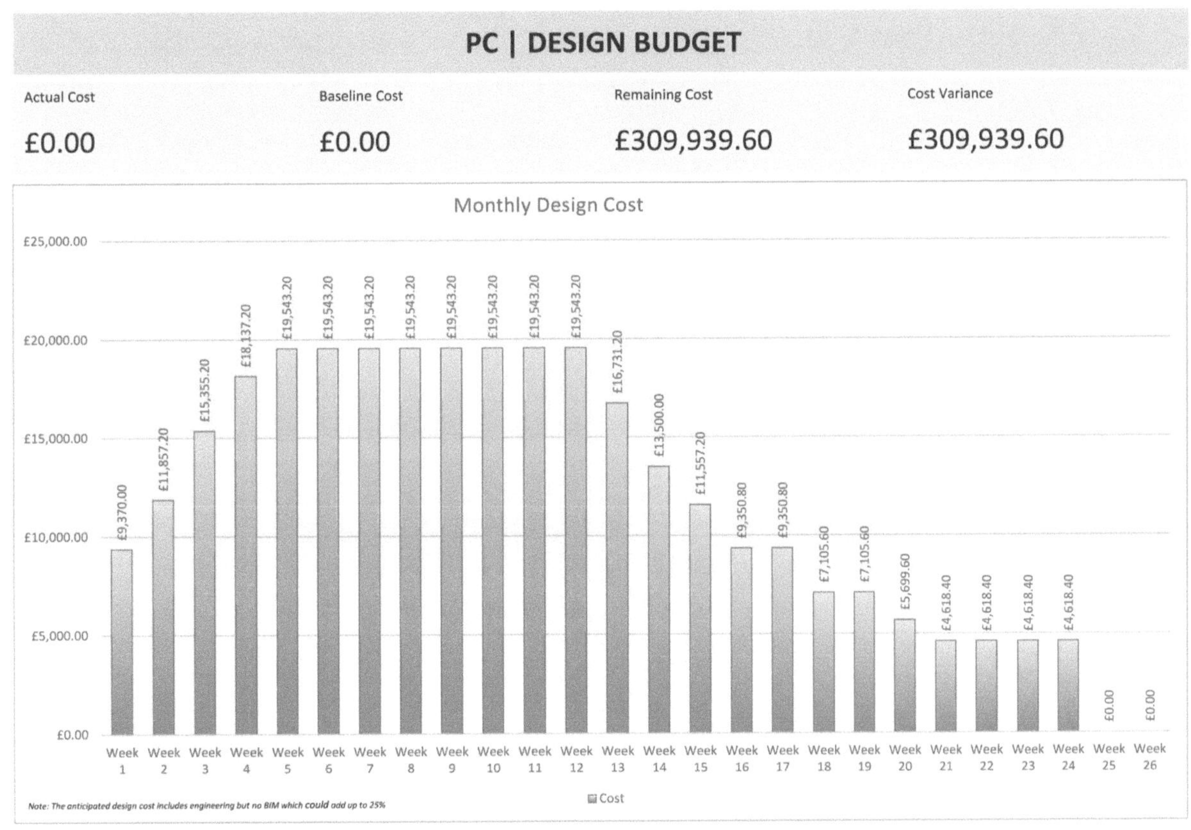

Cost Reporting

- Robust programme reporting, with true and accurate percentages, will provide automated cost reporting.
- In the example, you can see £103,853.60 spent to date with £14,464.48 remaining.

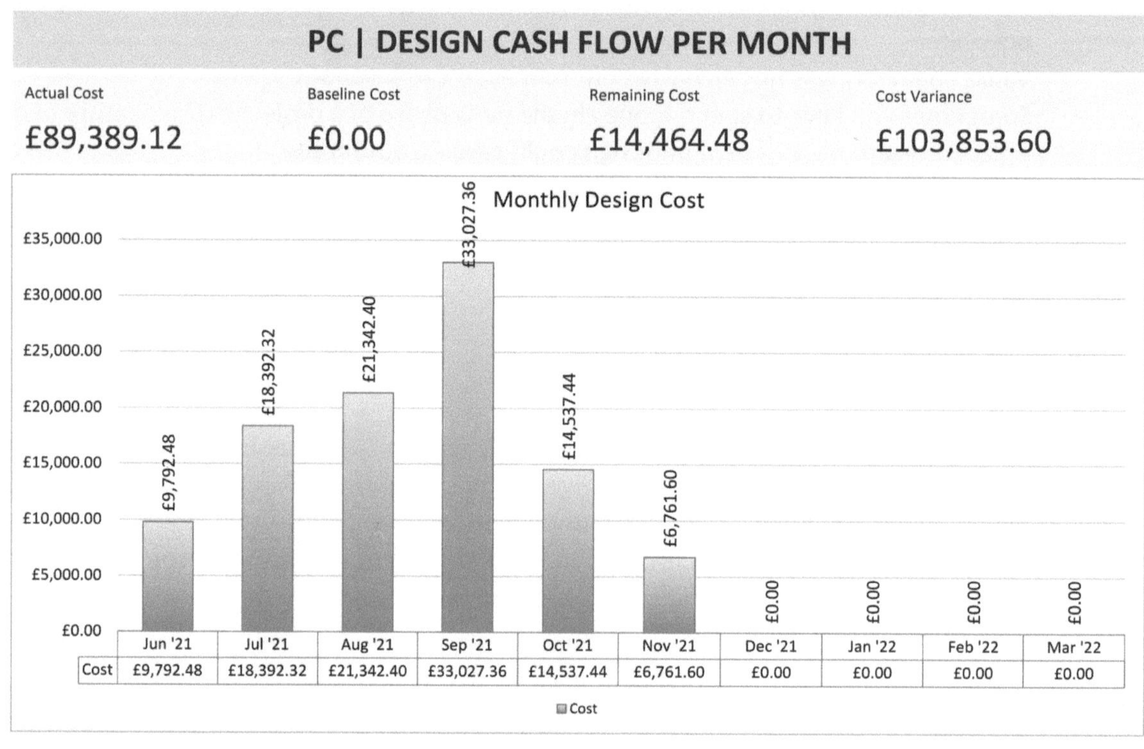

	Jun '21	Jul '21	Aug '21	Sep '21	Oct '21	Nov '21	Dec '21	Jan '22	Feb '22	Mar '22
Cost	£9,792.48	£18,392.32	£21,342.40	£33,027.36	£14,537.44	£6,761.60	£0.00	£0.00	£0.00	£0.00

Design Costs

- Overall project design costs should be recorded so trends can be identified, which may need feeding back to the front end of the business, especially to understand if, where and how design budgets have been exceeded.

PROJECT	Number	DM	CONTRACT SUM		FINAL ACCOUNT		DESIGN BUDGET		COST TO END OF MONTH		COST TO COMPLETE		SUB-TOTAL		COST AGAINST BUDGET		DESIGN VO COST		TOTAL		COST AGAINST BUDGET		DESIGN COST %
													PC | DESIGN COSTS										
Project 1	71	PC	£	361,921	£	361,921	£	139,000	£	-	£	-	£	-	£	139,000	£	-	£	-	£	139,000	0.0%
Project 2	70	PC	£	298,417	£	298,417	£	11,000	£	11,000	£	-	£	11,000	£	-	£	-	£	11,000	£	-	3.7%
Project 3	69	PC	£	578,269	£	608,450	£	51,675	£	52,175	£	5,000	£	57,175	-£	5,500	£	-	£	57,175	-£	5,500	9.9%
Project 4	68	PC	£	352,976	£	371,200	£	12,000	£	16,442	£	1,000	£	17,442	-£	5,442	£	-	£	17,442	-£	5,442	4.9%
Project 5	67	PC	£	23,697	£	53,791	£	300	£	300	£	-	£	300	£	-	£	-	£	300	£	-	1.3%
Project 6	66	PC	£	5,731,019	£	5,740,058	£	263,471	£	311,931	£	-	£	311,931	-£	48,460	£	39,347	£	272,584	-£	9,113	4.8%
Project 7	65	PC	£	3,105,178	£	3,124,589	£	194,485	£	139,876	£	-	£	139,876	£	54,609	£	5,000	£	134,876	£	59,609	4.3%
Project 8	64	PC	£	438,978	£	617,706	£	750	£	11,850	£	-	£	11,850	-£	11,100	£	-	£	11,850	-£	11,100	2.7%

- Robust and accurate design costs will allow an automated cost report and trending.

Model Coordination Variation [MCV]

- As a lot of design information received is in 3D, it is essential that, upon the receipt of new 3D information, a high-level review is carried out to identify any changes.
- Any changes identified should be recorded using a specific process and form.

<table>
<tr><td colspan="4" align="center">PC | MODEL COORDINATION VARIATION</td></tr>
<tr><td align="center">Contract No.</td><td align="center">MCV No.</td><td colspan="2" align="center">Project Name</td></tr>
<tr><td></td><td></td><td colspan="2"></td></tr>
</table>

DESIGN		
	Raised By	
	Date	
	Images	
	Brief Description of Variation	

COMMERCIAL		
	QS Review By	
	Project Manager	
	Date	
	Notes	
	Able to Proceed	☐ Proceed ☐ Do Not Proceed
	Variation No.	
	EWN / CE No.	

Potential Design Variation [PDV]

- Any design information received should be thoroughly reviewed to establish whether information is new, different or added.
- The designer is to complete a Potential Design Variation form immediately upon becoming aware of any varied and / or additional works that may require additional design time.
- It is often the case that this process will identify scope gaps for the Client and should be raised with the commercial department as soon as possible.

- This process will assist with control over design resource expenditure on varied and / or additional works.

PC | POTENTIAL DESIGN VARIATION		
Contract No.	**PDV No.**	**Project Name**

DESIGN	Raised By	
	Date	
	How Was Variation First Identified	☐ Drawing ☐ Spec ☐ RFI ☐ E-mail ☐ Minutes ☐ Other
	Document References	
	Area of Works	
	Brief Description of Variation	
	Anny Additional Design Time	
	Any Material Change / Addition	
	Any Programme Implications	

COMMERCIAL	QS Review By	
	Project Manager	
	Date	
	Notes	
	Able to Proceed	☐ Proceed ☐ Do Not Proceed
	Variation No.	
	EWN / CE No.	

- The form should be signed off by the appropriate commercial person, giving clear direction that the designer can proceed with the change or additional work.
- The commercial person should create a variation number for the agreed change on the Information Management System to allow the design team to book the relevant hours for the variation.
- The variation record is to be maintained by all parties to include all supporting documentation, including all relevant correspondence, drawings issued to us, drawings issued by you and any procurement schedules that show the varied and / or additional work and materials.
- Any additional materials should be marked with the relevant variation number so the Purchasing Department knows where the items do not form part of the original Tender.

CHECKING PROCESS

General

- A robust checking process for all documents should be in place. All design information should be ideally checked prior to release externally.
- Material procurement schedules should be issued by the Design Manager after they have been through the Review process. The schedules should be complete and accompanied by all relevant drawings.
- Schedules should be returned to the Design Manager if it is apparent they are not complete. Time should not be wasted checking schedules that are not ready to be checked.
- The relevant drawing numbers and detailed location are to be included by the designer on the procurement schedule. The Quantity Surveyor is to check the quantities of materials in these locations.

Checking of Materials

- The checking of material quantities for procurement is a fundamental responsibility of the Quantity Surveyor.
- A diligent review and check process is essential to minimise or to avoid the unnecessary costs arising from incorrect, insufficient, or too much material being delivered to site.

The unnecessary costs:

- Surplus materials, including the labour / plant cost of handling and disposal from site.
- Replacement materials for which we often pay premiums for small quantities, express delivery, etc.
- Downtime for labour.
- Wasted management time in dealing with the problem, identifying the cause, processing site materials requisitions, etc.
- Delay and / or disruption to our site installation programme.
- Loss of credibility.
- The cost of unnecessary waste has a significant effect on our net profit. For example, we must undertake in excess of £100,000 of profitable work to pay for a £2,000 error.

Timescale

- It is essential that the individual Designer allows a minimum of 5 days for the checking process. The Design Manager must ensure that this is sufficiently shown and allowed for in the design programme.

Wastage and Spares

- An allowance should be considered to procure additional materials to:
  - Ensure a sufficient amount of material is delivered to site to produce the required quantity of finished work.
  - Assess the amount of cutting waste together with the practicability of using off-cuts to make up full lengths.
  - Replace those materials damaged during off-loading, distribution and handling.
- The Designer is to ensure that the number of spares is clearly stated on procurement schedules.
  - Insulation – allow 5% wastage [be aware of roll / pack sizes or super cubes].
  - Vapour control layer – allow 20%, including laps.
  - Flashings – less on galvanised materials and more on coloured.
  - Optimisation – ensure that flat sheet sizes are utilised efficiently throughout the design process. Consider de-coiling where lead-in periods allow.
- Note – for larger or multi-phased projects, it is often better to allow stock-checking on site before calling in the last delivery.

Sheet Lengths

- The quality of design information and complexity of the building[s] will dictate whether or not a long hand check of the sheet lengths by the Quantity Surveyor is practicable. This will be assessed at the Technical Review Meeting, and a decision will be made on whether the sheet lengths are to be checked manually or subject to a CAD check.
- The rule of thumb is to allow 1 sheet in every 100. However, the Project Manager and Quantity Surveyor must be consulted on the spares allowance. Note that hips and valleys or complex shapes increase the risk of wastage.

Clips and Brackets

- The Designer will draw the clips, halters and brackets and then software can be used to count these. The fixings can then be easily counted from the clip quantities.
- Dynamic blocks are an excellent way of exporting data direct to spreadsheets.

Scheduling

- Ensure detailed locations are stated on Procurement Schedules and not just drawing numbers.

Flashing Schedule Checklist

- A checklist should be in place to ensure accurate and consistent production of information.
- Any checking carried out should be done in strict accordance with the checklist.

PC | Design Notes

Flashing Schedule Checklist

- ☐ Contract Number.
- ☐ Area Code.
- ☐ First [0] or consecutive Revision reference.
- ☐ Correct Project Title, with Area Description if applicable.
- ☐ Correct 'Originator' initials [must be the person who produced the schedule].
- ☐ Correct 'reviewed by' Design initials with date of review.
- ☐ 'Checked by' Commercial initials with date of checking.
- ☐ Correct 'Delivery Date' [never use 'asap' or 'urgent', and must be aligned with programme].
- ☐ 'Item Description' should be relevant to what is being scheduled [i.e. drip flashings to wall 1].
- ☐ List all relevant drawings which the item is identified on in the 'Reference Drawing No.' box.
- ☐ 'Tracker No.' box to have relevant Procurement Tracker No. added.
- ☐ Indicate if VO or Not [VO / PDV number must be stated].
- ☐ **Full** material specification to be listed in 'Material/Grade'.
- ☐ 'Finish/Colour' box completed with correct type & reference.
- ☐ Correct 'Gloss Level' and 'Microns'.
- ☐ Correct gauge [thickness] in mm.
- ☐ Add 'Girth' in mm.
- ☐ Add number of 'Bends' [note that welts are classed as 2 bends so this must be included].
- ☐ Correct length in mm.
- ☐ Accurate quantities including any spares required.
- ☐ Add 'Butt-Strap Quantity' if required and appropriate 'Butt-Strap Gauge'.
- ☐ Check 'CE Mark' box, typically "No", no execution class for all flashings. "Yes", execution class 2 for structural steel e.g. wind posts. Cladding Brackets - no CE.
- ☐ Correct 'Item Code'. Comprised of Area Code, Procurement Type and next consecutive number i.e. 13a-GAL001. Typically, this reference follows the same convention/number as the main Schedule ID.
- ☐ Complete 'Revision' boxes if required- A, B, C etc with initials of Design Reviewer and Commercial Checker and brief description of the changes made. These revision boxes to be left blank if first issue of the Schedule [Rev 0].
- ☐ Check all drawn/typed content for the item/material match the project drawings to which the schedule refers- section profile, length, fixing holes, side of visible finish etc.
- ☐ All required dimensions shown [include overall dimensions on thicker flashings] including diameter of any holes.
- ☐ Angles to 2 decimal places [where applicable].
- ☐ Locate icon where the item ID reference is to be marked by the manufacturer. Located so as not to be visible once item/material installed to the building face.
- ☐ Colour side identified with icon. Any grain to be identified with directional arrow.
- ☐ Hanging holes identified [if post coated or anodised].
- ☐ Titled relevant views with direction arrows and section lines with sections taken from the correct direction as drawn.
- ☐ Indicate internal and external butt straps with a dashed line to represent the profile and extent of the butt strap and label.
- ☐ State "welded with weld type" or "fully bonded" if applicable. State "linished" and "finished to architectural standard" if appearance is important.

Procurement Schedule Coding

- Ensure procurement schedules are coded accordingly, file names saved correctly and the correct references on the drawings.

			PC | MATERIAL SCHEDULING CODES	
Folder Number	Material Schedule Prefix	Folder Description	Item Code Prefix	Examples of items to be scheduled in this code
12.01	ALU	Aluminium Flashings	ALU-001 ALU-001-1 multiple items on same schedule ALU-001-2 multiple items on same schedule ALU-002	All mill finish aluminium flashings and extrusions [NO coloured items should be scheduled under this code]
12.02	BKT	Brackets	BKT-001 BKT-001-1 multiple items on same schedule BKT-001-2 multiple items on same schedule BKT-002	Brackets for curtain walling / glazing, generally welded bracket type assemblies
12.03	COL	Coloured Flashings	COL-001 COL-001-1 multiple items on same schedule COL-001-2 multiple items on same schedule COL-002	Flashing that are coloured coloured, i.e. steel , galv, alu & alu anodized with coloured faces
12.04	FIX	Fixing Schedules	FX***	Fixings, washers, nuts, anchors, bolts, etc.
12.05	GAL	Galvanised Flashings	GAL-001 GAL-001-1 multiple items on same schedule GAL-001-2 multiple items on same schedule GAL-002	Hot dipped and pre galv flashings, [NO coloured items should be scheduled under this code] Hot Dipped galv Steel fabrications and steel sections
12.06	GLS	Glass Schedules	GLS-001 GLS-001-1 multiple items on same schedule GLS-001-2 multiple items on same schedule GLS-002	Glass and spandrel panels
12.07	MAT	Material Schedules	MAT-001 MAT-001-1 multiple items on same schedule MAT-001-2 multiple items on same schedule MAT-002	All wall panels types e.g. composite and fabricated panel assemblies, roof sheets, insulation, accessories, black steel sections, curtain wall materials, louvres, Tapes, sealants, etc. Also you can use this MAT code to order from a specific drawing set using a MAT schedule as a cover sheet e.g. 'an MAT cover sheet to order gutters from a gutter layout drawing'.
12.08	RWG	Rain Water Goods	RWG-001 RWG-001-1 multiple items on same schedule RWG-001-2 multiple items on same schedule RWG-002	Gutters, outlets, gutter brackets, downpipes etc this code includes coloured rainwater items
12.09	SST	Stainless Steel Flashings	SST-001 SST-001-1 multiple items on same schedule SST-001-2 multiple items on same schedule SST-002	All stainless steel flashings
12.10	SMP	Samples	SMP-001 SMP-001-1 multiple items on same schedule SMP-001-2 multiple items on same schedule SMP-002	All samples
12.11	GLO	Global orders	GLO***	All materials requiring a global order, such as insulation, aluminium extrusions, coils, panels, sheeting etc

QUALITY MANAGEMENT

Non-Conformance Reports [NCRs]

- The quality issues observed in construction are addressed in a report called the Non-Conformance Report [NCR].
- An NCR explains the deviation of a specific construction work or task from the required standards, policies, procedures and specifications.
- There are a number of instances that require the issuing of an NCR:
  - Work that has been installed but is not in accordance with the approved 'Issued for Construction' drawings.
  - Work that fails to meet specified tolerances as established in the project specifications.
  - Work that is being performed using non-approved methods or standards.
  - Failure to follow the approved testing and inspection plan [ITPs].
  - Material used that has not been approved as a substitute.
  - Design is not accurate and does not represent on-site conditions.
  - Approved procedure was not followed, and quality defects have been identified.
- The NCR process is used as part of quality control processes by detailing:
  - The problem, including the:
  - Discipline.
  - Process.
  - Impact.
- How it occurred.
- How to prevent it from happening again.
- The NCR process is used to determine a resolution and document any corrective changes made through to the close out of the NCR, typically with acknowledgments of time and cost impacts.

- It is essential that there is an NCR process that supports the Workflow of the business.

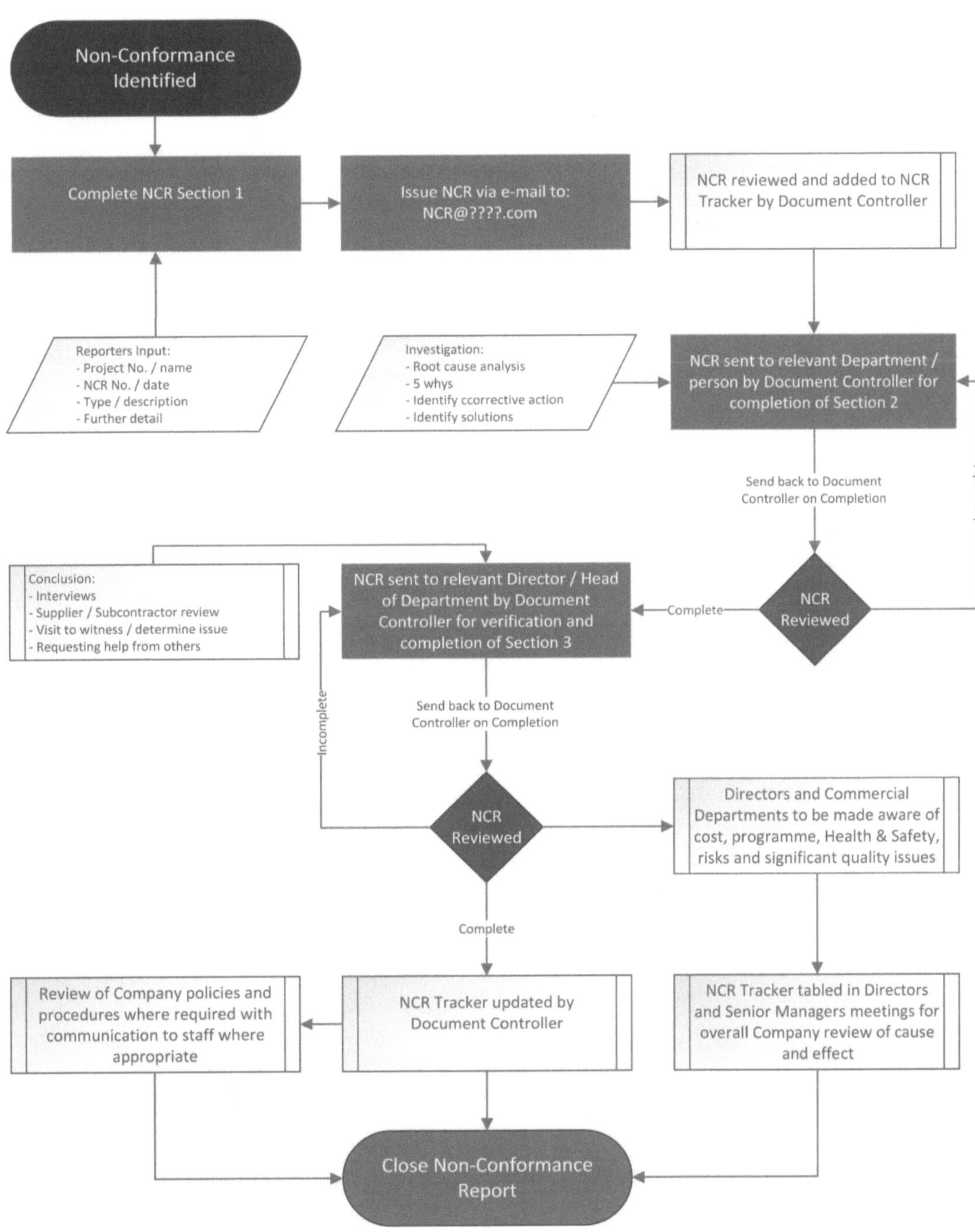

- An NCR example is below and should include description, root cause analysis, corrective action and close out.

PC | Non Conformance Report			
The objective of the NCR is to make an unambiguous, defensible, clear and concise definition of the problem so that corrective action can be initiated. This report is used as part of our quality control processes by detailing the problem, how it occurred, and how to prevent it from happening again.			
Project No.	**Project Name**	**NCR No.**	**Date of NCR**
Type of NCR	**Description**	**Client's Representative**	**Other**
	An incident relating to the client or main contractor affecting our work		
Section 1 - Details of Non-Conformity			
NCR Description	*Describe the NCR in enough detail that someone can read and understand where there has been a deviation from the project specification or where work fails to meet agreed quality standards*		
Raised By:		Date:	
Section 2 - Proposed Action Plan			
Root Cause Analysis	*Describe the root cause of the NCR including underlying reasons for why the non-conformance occurred and, how did it happen in the first place*		
Corrective Action	*Describe how this issue can be prevented from happening again and state what measures have been implemented to prevent recurrence*		
Completed By:		Date:	
Section 3 - Verification & Close Out			
Final Review & Close Out	*Describe what measures have been implemented to prevent this NCR from happening again and describe the method of communication*		
Closed Out By:		Date:	

- The NCRs should be added to a tracker document that allows monitoring of open and closed NCRs along with identify any common or reoccurring issues [i.e. trends].

PC | Non-Conformance Report Tracker			
Number of NCR's Total Raised	Number of NCR's Per Type	Type of NCR	Number of NCR's Total To Be Closed
10	2	Supplier	3
	2	Procurement	
	2	Design	
	2	Sub-Contractor	
	1	Site	
	0	Client	
	1	Other	

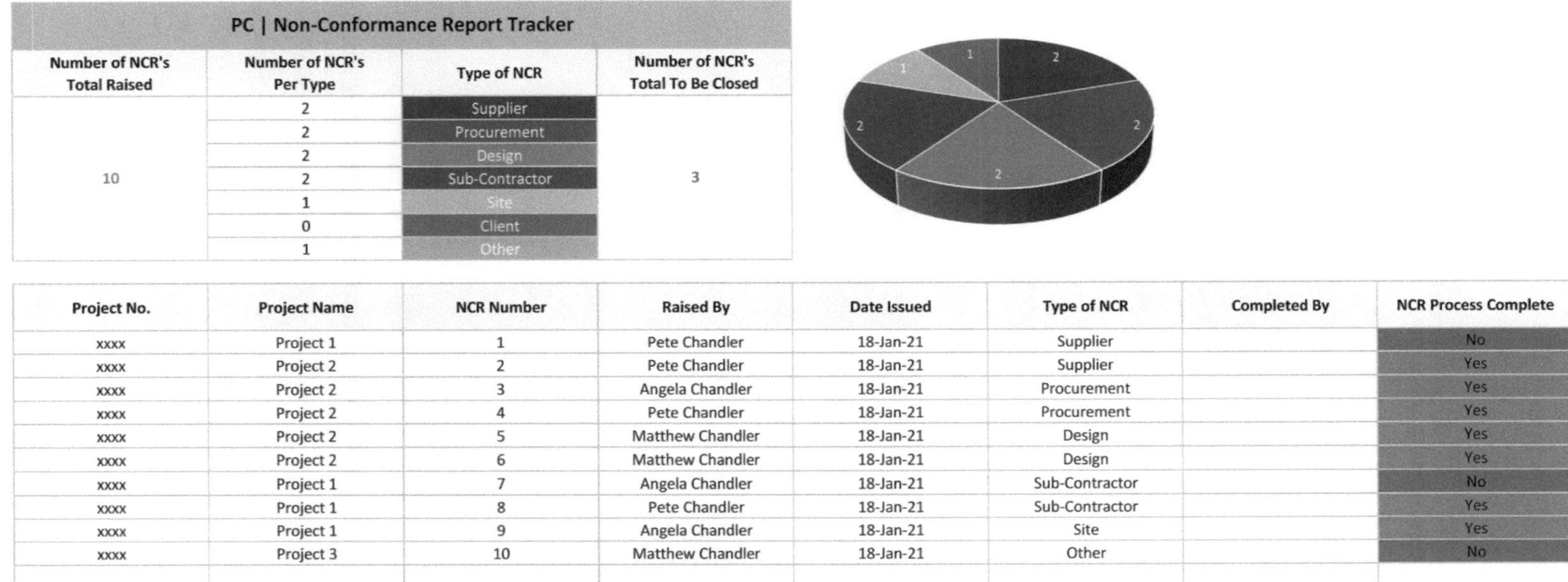

Project No.	Project Name	NCR Number	Raised By	Date Issued	Type of NCR	Completed By	NCR Process Complete
xxxx	Project 1	1	Pete Chandler	18-Jan-21	Supplier		No
xxxx	Project 2	2	Pete Chandler	18-Jan-21	Supplier		Yes
xxxx	Project 2	3	Angela Chandler	18-Jan-21	Procurement		Yes
xxxx	Project 2	4	Pete Chandler	18-Jan-21	Procurement		Yes
xxxx	Project 2	5	Matthew Chandler	18-Jan-21	Design		Yes
xxxx	Project 2	6	Matthew Chandler	18-Jan-21	Design		Yes
xxxx	Project 1	7	Angela Chandler	18-Jan-21	Sub-Contractor		No
xxxx	Project 1	8	Pete Chandler	18-Jan-21	Sub-Contractor		Yes
xxxx	Project 1	9	Angela Chandler	18-Jan-21	Site		Yes
xxxx	Project 3	10	Matthew Chandler	18-Jan-21	Other		No

Quality Assurance [QA]

- Carrying out on-site QA is a critical part of any business, not only to ensure quality, but to prevent future defects and legacy issues.
- As with all documentation, graphical data should be produced.

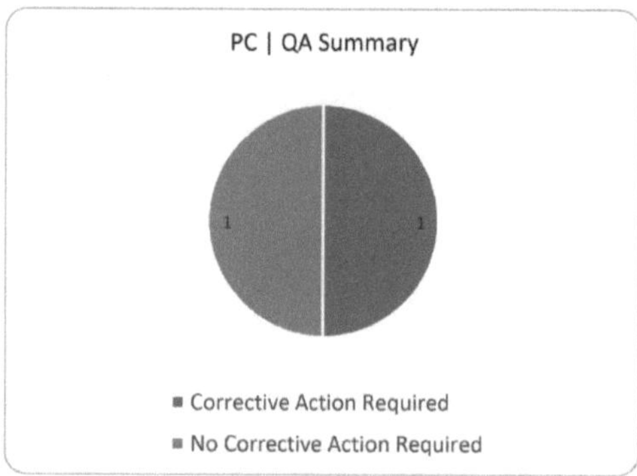

Item	Location / Description	Photograph	Action
	PC | QA OBSERVATIONS		
1	Block A, Grid Line B-C Sealant tape should cover the gap between the panel joints.		Corrective Action Required
2	Block B, Grid Line C-D Insulation was installed and tightly compressed around steel penetrations.		No Corrective Action Required

PC | QA Summary

Pie chart: 1, 1
- Corrective Action Required
- No Corrective Action Required

- This will also allow a checklist to be produced so corrective actions can be monitored.

TRAINING AND DEVELOPMENT

Design Competency Matrix

- The Design Competency Matrix should include:
  - Core software competency.
  - Policies and procedures.
  - Standards and regulations.
  - Contract requirements.
  - Planning and programming.
  - Management skills.
  - Product knowledge [i.e. roofing, cladding, glazing, rainscreen, louvres, doors].
  - Building envelope principles.
  - Materials and fabrications.
  - Understanding calculations.

PC | DESIGN COMPETENCT MATRIX																			
Anticipated Level of Competency / Assessed Level this review period / Assessed level 6 months previous / Assessed Level 12 months previous	Designer 1	Designer 2	Designer 3	Designer 4	Designer 5	Designer 6	Designer 7	Designer 8	Designer 9	Designer 10	Designer 11	Designer 12	Designer 13	Designer 14	Designer 15	Designer 16	Designer 17	Designer 18
Procedures and Standards	Score yourself between 1 and 10 to identify the level at which you feel to know each category																	
Design Procedures	1	1	3															
Procurement Issue	1	1	3															
Design Responsibilities	1	1	5															
Drawing Approval	2	1	5															
Checking Process	2	2	5															
Glass	2	2	5															
Doors	3	2	5															
Windows	3	3	5															
Building Information Modelling [BIM]	3	3	9															
Levels of Development [LOD]	4	3	9															
Workflows	4	4	9															
Drawing / CAD Standards	4	4	9															
Electronic filing system	5	9	9															
Information Management System [IMS]	5	9	9															
Procurement Issue	5	9	9															
Drawing Manager	5	9	9															
Drawing Filing	5	9	9															
Standards and Regulations	Score yourself between 1 and 10 to identify the level at which you feel to know each category																	
Building Regulations	6	8	2															
CE Marking	6	8	2															
Construction, Design and Management [CDM]	6	8	2															
CWCT Systemised Building Envelope Standards	6	8	6															
NFRC Standards	7	8	6															
Contract Requirements	Score yourself between 1 and 10 to identify the level at which you feel to know each category																	
Understanding Specifications	8	8	8															
Design life / Warranties	9	8	2															
Tender Documentation	10	8	2															
Design Responsibilities	8	8	2															
Contract processes and triggers [RFI's, IRS, EWN's, NCE's]	5	8	2															
Design risk management	4	8	2															
Planning and Programming	Score yourself between 1 and 10 to identify the level at which you feel to know each category																	
Read and Extract relevant data	7	8	1															
Design Programming	7	8	1															
Design Deliverables	7	8	1															
Design Delivery Schedule	7	8	3															
Information Required Schedule [IRS]	7	8	3															
Drop lining and progress reporting	7	8	3															
Lookaheads and blockers	7	8	3															
Resourcing	7	8	3															
Change control and impacting	7	8	3															
Understanding sequencing	7	8	3															

- Ensure Staff Development Reviews are carried out, which should be part of the business strategy.

<u>**Privacy Notice**</u>

The information recorded on this form is part of the Staff Development Review process. It will only be used for that purpose. It will be stored on our business systems and only be available to those with the correct access. The information will be removed from our business systems at the end of your employment. The information will not be shared with 3rd parties.

Your Details	
Name	Pete Chandler
Job Title	Design Director
Date	23rd March 2022

Achievements and Aspirations: Discuss employee's short, medium- and long-term plans:
Pete had another good year managing the combined design team during a period of considerable upheaval and change. Pete wants to maintain his position as default "go to" person for design, running the overall team and assisting in the development of the Regional Offices, using the control tools Pete has developed.

Areas for Development:
1. Maintain and develop the design Senior Management role taking an overall view of the design function without being specific to any project. 2. Maintain a view on pre-construction [bid support]. 3. Balance the demands of several projects and stakeholders, all of which Pete is involved in. This prioritisation and time management control will remain an area of focus.

- Individual and team objectives should be set using the **S**mart, **M**easurable, **A**chievable, **R**ealistic and **T**imescale principle.

Individual and Team Objectives and Goals			
Objective:	**Time Scale**	**Success Measured by:**	**Actual Outcome:**
1. Assist and develop the Design Manager in the Regional Office. Mentor and support him as he develops a generally inexperienced team into a functioning design resource	On-going	The development and progress of the Design Manager and the Regional Office	
2. Ensure that standards, procedures and quality are maintained across the design function irrespective of the office location and project.	On-going	1. Project delivery to budget and on time 2. Limited NCR' s/ redesigns	
3. Continue to manage, train, develop and retain the Head Office design team	On-going	Staff retention	

MANAGING YOURSELF

Management Skills

- Take responsibility.
- Provide reasonable support.
- Provide reasonable training.
- Lead by example.
- Remember, management is an "emotional bank account," you have to build up credit.
- Always remember impacts on behaviour.
- Save contentious e-mails to drafts rather than typing and sending in the 'heat of the moment'.
- Never use ASAP; specific dates must be identified.
- Standardise e-mails as inconsistency will devalue.
- Talk to people, do not always use e-mail. Phoning is better received.
- Make time for people.
- Take interest and listen to staff.
- Avoid answering the phone when talking to people – this is rude.
- Timed agenda in meetings and must start on time even if people are late.

Personal Development

- Communication.
- Confidence.
- Say what you think.
- Give regular feedback to Line Manager.
- Be proactive – tell your Line Manager what you are doing rather than asking permission.
- Tell your Line Manager anything you need or require to carry out your projects [i.e. new resources, maintaining current team etc].
- Be prepared to accept additional work and ask to take on extras rather than waiting. Always get in there first.
- Challenge your Line Manager and rise above others.
- Perform and project abilities to successfully execute the task.
- Keep records of any issues that arise with the team and advise your Line Manager accordingly.
- Challenge yourself and your Manager.

Planning and Programming

* Keep an overall resource programme and update regularly.
* Keep on top of resource requirements and always plan ahead.
* Update project programmes regularly; do not let them fall behind reality.
* Update reports and include all drawings / documents to understand overdue items.
* Keep records of all outstanding work and update regularly.
* Use personal action list and Calendar software.
* Costs of resources to be produced regularly and issued to relevant people.
* Ensure engineering is carried out where necessary and programmed accordingly.
* Ensure CDM is carried out on all projects.
* Identify and raise Request for Information [RFI] forms in a timely manner.
* Monitor costs of all projects and advise against budgets.
* Produce drawing list for all projects.
* Ensure that programmes are updated with percentages and issues, tracking is key.
* Introduce weekly work plans for specific team members where required.
* Carry out weekly team meetings to discuss progress, and only record actions.
* Challenge people in the correct manner if tasks are not complete.

Authorisation

* Understand limits of responsibilities. Can you authorise overtime and appointment of sub-contract staff providing it is within budget?
* Understand how much you can sign off for materials and equipment.
* Do not wait to be asked. Put forward proposals with costs so your Manager can see the whole picture.

Understand Yourself

* Evaluate yourself.
* Seek feedback from others.

Manage Effectively

* Be clear about what you are expected to achieve.
* Get the right balance between doing and managing.
* Get the right emphasis between your management activities.

Manage Efficiently

- Manage Time.
- Manage Paper.
- Manage to remember.
- Manage your support staff.

Delegate

- Plan what to delegate.
- Decide to whom to delegate.
- Delegate properly.

MANAGING OTHERS

Lead by Example

- Work hard to high standards.
- Be positive.
- Be corporate.
- Help out.
- Don't panic.
- Don't compromise yourself.
- Don't let things get you down.

Build Working Relationships

- Earn Trust and Respect.
- Be yourself.
- Be human.
- Be consistent.
- Be fair.
- Be trustworthy.
- Show trust and respect.
- Know your people.
- Be caring and considerate.
- Encourage involvement.
- Consult and explain.
- Help to achieve.
- Encourage openness.
- Be trusting.
- Make your staff feel valued and important. **Number 1 rule!**

Manage for Results

- Set high standards.
- Give clear direction.
- Make sound decisions.
- Face up to issues.
- Keep control.
- Recognise achievement.

Managing your Boss

- Develop understanding.
- Keep informed.
- Present solutions, not problems.
- Show initiative.
- Be businesslike.
- Give support.
- Disagree positively.
- Challenge them.

MANAGING PERFORMANCE

Plan Performance

- Identify goals.
- Set and agree objectives.
- Write a Performance Plan.
- Update the Performance Plan.

Track Performance

- Stay informed.
- Review progress.

Improve Performance

- Encourage.
- Help and Support.
- Give feedback.
- Appraise performance.
- Tackle poor performance positively.

MANAGING DISCIPLINE AND GRIEVANCES

Discipline Fairly

- Identify the standards required.
- Know and follow the Disciplinary Procedure.
- Act Promptly.
- Investigate and consult beforehand.
- Give a hearing.
- Determine the appropriate remedy.
- Summarise and identify next steps.
- Commit things to writing.
- Follow up.

Avoid Grievances

- Anticipate concerns.
- Listen Effectively.
- Act quickly and follow up.

MANAGING REWARD

Recognise Contribution

- Do it.
- Don't overdo it.
- Always be genuine.

Reward Fairly

- Match grade to job size.
- Relate total reward to performance.
- Aim for understanding.
- Stay objective.

MANAGING TRAINING AND DEVELOPMENT

Provide Proper Training

- Plan training.
- Produce a training matrix.
- Help people learn.
- Provide thorough induction.
- Develop the right attitude.
- Give effective instruction.
- Coach performance.
- Use courses selectively.
- Evaluate training given.

Support Individual Development

- Help self-development.
- Use abilities fully.
- Discuss aspirations.
- Establish a development process.
- Grow your own.
- Take a broad view.

MANAGING COMMUNICATION

Develop your Communication Skills

- Present effectively.
- Write thoughtfully.
- Listen carefully.
- Read Selectively.

Keep others Informed

- Establish a system.
- Aim for understanding.
- Brief your team.

Keep yourself in Touch

- Encourage openness.
- Be accessible.
- Be visible.

MANAGING DEPARTMENTS

Develop an Appropriate Structure

- Minimise levels.
- Optimise Spans of Control.
- Ensure clear accountability.

Build Teams and Teamwork

- Keep numbers tight.
- Ensure the right mix.
- Provide clear objectives.
- Give appropriate leadership.
- Foster team identity.
- Keep competition constructive.

Aim for Organisational Effectiveness

- Measure results.
- Improve performance.
- Increase resilience.

MANAGING QUALITY

Set Clear Standards

- Consult your customers.
- Decide on appropriate quality standards.
- Communicate quality standards.
- Review these standards.

Achieve the Standards Required

- Establish the procedures and methods.
- Determine and implement controls > Quality Assurance.
- Agree responsibility for quality.
- Write up and action training plans.

Track the Quality Achieved

- Install quality controls.
- Sound out your customers > Quality Control.
- Discuss quality with your staff.
- Ask for an audit.

Improve Quality

- Involve your staff.
- Address key vulnerabilities early.
- Develop the right approach.

MANAGING PRODUCTIVITY

Focus on Productivity

- Understand what productivity means.
- Explain why productivity is important.
- Aim for effectiveness.
- Aim for efficiency.

Plan to be Productive

- Assess your workload.
- Staff correctly.
- Provide the right tools for the job.
- Schedule projects.

Ensure Performance is Productive

- Manage your resources efficiently.
- Establish productivity measures.
- Track levels of productivity.

Maximise Productivity

- Involve your people.
- Look for better ways.
- Reduce costs.
- Seek outside help.

Build a Team

- Forming the team.
- Share the Vision.
- Give everyone a task.

The Storm

- Interfering.
- Distancing.
- Stifling enthusiasm.
- Refusing to delegate.
- Lacking trust.

The Final Straw

- Identifying the problem.
- Keep control.
- Keep to the agenda.
- Summarise the problem.

MANAGING MEETINGS

General

- Plan.
- Prepare.
- Chair.
- Record.

The Good Chair

- Establish the Chair.
- Set the agenda.
- Use tact.
- Keep control.

The Bad Chair

- Poor preparation.
- Poor Information.
- No time limits.
- The Chair shouldn't lecture.
- Inappropriate points.
- Loss of control.

The Post mortem

- The Chair must not become 'invisible'.
- The report should have been circulated before the meeting.
- Badly run meetings waste time and money.
- A record should be kept of what has happened.
- Conflict should be avoided whenever possible.

A Second Chance

- Set the Agenda.
- Stick to the Agenda.
- Keep Control.
- Avoid side-tracking.
- Maintain control.
- Avoid conflict.
- Be responsive.
- Sum up the meeting.

Decide

- Locations for meetings.
- Set the tone.
- State the purpose.
- Work to a pre-planned strategy.
- Be clear about the next step.
- Timely preparation / circulation of documents.
- Start on time / Indicate when expected to finish.
- Keeping the attenders in the picture before the meeting.
- Thank for input.
- Use visual aids.
- Keep control.
- Commitment means taking part in decision-making.
- Hidden agendas.
- Corridor preparation.
- Arguments make it more difficult to agree on decisions.
- The general effect of seating positions.
- Body language by Chair.
- Emotion antagonism well handled.
- Chairman has to control himself.
- Usefulness of a concluding Summary.

MANAGING NEGOTIATIONS

Preparing to Negotiate

- Establish your goals.
- Decide Roles.
- Research the Opposition.

Doing the Deal

- Probe for Information.
- Exchange Proposals.
- Start Bargaining.
- Close the Deal.

Breakdown

- A Serious Threat.
- Deadlock.
- Saving Face.

Getting the Brief

- Establish your Goals.
- Agree your limits.
- Check your Facts.

Negotiate

- Discuss Tactics.
- Present a United Front.

In the Balance

- Probe for Information.
- Exchange Proposals.
- Start Bargaining.
- Close the Deal.

Execution

- Composition of the Negotiating Team.
- Agreeing the Roles.
- Thinking about the Opposition.
- Ritual Shadow Boxing.
- The other side may be professional too.
- Words, Feelings and Reactions.
- The Role of Silence.
- Signalling.
- Summarising the Deal.
- Use of Threats.
- Avoiding Closing the Door.
- Establishing the Parameters.
- Need to take notes at meetings.
- Detailed Preparations.
- Establishing the Party line.
- Playing in the same team.
- Location of Meeting.
- Letting the Other Side say their Piece.
- Body Language.
- Closing the Deal – firmly.

MANAGING OTHER

Managing Holidays

- Ensure cover is maintained in the team at all times.
- Add your teams' holidays into your Calendar.
- Understand how holidays will impact programmes and adjust accordingly.

Managing Appraisals

- Appraisee must be prepared.
- Speak to individuals before meeting.
- Try to do appraisals off site.
- Only use 2-3 forms to discuss.
- Encourage two-way discussions.
- Avoid telling.
- Ask their thoughts.
- Avoid barriers [such as desks].
- Summarise at various stages.
- Avoid closed questions.
- Avoid silences for long periods.
- Allow silences for time to think.
- Body language and mannerisms.
- Explain structure.
- Avoid leading questions.
- Avoid leading in certain directions.
- Avoid reading and writing too long.
- Do not rush – if over-run then reschedule to continue.

Managing Feedback

- Little and often.
- Focus on behaviour, not beliefs.
- Balance positive and negative.
- Support rather than threaten.
- Ask rather than tell.
- Always back up with facts, evidence and examples.
- Plan when and where.
- Do not wait until appraisals to give feedback and praise.
- If you "give it", be prepared to "take it".

- Give specific examples and ask for specific examples.
- Never start on a negative.
- Should always be constructive.
- Body language and mannerisms.

Managing Recruitment

- Determine your needs.
- Plan your campaign.
- Aid self-selection.
- Select thoroughly.
- Treat people considerately.
- Offer appropriately.
- Do not wait for others; be proactive.
- Produce Organisational Charts to see what staff is required and at what level.
- Cost the requirements, including any fees, and present them to your Line Manager.

PRESENTATIONS

The Topic

- Your listeners will only ever be as excited about the topic as you are.
- Know what you are talking about; do not guess, do not assume.
- Read, listen, find facts and have an informed opinion.
- Think about your audience and tailor your topic to the way they think and prioritise.
- Have an answer to the question.

The Format

- There will be a time limit, and if there isn't, make one. Then aim to fill three quarters of it, and leave time for questions.
- Plan on paper – mind mapping is ideal.
- Presentation software is to be used all the way through [10/20/30 rule – 10 slides, 20 minutes, 30-point font minimum].
- Slides should keep you going, not hold you up.
- Don't fall back onto boring stock photography and clip art. Consider using your own personal photographs.

The Content

- Keep it short and sweet.
- Stick to words and avoid jargon.
- Give it focus – no one is impressed by rambling.
- Tell compelling stories – there must be a reason you are presenting to these people.
- Use examples and keep your points grounded.
- Pre-empt questions.
- Know what you can leave out if things do not run to plan.

The Preparation

- Rehearse and be familiar enough to deliver it if the power goes out.
- Try and get in the room and familiarise yourself with the surroundings in advance.

The Day

- Take everything you need and a backup.
- Arrive early so you do not get flustered.
- Warm up and relax.
- Give an entertaining performance – give them an awesome experience.
- Use media only to enhance – avoid death by PowerPoint.
- Create a worthy leave behind – give them something to remember you by.

TOP 10 DESIGN MANAGEMENT MISTAKES – AND HOW TO AVOID THEM

Having your plan in your head

- When things start off simple, we think we can do it all in our heads, but even if you can remember it all, you'll find it much more stressful to keep it in your head as it gradually gets more complicated.

- More importantly, when it's all in your head, you can't show the plan to your boss, your customer [to justify the cost and time and to show that you are scientific and reliable], or to the team who are going to help carry it out.

- Solution: Have a Gantt chart, which shows everyone who will do what and when, all in a nice simple format that anybody can immediately understand.

Agreeing to an impossibly short time frame by saying, "Maybe I can do it" or "I'll try".

- The second mistake, which is partly your boss's fault, is Saying "Maybe" or "I'll try" when asked if the project can be done in a ridiculously short timescale.

- You might think that being vague will get you off the hook later, but be careful because "maybe" sounds like "yes" to customers and bosses. So does "If it doesn't rain and the IT works right the first time, and nobody gets sick, and the subcontractors deliver on time, then we just might get it done." The only thing that doesn't sound like "yes" is "NO"!

Promising the best outcome possible

- Bosses love to ask, "What's the best you can do if it all goes really well?" They might as well be asking, "Please can you make up a number that you'll never achieve, so that I can promise it to the customer and we can both look bad in a few months' time when you fail?"

- From the moment you mention that optimistic number, they are expecting it – and you're both goosed!

- Solution: Instead of "I might be able to do it in 3 weeks," say, "Well, it's a pretty tricky job, we're trying out a new supplier, and the IT is unproven, so it could easily take as many as 8 weeks." [Give them a number that you can be 90% sure of achieving – you can never be 100% certain.]

Forgetting to involve your team

- Project Managers who have strong personalities and who have lots of knowledge can sometimes be prone to forgetting that their team have ideas, too.

- When listing the tasks required in the project, right at the start.

- When planning the running order of the tasks, ideally as a flow diagram using notes.

Mistaking a task list for a project plan

- If I have one top pet hate, it's when a project manager shows me their "Project Plan", and it's just a list of tasks [with start and finish dates].

- A task list is not visual. Unlike with a proper Gantt chart, you can't see what depends on what, which things are happening at the same time, and therefore how busy you are going to be at that moment, and you can't see how much you can move one task without it affecting another, etc. A list is RUBBISH!

- Solution: Make a proper plan, starting off as a Post-it notes flow diagram and then becoming, you guessed it, a Gantt chart.

Forgetting about other projects

- Always remember that other projects are going to come in and affect your project by taking away some of your carefully planned resources.

- Solution: To be fair, this is a difficult one to solve. The only way, really, is to have a Gantt of Gantts which capture all projects.

Listening to people's stories

- The next pitfall is to let people tell you stories: "We've had terrible trouble with the concrete not setting in this cold weather", or "We worked all night to get it fixed." Great, you've finished tasks A and B, but should you have done more than that by now, ... I don't know?

- The stories tell us what they've DONE, but not what they SHOULD have done by now, so we still don't know how they are doing compared to the plan: will they be finished on time or not?

- Solution: A coloured-in Gantt chart, which allows you to immediately see the state of play. It's much quicker and shows you what they SHOULD have done as well as what they have ACTUALLY.

Thinking that Underspending is OK!

- This mistake is made more by accountants than by project managers. If your project has used up less money than you expected so far, then yes, it could be happening more cheaply than you expected. But more likely, it's happening more slowly than you expected.

- Lateness means you've had some problems, which means that in the end you'll have overspent—especially if you'll have to spend even more money to speed it back up.

- Solution: When faced with an apparent underspend, your first thought should be to check the progress using the coloured-in Gantt chart. For example, suppose we planned to spend 50 by now and we have actually spent only 40, you might think that's OK.

- But when you look at the chart, you should clearly see that although we might think we're underspent, we are so far behind the Now Line, we've done SO little [probably only about 20's worth], that we are almost certainly over spent. We've spent 40 doing 20's worth!

Rescheduling too late

- When a project is running late, it's tempting to HOPE that you'll find a way to save it, or that a bit of LUCK will come along. But eventually, when it's nearly due to be delivered, you'll have to come clean and confess that you're way behind.

- This is a bad thing to do! Customers don't like surprises, especially when there's not much time left to do anything about them.

- Solution: Confess at about the halfway point and ask for more time and / or money. Take the pain early; trust me, it'll hurt less in the long run!

Not reviewing your completed project

- This mistake is very commonly made and yet easily rectified. "We don't have time for a review! We don't want to re-live the pain a second time! We're never going to do a similar project to that again! I don't want to admit my mistakes publicly! It's OK, I've got all the learning points in my head now!"

- But unless you do a review, you won't remember the learning points, and certainly nobody else in the organisation will reap the benefits of your pain. So reviews are vital, and management should make sure that project managers have them.

- Solution: Have a review, ask what was good that we can repeat, what we should avoid, and what could have been done better.

- Record it on a single sheet of paper and keep all your reviews in a file. If you're a manager, ask that this be done at the end of each project. Ask to see the file where all the reviews are stored…

Avoid these 10 mistakes and your projects will have to try pretty hard in order to go wrong!

Key Points

- We all make mistakes, and there are some mistakes that leaders and managers make in particular. These include not giving good feedback, being too "hands-off," not delegating effectively, and misunderstanding your role.

- It's true that making a mistake can be a learning opportunity. But, taking the time to learn how to recognise and avoid common mistakes can help you become productive and successful, and highly respected by your team.

KEY PERFORMANCE INDICATORS [KPIS]

Introduction

- KPIs are performance measures that evaluate the success of your business or a particular activity. The following set out some KPIs in the design world.
    - o Design programme planned v actual.
    - o Design deliverables schedule and graphs on progress.
    - o Design cost budget v actual.
    - o Request for Information [RFIs] raised.
    - o Potential Design Variations [PDVs] raised.
    - o Cost per drawing [based on budget v number].

PC	KPI's			
Project	**Requests for Information**	**Potential Design Variations**	**Drawings**	**Schedules**
Project 1	96 No.	56 No.	500 No. £810k / £1620 per drawing	1000 No.
Project 2	380 No.	180 No.	1400 No. £1.2m / £860 per drawing	970 No.
Project 3	24 No.	22 No.	114 No. £110k / £960 per drawing	294 No.

- It often assists if the drawings are categorised into complexity.

PC	DRAWING COMPLEXITY	
Category A	**Category B**	**Category C**
Small Product Mix [small flat roof]	Medium Product Mix [roof, cladding, glazed entrance]	High Product Mix roof 1, roof 2, cladding, curtain walling, glazed screen, louvres]
Small Areas of Design [roof only]	Medium Areas of Design [roof and walls]	Large Areas of Design [several buildings]
Low Complexity [standard duo-pitch roofs]	Medium Complexity [curved roof, simple glazed screen]	High Complexity [curved, tapered, facetted]
0-25 Requests for Information	26-50 Requests for Information	50+ Requests for Information

Drawing Costs

- The following table is an example of drawing costs. This is subject to individual companies and is project specific.

Ref	Drawing/Activity Cost	Quantity	Rate Category A	Rate Category B	Rate Category C	Total
	Drawings:					
1	Liner Layout	1	£ 250.00			£ 250.00
2	Top Sheet Layout	1	£ 250.00			£ 250.00
3	Gutter Layout	2	£ 250.00			£ 500.00
4	Soffit Layout	1	£ 250.00			£ 250.00
5	Eaves Detail	3	£ 125.00			£ 375.00
6	Verge Detail	4	£ 125.00			£ 500.00
7	Ridge Detail	2	£ 125.00			£ 250.00
8	Junction Detail	2	£ 125.00			£ 250.00
9	Valley Detail	2	£ 125.00			£ 250.00
10	Standard Liner Lap	1	£ 125.00			£ 125.00
11	Down Pipe Detail	2	£ 125.00			£ 250.00
	Schedules:					
12	Top sheets	2	£ 120.00			£ 240.00
13	Accessories	2	£ 90.00			£ 180.00
14	Liner	2	£ 120.00			£ 240.00
15	Insulation	2	£ 90.00			£ 180.00
16	VCL	1	£ 90.00			£ 90.00
17	General Materials	4	£ 90.00			£ 360.00
18	Flashings	20	£ 120.00			£ 2400.00
19	Fixings	2	£ 90.00			£ 180.00
20	RFIs	6	£ 40.00			£ 240.00
21	Site Meetings/Visits	2	£ 240.00			£ 480.00
22	Drawing Amendments	32	£ 25.00			£ 800.00
	Total					**£ 8640.00**

Formula

Design cost in month
[From individual costs / time sheets]

Number of drawings in month

Design cost in month
[From individual costs / time sheets]

DESIGN SESSION

Current Workload and Resources

- Green – allocation.
- Orange – new projects.
- Red – potential allocation [to be resolved].
- Costs – individual projects.
- Questions.

Programming and Planning

- Use Project 1 example.
- Show how resources are allocated.
- Explain contractual requirements [week minus, key dates].
- Look at Design Report.
- Swapping resources.
- Making sure items have been ordered.
- Use of calendar.
- Phone people.
- Chase people [pick up the phone].
- Honesty.
- Done is done [not sent to printer, etc.].
- Pete's finished [task is 100% complete].
- Questions.

Checking and Reviewing

- Flashing schedule checklist.
- Ownership [not he checked it / he updated it].

Procurement Tracker

- Items.
- Resources.
- Visibility.
- Issued every Monday.

Commercial Awareness

- Drawing changes.
- Variations.
- The best designers [those who have commercial awareness].
- Item Rate Analysis / material allowances.
- What has been bought / baseline?

Relationships

- Pick up the phone to people.
- We are in it together.

Training / Skills Matrix

- Identify areas for development.
- Consistency.
- In-house sessions.

New Projects

- Table new projects and give clear visibility to the department.

What's on your mind?

- If there is something to say, then say it!

AOB

- Time keeping.
- Dress code.
- Headphones.
- Technical or regulation updates.

RESEARCH AND DEVELOPMENT [R&D]

What is R&D?

- When we are developing Easier, Safer, Greener, More Efficient details or products that are bespoke or specifically developed for the project.

- To Research and provide a solution to a problem that has arisen on either a tender or a live project that can't be solved with an off-the-shelf solution.

- This may be the production of a BIM model for tender presentations to demonstrate that we have understood the challenges of the works being integrated together, or on a live project, solving a technical challenge like the development of a cladding build-up in a space-constrained wall thickness.

- Mock-ups, the design, planning, procurement and erection of mock-ups are all allowable against R&D and should all be claimed as per the rules noted above and below; most time should be able to be claimed to their inherently unique requirements.

What is not R&D?

- Once the problem has been solved and the solution developed as a set of standard details, the detailing of this onto GA's etc., would not be considered to be R&D.

- However, if all details and products are developed especially for the project, most of the individuals time would be R&D acceptable other than-day-to-day admin, document control, etc. which may be as high as 80%. This scenario is rare but was the reality on the some projects.

- As an example, developing a fixing detail and researching what fixing to use to fix a bracket, then adding this to our standard project details and briefing other team members on this research is allowable, then once the designer starts adding these references to drawings, this is not an allowable cost as this is our core work.

Who is likely to do R&D?

- Simple answer, anybody whose work is covered by the explanation above. Pre Construction and Design have an especially high percentage of R&D in their day-to-day activities.

- Project Managers and Site Managers may have significant claimable time at the beginning of projects whilst solving site issues and documenting new and innovative ways to safely fit the works on site.

- A Senior Design Manager should more likely be producing R&D qualifying work than a Graduate designer, with the scale of R&D sliding down from Senior Design Manager.

Key Words to use in R&D claims:

- What   [... were we doing, solving, producing or developing?].
- Why   [... was it necessary to solve the problem or develop a new solution?].
- How   [... did we produce the answer?].

Examples of R&D

- An initial examination of the specification for this cladding led to concern over the suitability of the material proposed. The material stated, even in FR grade, would not meet the fire classification requirements for the project.

- Thus, the proposal is to use 3mm aluminium, which would then be polyester powder coated in the specified paint finishes.

- As seen below, a bespoke mock-up was built to demonstrate the products and systems being used, interfaces and workmanship, whilst ensuring specification compliance.

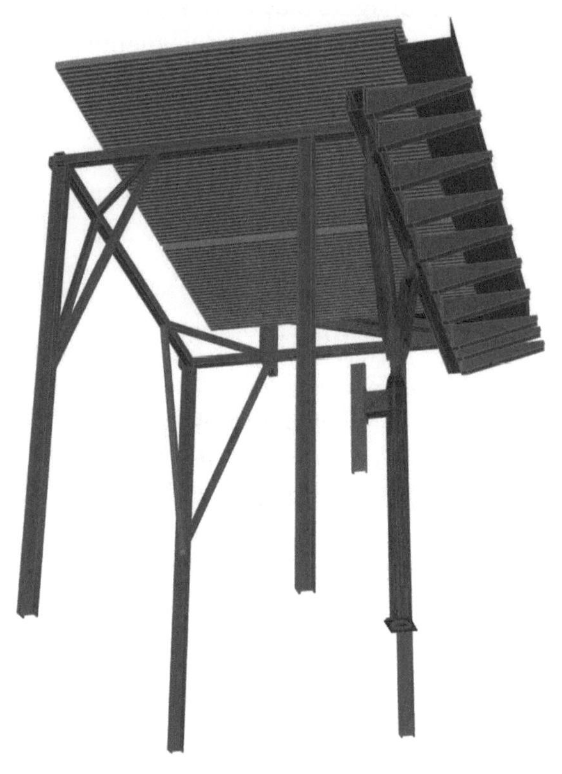

Recording of R&D

- Timesheets – these must be completed in the usual manner through the Information Management System [IMS].

- We need to enter R&D information by adding a new line for the project and amending the analysis to R&D, then adding a Day Note in the normal way.

- This will allow the R&D costs to be recorded in the same way as Variations and will allow costs to be allocated to the correct project.

- This also means that when the data is exported from the Information Management System prior to uploading to the accounting system, the correct Cost Code will be automatically applied.

PC | TIMESHEET						
Time	**Analysis**	**Mon**	**Tue**	**Wed**	**Thu**	**Fri**
Project 1	Project Time	2	3	2	2	1
Project 2	R&D	1	1	2	2	1
Project 3	R&D	4	2	2	2	3
Project 4	Project Time	1	2	2	2	3
		8	**8**	**8**	**8**	**8**

R&D - working on the bespoke mock-up, developing the façade and roof design with the system suppliers, researching alternative products, innovation throughout the design to enhance the efficiency of the programme and build.

- Keep evidence of the above within the project folder on the relevant drive under the relevant section where it should be stored for future use. This must include example drawings and a brief 'Example Description Sheet'.

- Remember, R&D is:

Innovation, Unique, Bespoke, Developed, Iterations, Research, Problem Solved, Efficient

WHAT'S NEXT?

Lessons Learnt

- As part of the complete design process, it is essential to carry out a lessons learnt exercise.

- This should be done as a design team and should address the good, the bad and the ugly.

PC | Design Notes

Lesson Learnt

Project 1

- Face fixed louvres with plenums as part of the cladding package. Project 1 had integral louvres into the panel joints with bespoke profiles.
- Doors were flush with cladding which required cantilevered hot-rolled steel extension plates due to double-skin wall build up.
- Windows were punched with 900mm between them. Ribbon windows would be beneficial with less welded 'pods.
- Anti-climb rainwater pipe covers were too thin as they had to be in the same material as the cladding.

Project 2

- Timber was high spec [cut type, random pattern, and knot %] which resulted in significant wastage.

Project 3

- Brise solei had a traditional large bracket.
- Canopy steelwork penetrated spandrel panels in curtain walling.
- Vertical glazing around rooflight was only 300mm and in glass. This would be better in metal.
- Glazing corners did not work. Distance at corner was too small for depth of mullions and bespoke inserts were required.
- Internal finishes were flush with edge of mullion as opposed to centre of profile. This caused visual issues due to tolerances.
- Steelwork was not adequate for glazed rooflights. We had to provide structural brackets 700mm high.
- Louvres had 7 different configurations i.e. single, double, blanking, no blanking and different performances.

- The Lessons Learnt should include, but not be limited to, the following:
  - Pre-Construction – handover, quality of documents, understanding our scope.
  - Design Responsibility – what was our responsibility? / how did it affect us?
  - Design Programme – was it accurate? / was it used effectively?
  - Design Deliverables – was it accurate? / was it used effectively?
  - Samples and Benchmarks – were there any? / how effective were they?
  - Testing – was there any? / how effective was it?
  - Lines of Communication – what was it? / how successful was it?
  - Engineering – who did we use? / how did they perform? / would we use them again?
  - Design Team – was it the right team? / were the skill sets correct? / what strengths have we gained? / use of 3D / document control protocols / technical challenges / relationships.
  - Buying Team – queries on design information / supplier changes which affected design / relationships.
  - Site Team – document control / review of drawings during design / buildability reviews / accuracy of the build against the drawings / installation quality / non-conformances / relationships.
  - Commercial Team – sub-contractor order placement on time / action of variations / checking support / relationships.
  - Technical challenges – what were they? / new legislation / shared learning with others.
  - Software – key issues / new software / shared learning.
  - Design Costs should be identified.

Project value	
Design budget	
Design variations	
Total design budget	
Total design cost	
Design cost variance	
Design cost as a percentage	

  - Key Performance Indicators [KPIs] should be identified

Number of drawings planned	
Number of drawings produced	
Total design cost	
Average cost per drawing	
Number of RFIs issued	
Number of PDVs issued	

- o   Conclusion – what would we change? / what would we do differently? / what did you enjoy? / what was good? / what would we do again?
- o   Exit – has the project finished in? / what is the close out strategy?
- o   Training / Development Identified – shared learning / Technical Bulletins required / external training required / personal development required.

Post Contract Review

- The next stage should be to carry out a full Post Contract Review [PCR] meeting.
- The purpose of this is to understand what went well, what went wrong, what we would do again, what we would do differently and overall design costs. This is not a blame or finger pointing exercise, but we must understand the end-to-end effectiveness in order to develop as individuals and as a team.
- A Post Contract Review should include the following:
  - o   Programme – tender v actual.
  - o   Did we meet the Client's expectations?
  - o   Was the job successful?
  - o   Main changes form handover.
  - o   Non-Conformance Reports.
  - o   Estimating – issues and actions.
  - o   Design – issues and actions.
  - o   Procurement – issues and actions.
  - o   Contracts – issues and actions.
  - o   Health and Safety – issues and actions.
  - o   Commercial – issues and actions.
  - o   Sub-Contractors – issues and actions.
  - o   What did we do right?
  - o   Areas for improvement.
  - o   Good ideas for next Contract.
- This should be carried out with all members of the team [i.e. Estimator, Design Manager, QS, Project Manager and Buyer] to understand how the project went overall, what could be done differently through all the disciplines.

PC | Post Contract Review Meeting

Project 1

Introduction

To understand what went well, what went wrong, what we would do again, what we would do different and overall design costs. This is not a blame or finger pointing exercise but we must understand the end-to-end effectiveness in order to develop as a design team.

Attendees	
Name	**Role**

Client Details	
Main Contractor	
Architect	
Structural Engineer	

General Observations

Did we meet the Client's expectations?	
Was the project successful for us?	
Was the project successful for the Client?	

Materials

Please list any main changes from the project handover and why?

Senior Management Reporting

- Communication with the Senior Management and directors is key, and there should be monthly Senior Management Meetings held.
- These meetings provide opportunity for Senior Staff to come together and discuss key issues, departmental challenges and contribute to the ongoing strategy of the business.
- You will not be able to cover and resolve every issue as these should be captured during Project Coordination Meetings. Any key actions should be taken for separate workshops.
- The Agenda should cover the following:
  - Introduction and Previous Minutes.
  - Sales and Estimating.
  - Design.

o   Purchasing.

o   Contracts.

o   Commercial.

o   Health, Safety and Quality.

o   HR and Training.

o   Finance.

o   Any Other Business.

- These meetings should have a report produced by the Head or Director of the department, and all reports should be standardised.

PC | Senior Management Meeting

Report Produced By	Department	Date
Pete Chandler	Design	XX/XX/XXXX

Pre-Construction

- Regular sales / pipeline meetings required to understand workload, timescales, resourcing, support required and establish roles and responsibilities throughout the BID Process.
- BID review process and integration of Operations to be reviewed i.e. programme, sequence, methodology and logistics.

Personnel / Training / HR

- Designer 1 is at Project A 2-days per week. Designer 2 is full-time at Project B.
- Working from home strategy to be reviewed [especially Fridays' – everyone should be in].
- Mental health awareness to be raised [H & S corner created but needs developing].

High Level Project Issues

Project A

- Design close out of doors remains a challenge but significant progress made.
- O & M process and As-built drawings is underway.

Project B

- Change, change management, impact on resources and programme remain a concern.
- Sequencing and programme are being reviewed with draft completion programme produced, meeting with Client to be held.
- Plant Room design is well underway with 'construction' drawings already available.
- Interim 'lessons learnt' meeting to be held, final one to be carried out at a later stage.

BIM / 3D Strategy

- BIM will be a major issue should we win Project C [high level discussion should be had with Client in respect of our deliverables, Director support required].

KPI's

- Design programme planned v actual.
- Design cost budget v actual.
- RFI's raised.
- PDV's raised.
- Cost per drawing [based on budget v number].

Other

- Space with 'standing desks' for ad-hoc meetings to be set in the old storage area.
- R & D is on-going and hours are continuing to be booked.

Technical Bulletins

- Regular technical updates, legislation updates and company standards should be communicated through the Company.
- This is best carried out by the issuing of Technical Bulletins.

TB No.	0001 Rev B
Date	XX/XX/2023
Page No:	Page 1 of 1
Doc Ref:	TB 0001

Flat Sheet Material for Flashings & Pressed Panels

General

Flashings and pressed panels are fabricated from flat sheets of steel and aluminium. These flat sheets are de-coiled from standard coil sizes. For the most cost effective flashing and panel design, we are aiming to minimise the waste from the coil width. This is particularly important for repetitive soffit panel modules and long runs of fascia flashings.

The aim is for the total girth of the flashing to be a multiple of the coil width with as little waste as possible left over. Therefore flashings that have girths of 1/2, 1/3 of the coil widths etc, are very economical. Note bends generally decrease the flashing girth slightly so are ignored for this purpose. It is not worth worrying about flashings of less than 250mm girth.

Generally mill finish aluminium, pre coated aluminium and pre coated steel flat sheet are available in: - 1500mm Flat [Blanks] & 1250mm coil widths.

Flat sheet as standard is de-coiled in 3m lengths. Mill finish Aluminium and galv are available in 4m lengths. Please note that if 4m Lengths are required you will need to globally order with Fabricators to allow for de-coiling.

Special situations

1000mm coils are sometimes available as a special order. These should only be considered for larger jobs where this girth would be particularly efficient.

It may also be possible to de-coil pre-coated flashing material in other lengths up to 4m if this helps the efficiency. These options are subject to long lead-ins and would need to be carefully planned at the start of the project.

When special colours are specified please ensure that the flashings are sourced from the same supplier as the main panel to ensure colour match.

Weights of Flat Sheets

For weights of material please refer to the relevant Technical Bulletin for this information.

PSYCHOLOGY

Think, Feel and Act

- Thinking differently = you will act differently.
- E + R = O [Event + Reaction = Outcome].
- Small changes = bigger outcome, target small things first.

Success

- Success is two connections that come together and are unconnected.
- Talk, argue, debate and share breeds success.

Motivation

- Be motivated by good and what is going to happen, or be motivated by what you need to avoid.
- Be motivated by what you want to create and achieve [i.e. something purposeful].
- Define yourself by contributions and not titles, job descriptions, etc. > bring value.
- The future demands us to be different.
- Define yourself by the value you create.
- Succeed by being different, not just good.
- Believe in choice.
- Focus on what you can do.
- Attitude is more important than intelligence.
- Blame looks backward – responsibility looks forward.
- Opportunities are never lost.

Belief System

- Your belief system deletes, distorts and filters information.

MAXIMUM VALUE MINIMUM COST

Introduction

- An essential part of any team or business is to review the various departments and conduct an honest and robust review.
- This works best when carried out off the premises with a beer afterward!

Resources

- Trainee programme to be structured.
- Shared resources between offices to prevent silos.
- Shared Design Managers.
- SWOT [Strengths, Weaknesses, Opportunities and Threats] analysis of design staff across regions.
- Experience of Design Managers, are they just good designers?

Design / Drawings

- CDM to be identified on drawings.
- In-house training on specific software.
- Review Key Technical Points in coordination meetings.
- Standard Details to be produced.
- Enlarged programmes to be placed on white boards.
- Technical Bulletins to be produced [6 month review].
- Shared learning / experiences / new projects [list of projects with products].
- Toughen up on mistakes.
- Toughen up on "playful behaviour".
- Site visits at the start of key areas.
- Internal training on "back to basics" [tolerances, fixings, procedures, IMS, types of contracts, commercial, material savings [i.e. 25mm increments].
- Review content on drawings [too much info, not enough, specification drawings].
- Closer relationship in Design and Contracts.
- Sites to have access to Extranet sites.
- Electronic passage of information / IMS review / Procurement issuing.
- Clarification of job roles.
- Door scheduling / procurement procedure.
- CDM procedure.
- Introduce / produce procurement check lists on all products.
- Introduce flashing list / schedule to avoid items being missed or duplicated.

- Design meetings to be reinstated.
- More time to be spent speaking to design staff from Senior Managers / other departments.
- Design progress / resources to be discussed more frequently.
- Training on Regulations and Standards.
- Identify air sealing on drawings.
- Identify VOs on drawings better – mark "extra to contract" or "VO".
- Monitor errors on procurement schedules.

Programming

- Combined site and design programmes [put up on white boards].
- Structure of coordination meetings for consistency [programme must be the focus].
- Weekly work plans [put up on white boards].
- Programmes to be updated with percentages ready for coordination meetings.
- Introduce KPIs and monitor [especially procurement errors].
- Placing of orders to be shown on programmes.
- VOs to be shown on programmes.
- Use baseline on first issue to save master and original planned dates.
- Allocate resources accordingly and use software to cost.

Contracts

- Early construction programmes.
- Establish sequencing early.
- Identify maximum lengths of materials.
- Project Managers to remain on project until end.
- Feedback quality into sales and design [especially Quality Reports].
- Post Contract Reviews [PCRs] to be held on all projects [with correct staff].
- Project Managers to get more involved in design and assist in resolving issues.
- Every drawing to be reviewed for buildability.
- Do not have several copies of site programmes [revision / names].

Procurement

- Quantities on schedules and take-offs must get better.
- Identify "must go to" suppliers.
- Site Requisitions must not be signed off by any Designer. Manager to sign all.
- Easy to bypass checking and reviewing due to electronic initials.
- Alternative materials / cost updates from Buying.
- All checking and reviewing to pass through Manager.

- Girths of materials to be added to schedules.
- Get "into bed" with key suppliers on certain products [i.e., gutters].

Sales and Estimating

- Programming front end of the business.
- Technical review on all projects.
- Completion of technical handover document.
- Identify shortfalls / material changes and feed back to Sales Team.
- Technical handovers after "normal" handover.
- Drawing Lists to be produced on all projects and early.

Commercial

- More information from QSs regarding design costs allocated to VOs.
- Updates on instructions received.
- Updates on outstanding instructions.
- Design to identify time spent on design issues [i.e. positioning steelwork].
- Project strategy meeting.
- Closer coordination with QSs [i.e. samples].
- Design to avoid "sitting down" with QSs to help with checking.
- Checked schedules not to be returned to individual designers.
- QSs to check schedules against tender quantities.

Design Manager Role

- Review all drawings before being issued.
- Review and sign off all site requisitions.
- Be copied in on all design-related e-mails.
- Attend every coordination meeting.
- All checking and reviewing to pass through DM.
- Design meetings to be reinstated.
- Speak to designers more.
- Manage the department more and less "day-to-day" managing of projects.
- Planning – star managers develop results-focused plans of action.
- Organisation – great management requires the ability to multi-task.
- Communication – effective managers communicate clearly and listen.
- Delegation – managers must efficiently and effectively delegate tasks.
- Confident decision-making – successful managers accept responsibility and are decisive.
- Optimism – effective managers have a contagious positive outlook.

- Flexibility – successful managers stay focused on the big picture.
- Candid self-evaluator – effective managers recognise their own flaws.
- Team player – great managers pitch-in to help their staff.
- Lead by example – respected managers 'practice what they preach'.

PROMOTE A DESIGN LED BUSINESS

Introduction

- What makes us a Design Led Business, and how do we support this as a Unique Selling Point [USP]?

Website

- Easy to read "about" content that represents our design function.
- Showcase our best work [drawings, photos, 3D images].
- Make it easy for visitors and potential Clients to contact us directly.

Word of mouth

- Let your family and friends know what it is you're doing.

Early design engagement

- Early engagement in design is working well [Design Manager is attending several Pre-Con meetings].

Experiment with social media

- Actively use your social media accounts.
- Share useful links and converse with others online.

... AND THEN WHAT?

Team Building Skills

- Solving the problem.
- Performing.
- Setting the goals.
- Establishing the aims.
- Delegating.
- Failing to build a positive climate.
- Storming.
- Joint ownership of goals.
- Unclear organisation roles.
- Unhelpful criticism of team members.
- Involving the group.
- Body language.
- Encouraging openness.
- Continuing restatement of the goal.
- The beginnings of good intergroup relationships.
- Gaining and building commitment through consultation.
- Allow individuals to develop their own methods.
- Accept comments on blind spots.
- Learn from mistakes.
- Caring for the team.

Easy Mistakes

- Not providing feedback.
- Not making time for your team.
- Being too 'hands-off'.
- Being too friendly.
- Failing to define goals.
- Misunderstanding motivation.
- Hurrying recruitment.
- Not 'walking the walk'.
- Not delegating.
- Misunderstanding your role.

Plan – Do – Check – Act

- The PDCA cycle is a continuous loop of planning, doing, checking and acting.
- It provides a simple and effective approach to solving problems and managing change.
- The model is useful for testing improvement measures on a small scale before updating procedures and working practices.

Personal Development

- What is in it for me? Never go to a meeting unless you know what it is about, that you are prepared and what you need to get out of it.
- Programming and planning.
- Technical knowledge of product and systems.
- Commercial [costs, budgets, item rate, allowance].
- Action plans, weekly work plans, tasks, use of software [What? When? How?].
- The best designers do not necessarily make the best managers.
- Proactive approach.
- Office and third-party awareness.
- Aspire to be like someone [Who and why? Take the good and make it your own, leave out the bad].
- Ownership.
- Build your own tool kit.
- Negative v constructive – is the only way to learn [in fact, in my experience you only learn through pain].
- Pressure – more productivity, less time, put yourself under your own pressure.
- Plan, Do, Check, Act [PDCA].
- Can't 'live' in the moment.
- When does reporting happen? – admin day.
- What? Why? When? Who? Where? How?
- Do not plan to fail.
- Make time for yourself.
- Follow the process.
- The Business – what is right for the business.

Rugby [My Passion]

- I am a Level 2 RFU rugby coach and referee. I have been coaching for 10 years and find that my management and leadership roles complement my coaching skills and vice versa.
- My personal philosophy is 'and then what', meaning I am always looking at how I can develop people, processes, systems, procedures and designs. I always look for more efficient ways of working and believe there is a glass ceiling you need to get to and crash through.
- And remember:

Rugby, as with any sport, is a game all about teamwork and support.

END

My First Drawing

- Make sure to take time to stop and look at where you have come from, how you have developed, how your skills have changed and how your knowledge has increased.
- It is often a very steep curve we follow during our careers, and it is important that we stay grounded.
- Below is my first ever drawing, which reminds me of exactly where it all started back on September 5th 1994.

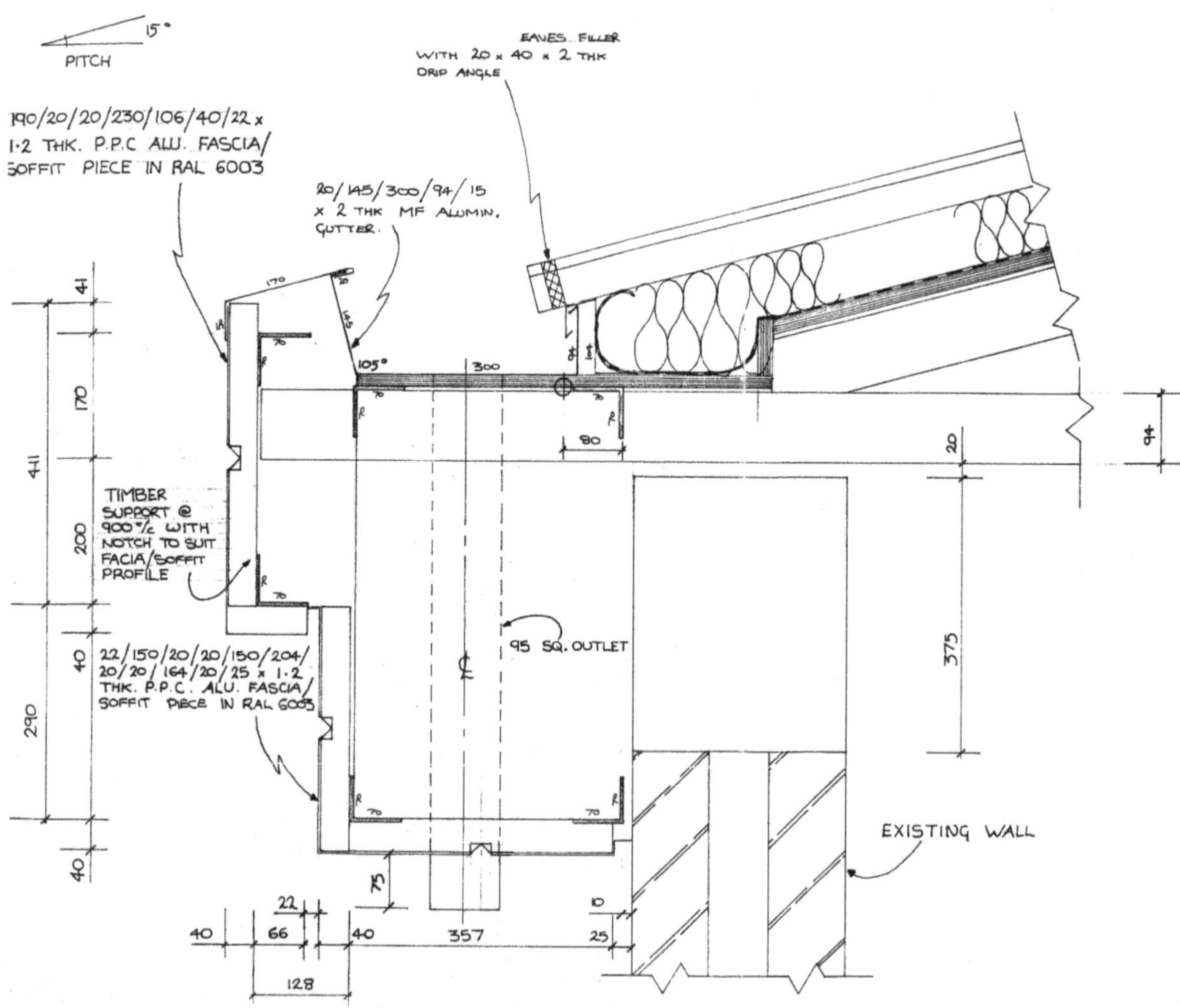

Good Phrases

- Deliver what is promised.
- Do not accept below standard output.
- You can't eat an elephant whole – break up into smaller parts.
- Add value, eliminate waste.
- Description not judgement.
- Cause not blame.
- Never underestimate the quiet man.
- Feel the fear and do it anyway.
- I'll handle it.
- Anger is poisonous.
- Fear will not go away.
- If it feels wrong then it probably is.
- Out talk your negativity.
- Do not listen to your inner chatterbox.
- Stress is good [stress causes adrenalin and adrenalin is required for optimum performance].
- If you shoot for the moon and miss, you will still land amongst the stars.
- Train hard, fight easy.
- Bad news is best delivered early.
- Better to make a bad decision than not make one at all.
- Better to ask for forgiveness than permission.
- F.I.S.H.M.O – F*ck it, sh*t happens, move on.
- Leadership, drive and ambition.
- Gather success in incremental parts.
- Risk analysis [go or no go].
- Uncomplicate it.
- Create energy.
- Experience and judgement.
- Acid test the process.
- What would Pete do?

5 Ps: **P**reparation and **P**lanning **P**revents **P**oor **P**erformance

Get the design right first time

- Management Rule Number. 1:

Make your staff feel valued and important

- And remember:

Building relationships with people is the key to success

Standing Operating Procedures

- Standing Operation Procedures [SOPs] are critical to any department and any business. In the Army, SOPs not only save your backside, they save your life. In business, when the going gets tough, workload is high and deadlines need to be met, SOPs and procedures seem to drop away.
- This is not good enough. Pete's Arse Saving Documents [ASDs] are:
  - Design Programme.
  - Design Report.
  - Design Deliverables.
  - Design Blockers.
  - Procurement Tracker.
  - Change / variation register.
  - 3D model progress.
  - Scope / allowance / baseline position.
- You need to earn your own stripes, claw through a few years of shit jobs and learn how to get through them no matter what.
- You need to face projects head on and show the team that you are there in the trenches with them. That is leadership.
- And remember:

In the middle of every difficulty lies opportunity

Rate this book on our website!

www.novum-publishing.co.uk

EIN HERZ FÜR AUTOREN A HEART FOR AUTHORS À L'ÉCOUTE DES AUTEURS ΜΙΑ ΚΑΡΔΙΑ ΓΙΑ ΣΥΓΓΡΑΦΕΙΣ UN CUORE PER
HJÄRTA FÖR FÖRFATTARE UN CORAZÓN POR LOS AUTORES YAZARLARIMIZA GÖNÜL VERELIM SZÍVÜNKET SZERZŐINKÉF
CUORE PER AUTORI ET HJERTE FOR FORFATTERE EEN HART VOOR SCHRIJVERS TEMOS OS AUTORES NO CORAÇÃO BCI
SZERZŐINKÉRT SERCE DLA AUTORÓW EIN HERZ FÜR AUTOREN A HEART FOR AUTHORS À L'ÉCOUTE DES AUTEURS ΜΙΑ
CORAÇÃO ВСЕЙ ДУШОЙ К АВТОРАМ ETT HJÄRTA FÖR FÖRFATTARE Á LA ESCUCHA DE LOS AUTORES YAZARLARIMIZA G
AUTEURS ΜΙΑ ΚΑΡΔΙΑ ΓΙΑ ΣΥΓΓΡΑΦΕΙΣ UN CUORE PER AUTORI ET HJERTE FOR FORFATTERE EEN HART VOOR SCHRIJVE
YAZARLARIMIZA GÖNÜL VERELIM SZÍVÜNKET SERCE DLA AUTORÓW EIN HERZ FÜR AUTOREN A HEART FC
VOOR SCHRIJVERS TEMOS OS AUTORES NO CORAÇÃO ВСЕЙ ДУШОЙ К АВТОРАМ ETT HJÄRTA FÖR FÖRFATTARE Á LA ES

The author

Pete Chandler is a seasoned Design Director boasting an impressive career over 30 years in the construction industry, focusing particularly on roofing, cladding and glazing for both commercial and residential projects. With a passion for excellence and an unwavering commitment to delivering exceptional results, Pete has built a solid track record of successfully managing and executing complex projects. His exceptional ability to navigate the intricacies of the design process has led him to oversee multi-million-pound developments, receiving prestigious accolades and awards, solidifying his standing as a key player in the industry. Outside of work, he immerses himself in the world of rugby, being an avid follower of the sport. Pete shares his life with his wife and 19-year-old son in Hampshire, England.

novum PUBLISHER FOR NEW AUTHORS

The publisher

He who stops getting better stops being good.

This is the motto of novum publishing, and our focus is on finding new manuscripts, publishing them and offering long-term support to the authors.
Our publishing house was founded in 1997, and since then it has become THE expert for new authors and has won numerous awards.

Our editorial team will peruse each manuscript within a few weeks free of charge and without obligation.

You will find more information about novum publishing and our books on the internet:

www.novum-publishing.co.uk